Acclaim for Orhan Pamuk's **ISTANBUL**

**A *San Francisco Chronicle*, *Financial Times*,
and *Washington Post Book World*
Best Book of the Year**

"Insightful, eclectic, whimsical. . . . Pamuk is not writing about it, he is painting it."

"Brilliantly constructed. . . . Pamuk has opulent muse. This quietly instructive redeemed childhood and to Istanbul itself will bring the world to his feet."   —*The Observer* (London)

"Masterful. . . . A three-pronged book: an anatomy of the city's body and soul; a compelling account of family politics, war and diplomacy; and a study of the youthful writer's gropings through the dark towards his true vocation."   —*The Guardian* (London)

"*İstanbul* is equal parts autobiography, travel essay, sociology and criticism. . . . As evocative as Joyce's *A Portrait of the Artist as a Young Man*."   —*The Miami Herald*

"Fascinating. . . . A deeply inward memoir of a city."   —*The Sun*

"Essential reading for devoted fans of his novels."
                                   —*The Independent* (London)

"Engaging. . . . A rich and quirkily faceted portrait of a city."
                                   —*Los Angeles Times Book Review*

"A fascinating literary adventure. . . . Rich in details and research."
—*San Francisco Chronicle*

"Elegant. . . . Paints an absorbing portrait of this complex and singular place." —*Town & Country*

"With *İstanbul*, Orhan Pamuk may have written the most haunting, heartbreaking, gorgeous book ever about a city."
—*The San Diego Union-Tribune*

"Entrancing. . . . Brilliant. . . . Pamuk will be identified with Istanbul just as Lawrence Durrell is with Alexandria and James Joyce with Dublin." —*San Jose Mercury News*

"*İstanbul* is full of byways that lead the reader into Pamuk's fiction—sometimes with a jolting literalness."
—*The New York Times Book Review*

"Remarkable. . . . Even those of us who have never set foot in [Istanbul] will be transformed by reading Pamuk's extraordinary and moving book." —*The Financial Times*

"Far from a conventional appreciation of the city's natural and architectural splendors, *İstanbul* tells of an invisible melancholy and the way it acts on an imaginative young man, aggrieving him but pricking his creativity." —*The New York Times*

"A fascinating read for anyone who has even the slightest acquaintance with this fabled bridge between east and west."
—*The Economist*

Orhan Pamuk

İSTANBUL

Orhan Pamuk is the winner of the Nobel Prize in Literature for 2006. His novel *My Name is Red* won the 2003 IMPAC Dublin Literary Award. His work has been translated into more than fifty languages. He lives in Istanbul.

INTERNATIONAL

ISTANBUL

ISTANBUL

Memories and the City

Orhan Pamuk

Translated from the Turkish by Maureen Freely

VINTAGE INTERNATIONAL

VINTAGE BOOKS

A DIVISION OF RANDOM HOUSE, INC.

NEW YORK

FIRST VINTAGE INTERNATIONAL EDITION, JULY 2006

Translation copyright © 2004 by Alfred A. Knopf, a division of Random House, Inc.

Published in the United States by Vintage Books, a division of Random House, Inc.,
New York, and in Canada by Random House of Canada Limited, Toronto.
Originally published in Turkey as *İstanbul Hatıralar ve Şehir* by Yapı Kredi Yayınları,
İstanbul, in 2003. Copyright © 2003 Yapı Kredi Kültür Sanat Yayıncılık Ticaret ve
Sanayi A.Ş. This translation originally published in hardcover in the United States
by Alfred A. Knopf, a division of Random House, Inc., New York, in 2005.

Vintage is a registered trademark and Vintage International and colophon are
trademarks of Random House, Inc.

The Library of Congress has cataloged the Knopf edition as follows:
Pamuk, Orhan, [date]
Istanbul: memories and the city/Orhan Pamuk;
translated from the Turkish by Maureen Freely.
p. cm.
Originally published as İstanbul: hatiralar ve sehir.
1. Istanbul (Turkey)—Description and travel.   I. Title.
DR723.P36 2005
949.61'803'092—dc22 2004061537

Vintage ISBN-10: 1-4000-3388-8
Vintage ISBN-13: 978-1-4000-3388-1

Book design by Robert C. Olsson

www.vintagebooks.com

Printed in the United States of America
22 24 26 28 30 29 27 25 23 21

To my father, Gündüz Pamuk (1925–2002)

The beauty of a landscape resides in its melancholy.

—Ahmet Rasim

CONTENTS

İSTANBUL

CHAPTER ONE

Another Orhan

From a very young age, I suspected there was more to my world than I could see: Somewhere in the streets of Istanbul, in a house resembling ours, there lived another Orhan so much like me that he could pass for my twin, even my double. I can't remember where I got this idea or how it came to me. It must have emerged from a web of rumors, misunderstandings, illusions, and fears. But in one of my earliest memories, it is already clear how I've come to feel about my ghostly other.

When I was five I was sent to live for a short time in another house. After one of their many stormy separations, my parents arranged to meet in Paris, and it was decided that my older brother and I should remain in Istanbul, though in separate places. My brother would stay in the heart of the family with our grandmother in the Pamuk Apartments, in Nişantaşı, but I would be sent to stay with my aunt in Cihangir. Hanging on the wall in this house—where

I was treated with the utmost kindness—was a picture of a small child, and every once in a while my aunt or uncle would point up at him and say with a smile, "Look! That's you!"

The sweet doe-eyed boy inside the small white frame did look a bit like me, it's true. He was even wearing the cap I sometimes wore. I knew I was not that boy in the picture (a kitsch representation of a "cute child" that someone had brought back from Europe). And yet I kept asking myself, Is this the Orhan who lives in that other house?

Of course, now I too was living in another house. It was as if I'd had to move here before I could meet my twin, but as I wanted only to return to my real home, I took no pleasure in making his acquaintance. My aunt and uncle's jovial little game of saying I was the boy in the picture became an unintended taunt, and each time I'd feel my mind unraveling: my ideas about myself and the boy who looked like me, my picture and the picture I resembled, my home and the other house—all would slide about in a confusion that made me long all the more to be at home again, surrounded by my family.

Soon my wish came true. But the ghost of the other Orhan in another house somewhere in Istanbul never left me. Throughout my childhood and well into adolescence, he haunted my thoughts. On winter evenings, walking through the streets of the city, I would gaze into other people's houses through the pale orange light of home and dream of happy, peaceful families living comfortable lives. Then I would shudder to think that the other Orhan might be living in one of these houses. As I grew older, the ghost became a fantasy and the fantasy a recurrent nightmare. In some dreams I would greet this Orhan—always in another house—with shrieks of horror; in others the two of us would stare each other down in eerie merciless silence. Afterward, wafting in and out of sleep, I would cling ever more fiercely to my pillow, my house, my street, my place in the world. Whenever I was unhappy, I imagined going to the other house, the other life, the place where the other Orhan lived, and in spite of everything I'd half convince myself that I was he and took pleasure in imagining how happy he was, such pleasure that, for a time, I felt no need to go to seek out the other house in that other imagined part of the city.

Here we come to the heart of the matter: I've never left Istanbul, never left the houses, streets, and neighborhoods of my childhood. Although I've lived in different districts from time to time, fifty years on I find myself back in the Pamuk Apartments, where my first photographs were taken and where my mother first held me in her arms to show me the world. I know this persistence owes some-

thing to my imaginary friend, the other Orhan, and to the solace I took from the bond between us. But we live in an age defined by mass migration and creative immigrants, so I am sometimes hard-pressed to explain why I've stayed, not only in the same place but in the same building. My mother's sorrowful voice comes back to me: "Why don't you go outside for a while? Why don't you try a change of scene, do some traveling . . . ?"

Conrad, Nabokov, Naipaul—these are writers known for having managed to migrate between languages, cultures, countries, continents, even civilizations. Their imaginations were fed by exile, a nourishment drawn not through roots but through rootlessness. My imagination, however, requires that I stay in the same city, on the same street, in the same house, gazing at the same view. Istanbul's fate is my fate. I am attached to this city because it has made me who I am.

Gustave Flaubert, who visited Istanbul 102 years before my birth, was struck by the variety of life in its teeming streets; in one of his letters he predicted that in a century's time it would be the capital of the world. The reverse came true: After the Ottoman Empire collapsed, the world almost forgot that Istanbul existed. The city into which I was born was poorer, shabbier, and more isolated than it had ever been before in its two-thousand-year history. For me it has always been a city of ruins and of end-of-empire melancholy. I've spent my life either battling with this melancholy or (like all *İstanbullus*) making it my own.

At least once in a lifetime, self-reflection leads us to examine the circumstances of our birth. Why were we born in this particular corner of the world, on this particular date? These families into which we were born, these countries and cities to which the lottery of life has assigned us—they expect love from us, and in the end we do love them from the bottom of our hearts; but did we perhaps deserve better? I sometimes think myself unlucky to have been born in an aging and impoverished city buried under the ashes of a ruined empire. But a voice inside me always insists this was really a piece of luck. If it is a matter of wealth, I can certainly count myself fortunate to have been born into an affluent family at a time when the city was at its lowest ebb (though some have ably argued the contrary). Mostly, I am disinclined to complain; I've accepted the city into which I was born in the same way that I've accepted my body (much as I would have preferred to be more handsome and better built) and my gender (even though I still ask myself, naïvely, whether I might have been better off had I been born a woman). This is my fate, and there's no sense arguing with it. This book is concerned with fate.

I was born in the middle of the night on June 7, 1952, in a small private hospital in Moda. Its corridors, I'm told, were peaceful that night, and so was the world. Aside from the Strambolini volcano's having suddenly begun to spew flames and ash two days earlier, relatively little seems to have been happening on our planet. The newspapers were full of small news: a few stories about the Turkish troops fighting in Korea; a few rumors spread by Americans stoking fears that the North Koreans might be preparing to use biological weapons. In the hours before I was born, my mother had been avidly following a local story: Two days earlier, the caretakers and "heroic" residents of the Konya Student Center had seen a man in a terrifying mask trying to enter a house in Langa through the bathroom window; they'd chased him through the streets to a lumberyard, where, after cursing the police, the hardened criminal had committed suicide; a seller of dry goods identified the corpse as a gangster who the year before had entered his shop in broad daylight and robbed him at gunpoint.

When she was reading the latest on this drama, my mother was alone in her room, or so she told me with a mixture of regret and annoyance many years later. After taking her to the hospital, my father had grown restless and, when my mother's labor failed to progress, he'd gone out to meet with friends. The only person with her in the delivery room was my aunt, who'd managed to climb over the hospital's garden wall in the middle of the night. When my mother first set eyes on me, she found me thinner and more fragile than my brother had been.

I feel compelled to add *or so I've been told.* In Turkish we have a special tense that allows us to distinguish hearsay from what we've seen with our own eyes; when we are relating dreams, fairy tales, or past events we could not have witnessed, we use this tense. It is a useful distinction to make as we "remember" our earliest life experiences, our cradles, our baby carriages, our first steps, all as reported by our parents, stories to which we listen with the same rapt attention we might pay some brilliant tale of some other person. It's a sensation as sweet as seeing ourselves in our dreams, but we pay a heavy price for it. Once imprinted in our minds, other people's reports of what we've done end up mattering more than what we ourselves remember. And just as we learn about our lives from others, so too do we let others shape our understanding of the city in which we live.

At times when I accept as my own the stories I've heard about my city and myself, I'm tempted to say, "Once upon a time I used to paint. I hear I was born in Istanbul, and I understand that I was a somewhat curious child. Then, when I was twenty-two, I seem to have begun writing novels without knowing why." I'd have liked to write my entire story this way—as if my life were something that happened to someone else, as if it were a dream in which I felt my voice fading and my will succumbing to enchantment. Beautiful though it is, I find the language of epic unconvincing, for I cannot accept that the myths we tell about our first lives prepare us for the brighter, more authentic second lives that are meant to begin when we awake. Because—for people like me, at least—that second life is none other than the book in your hand. So pay close attention, dear reader. Let me be straight with you, and in return let me ask for your compassion.

CHAPTER TWO

The Photographs in
the Dark Museum House

My mother, my father, my older brother, my grandmother, my uncles, and my aunts—we all lived on different floors of the same five-story apartment house. Until the year before I was born, the different branches of the family had (as with so many large Ottoman families) lived together in a stone mansion; in 1951 they rented it out to a private elementary school and built on the empty lot next door the modern structure I would know as home; on the facade, in keeping with the custom of the time, they proudly put up a plaque that said PAMUK APT. We lived on the fourth floor, but I had the run of the entire building from the time I was old enough to climb off my mother's lap and can recall that on each floor there was at least one piano. When my last bachelor uncle put his newspaper down long enough to get married, and his new wife moved into the first-floor apartment, from which she was to spend the next half century gazing out the window, she brought her piano with her. No one ever played, on this one or any of the others; this may be why they made me feel so sad.

But it wasn't just the unplayed pianos; in each apartment there was also a locked glass cabinet displaying Chinese porcelains, teacups, silver sets, sugar bowls, snuffboxes, crystal glasses, rosewater ewers, plates, and censers that no one ever touched, although among them I sometimes found hiding places for miniature cars. There were the unused desks inlaid with mother-of-pearl, the tur-

ban shelves on which there were no turbans, and the Japanese and Art Nouveau screens behind which nothing was hidden. There, in the library, gathering dust behind the glass, were my doctor uncle's medical books; in the twenty years since he'd emigrated to America, no human hand had touched them. To my childish mind, these rooms were furnished not for the living but for the dead. (Every once in a while a coffee table or a carved chest would disappear from one sitting room only to appear in another sitting room on another floor.)

If she thought we weren't sitting properly on her silver-threaded chairs, our grandmother would bring us to attention. "Sit up straight!" Sitting rooms were not meant to be places where you could lounge comfortably; they were little museums designed to demonstrate to a hypothetical visitor that the householders were westernized. A person who was not fasting during Ramadan would perhaps suffer fewer pangs of conscience among these glass cupboards and dead pianos than he might if he were still sitting cross-legged in a room full of cushions and divans. Although everyone knew it as freedom from the laws of Islam, no one was quite sure what else westernization was good for. So it was not just in the afflu-ent homes of Istanbul that you saw sitting-room museums; over the next fifty years you could find these haphazard and gloomy (but sometimes also poetic) displays of western influence in sitting rooms all over Turkey; only with the arrival of television in the 1970s did they go out of fashion. Once people had discovered how pleasurable it was to sit together to watch the evening news, their sitting rooms changed from little museums to little cinemas— although you still hear of old families who put their televisions in their central hallways, locking up their museum sitting rooms and opening them only for holidays or special guests.

Because the traffic between floors was incessant, as it had been in the Ottoman mansion, doors in our modern apartment building were usually left open. Once my brother had started school, my mother would let me go upstairs alone, or else we would walk up together to visit my paternal grandmother in her bed. The tulle curtains in her sitting room were always closed, but it made little difference; the building next door was so close as to make the room very dark anyway, especially in the morning, so I'd sit on the large heavy carpets and invent a game to play on my own. Arranging the miniature cars that someone had brought me from Europe into an obsessively neat line, I would admit them one by one into my garage. Then, pretending the carpets were seas and the chairs and tables islands, I would catapult myself from one to the other without ever touching water (much as Calvino's Baron spent his life jumping from tree to tree without ever touching ground). When I was tired of this airborne adventure or of riding the arms of the sofas like horses (a game that may have been inspired by memories of the horse-drawn carriages of Heybeliada), I had another game that I would continue to play as an adult whenever I got bored: I'd imagine that the place in which I was sitting (this bedroom, this sitting room, this classroom, this barracks, this hospital room, this government office) was really somewhere else; when I had exhausted the energy to daydream, I would take refuge in the photographs that sat on every table, desk, and wall.

Never having seen them put to any other use, I assumed pianos were stands for exhibiting photographs. There was not a single surface in my grandmother's sitting room that wasn't covered with frames of all sizes. The most imposing were two enormous portraits that hung over the never-used fireplace: One was a retouched photograph of my grandmother, the other of my grandfather, who died in 1934. From the way the pictures were positioned on the wall and the way my grandparents had been posed (turned slightly toward each other in the manner still favored by European kings and queens on stamps), anyone walking into this museum room to meet their haughty gaze would know at once that the story began with them.

They were both from a town near Manisa called Gördes; their family was known as Pamuk (cotton) because of their pale skin and white hair. My paternal grandmother was Circassian (Circassian girls, famous for being tall and beautiful, were very popular in Ottoman harems). My grandmother's father had immigrated to Anatolia during the Russian-Ottoman War (1877–78), settling first in Izmir (from time to time there was talk of an empty house there) and later in Istanbul, where my grandfather had studied civil engineering. Having made a great deal of money during the early 1930s, when the new Turkish Republic was investing heavily in railroad building, he built a large factory that made everything from rope to a sort of twine to dry tobacco; the factory was located on the banks of the Göksü, a stream that fed into the Bosphorus. When he died in 1934 at the age of fifty-two, he left a fortune so large that my father and my uncle never managed to find their way to the end of it, in spite of a long succession of failed business ventures.

Moving on to the library, we find large portraits of the new generation arranged in careful symmetry along the walls; from their pastel coloring we can take them to be the work of the same photographer. On the far wall is my fat but robust Uncle Özhan, who went to America to study medicine without first doing his military service and so was never able to return to Turkey, thus paving the way for my grandmother to spend the rest of her life assuming mournful airs. There is his bespectacled younger brother Aydın, who lived on the ground floor. Like my father, he studied civil engineering and spent most of his life involved in big engineering projects that never quite got off the ground. On the fourth wall is my father's sister, who spent time in Paris studying piano. Her husband was an assistant in the law faculty and they lived in the penthouse apartment, to which I would move many years later and where I am now writing this book.

Leaving the library to return to the main room of the museum, stopping briefly by the crystal lamps that only add to the gloom, we find a crowd of untouched black-and-white photographs that tell us life is gaining momentum. Here we see all the children posing at their betrothals, their weddings, and the other great moments of their lives. Next to the first color photographs that my uncle sent from America are snapshots of the extended family enjoying holiday meals in various city parks, in Taksim Square, and on the shores of the Bosphorus; next to a picture of me and my brother with our parents at a wedding is one of my grandfather, posing with his new

car in the garden of the old house, and another of my uncle, posing with his new car outside the entrance to the Pamuk Apartments. Except for extraordinary events like the day my grandmother removed the picture of my American uncle's first wife and replaced it with a picture of his second, the old protocols prevailed: Once assigned its place in the museum, a photograph was never moved; although I had looked at each one hundreds of times, I could never go into that cluttered room without examining all of them again.

My prolonged study of these photographs led me to appreciate the importance of preserving certain moments for posterity, and in time I also came to see what a powerful influence these framed scenes exerted over us as we went about our daily lives. To watch my uncle pose my brother a math problem, and at the same time to see him in a picture taken thirty-two years earlier; to watch my father scanning the newspaper and trying, with a half smile, to catch the tail of a joke rippling across the crowded room, and at that very same moment to see a picture of him at five years old—my age—with hair as long as a girl's, it seemed plain to me that my grandmother had framed and frozen these memories so we could weave them into the present. When, in the tones ordinarily reserved for discussing the founding of a nation, my grandmother spoke of my grandfather, who had died so young, and pointed at the frames on the tables and the walls, it seemed that she—like me—was pulled in two directions, wanting to get on with life but also longing to capture the moment of perfection, savoring the ordinary but still honoring the ideal. But even as I pondered these dilemmas—if you pluck a special moment from life and frame it, are you defying death, decay, and the passage of time or are you submitting to it?—I grew very bored with them.

In time I would come to dread those long festive lunches, those endless evening celebrations, those New Year's feasts when the whole family would linger after the meal to play lotto; every year, I would swear it was the last time I'd go, but somehow I never managed to break the habit. When I was little, though, I loved these meals. As I watched the jokes travel around the crowded table, my uncles laughing (under the influence of vodka or rakı) and my grandmother smiling (under the influence of the tiny glass of beer she allowed herself), I could not help but notice how much more fun life was outside the picture frame. I felt the security of belonging to a large and happy family and could bask in the illusion that we were put on earth to take pleasure in it. Not that I was unaware that these relatives of mine who could laugh, dine, and joke together on holidays were also merciless and unforgiving in quarrels over money and property. By ourselves, in the privacy of our own apartment, my mother was always complaining to my brother and me about the cruelties of "your aunt," "your uncle," "your grandmother." In the event of a disagreement over who owned what, or how to divide the shares of the rope factory, or who would live on which floor of the apartment house, the only certainty was that there would never be a resolution. These rifts may have faded for holiday meals, but from an early age I knew that behind the gaiety there was a mounting pile of unsettled scores and a sea of recriminations.

Each branch of our large family had its own maid, and each maid considered it her duty to take sides in the wars. Esma Hanım, who worked for my mother, would pay a visit to İkbal, who worked for my aunt. Later, at breakfast, my mother would say, "Did you hear what Aydın's saying?"

My father would be curious to know, but when the story was over he'd say only, "For God's sake, just stop worrying about it," and return to his newspaper.

If I was too young to understand the underlying cause of these disputes—that my family, still living as it had done in the days of the Ottoman mansion, was slowly falling apart—I could not fail to notice my father's bankruptcies and his ever-more-frequent absences. I could hear in more detail how bad things were whenever my mother took my brother and me to visit our other grandmother in her ghost-ridden house in Şişli. While my brother and I played, my mother would complain and my grandmother would counsel patience. Worried, perhaps, that my mother would want to return to this dusty three-story house, my grandmother, who now lived all alone, would again draw our attention to its many defects.

Apart from the occasional show of temper, my father found little to complain about; he took a childish delight in his good looks, his brains, and the good fortune he never tried to hide. Inside, he was always whistling, inspecting his reflection in the mirror, rubbing a wedge of lemon like brilliantine on his hair. He loved jokes, word games, surprises, reciting poetry, showing off his cleverness, taking planes to faraway places. He was never a father to scold, forbid, or

punish. When he took us out, we would wander all over the city, making friends wherever we went; it was during these excursions that I came to think of the world as a place made for taking pleasure.

If evil ever encroached, if boredom loomed, my father's response was to turn his back on it and remain silent. My mother, who set the rules, was the one to raise her eyebrows and instruct us in life's darker side. If she was less fun to be with, I was still very dependent on her love and attention, for she gave us far more time than did our father, who seized every opportunity to escape from the apartment. My harshest lesson in life was to learn I was in competition with my brother for my mother's affections.

It was, perhaps, because my father exerted so little authority that relations with my brother took on the significance they did: He was the rival for my mother's love. As we of course knew nothing of psychology, the war was initially dressed up as a game, and in the game we would both pretend to be other people. It was not Orhan and Şevket locked in deadly combat but my own favorite hero or soccer player versus my brother's. Convinced that we had become our heroes, we gave the game all we had; and when it ended in blood and tears, the anger and jealousy would make us forget we were brothers.

Whenever my mood dipped, whenever I became unhappy or bored, I'd leave our apartment without a word to anyone and go either to play with my aunt's son downstairs or, more often, upstairs to my grandmother's. Although all the apartments looked very

much alike, with chairs and dining sets, sugar bowls and ashtrays all bought from the same stores, every apartment seemed like a different country, a separate universe. And in the cluttered gloom of my grandmother's sitting room, particularly in the shadow of its coffee tables and glass cabinets, its vases and framed photographs, I could dream I was somewhere else.

In the evenings when we gathered in this room as a family, I often played a game wherein my grandmother's apartment became the bridge of a large ship. This fantasy owed much to the traffic passing through the Bosphorus, those mournful horns making their way into my dreams as I lay in bed. As I steered my imaginary craft through the storm, my crew and passengers ever more troubled by the rising waves, I took a captain's pride in knowing that our ship, our family—our fate—was in my hands.

Although my brother's adventure comics may have inspired this dream, so too did my thoughts about God. God had chosen not to bind us to the city's fate, I thought, simply because we were rich. But as my father and my uncle stumbled from one bankruptcy to the next, as our fortune dwindled and our family distintegrated and the quarrels over money grew more intense, every visit to my grandmother's apartment became a sorrow and took me a step closer to a realization: It was a long time coming, arriving by a circuitous route, but the cloud of gloom and loss spread over Istanbul by the fall of the Ottoman Empire had finally claimed my family too.

CHAPTER THREE

"Me"

When I was four, my brother, then six, started school, and over the next two years the intense ambivalent companionship that had built up between us began to fade. I was free of our rivalry and of the oppression of his superior strength; now that I had the Pamuk Apartments and my mother's undivided attention for the entire day, I grew happier, discovering the joys of solitude.

While my brother was at school I'd take his adventure comics and, guided by my recollections of what he'd read to me, "read" them to myself. One warm and pleasant afternoon, I'd been put to bed for my daily nap but finding myself too animated for sleep, I turned to an issue of Tom Mix, and soon I felt the thing my mother called my "bibi" going hard. I was looking at a picture of a half-naked redskin with the thinnest of strings around his waist and, draped over his groin like a flag, a piece of straight white cloth with a circle drawn at its center.

Another afternoon, as I was lying under the covers in my pajamas talking to a bear I'd owned for some time, I felt the same hardening. Curiously, this strange and magical event—which, though pleasurable, I felt compelled to conceal—occurred just after I told my bear, "I'm going to eat you!" But it wasn't owing to any great attachment to this bear: I was able to produce the same effect almost at will, just by repeating the same threat. It happens that these were the words that made the greatest impression on me in the stories my mother told me—"I am going to eat you!"—which I understood to mean not merely to devour but to annihilate. As I

was later to discover, the daevas of classical Persian literature—
those terrifying tailed monsters who were related to devils and jinns
and frequently painted by miniaturists—became giants when they
found their way into tales told in Istanbul Turkish. I got my image of
a giant from the cover of an abridged version of the classic Turkish
epic *Dede Korkut*. Like the redskin, this particular giant was half
naked, and to me he looked as if he ruled the world.

My uncle, who around this same time had purchased a small film
projector, would go during the holidays to the local photography
shop, where he rented film shorts: Charlie Chaplin, Walt Disney,
Laurel and Hardy. After ceremoniously removing my grandparents'
portraits, he would screen the films on the white wall above the fireplace. In my uncle's permanent film collection there was a Disney
film he showed only twice; this short run was on account of me.
The film featured a primitive, heavy, retarded giant who was as big
as an apartment; when he chased Mickey Mouse into the bottom of
a well, the monster tore the well from the ground with one sweep of
his hand and drank from it like a cup; just as Mickey fell into his
mouth, I would cry with all my might. There's a painting by Goya in
the Prado called *Saturn Devouring His Son* in which a giant thrusts a
little man he has scooped from the ground into his mouth, and it
terrifies me to this day.

One afternoon, as I was threatening my bear in the usual way but
also feeding him with a strange compassion, the door opened, and

my father caught me with my underpants down. He closed the door just a bit more softly than he had opened it, and (even I could tell) with some respect. Until then, when he came home for lunch and a brief rest, he had been in the habit of coming in to give me a kiss before returning to work. I worried that I had done something wrong or, even worse, that I had done so for pleasure: It was then that the very idea of pleasure became poisoned.

This sense was confirmed just after one of my parents' more prolonged quarrels, when my mother had left the house and the nanny who had come to look after us was giving me a bath. In a voice devoid of compassion, she scolded me for being "like a dog."

I could not control my body's responses; to make things worse, it was fully six or seven years, when I found myself in an all-boys junior school, until I discovered they were not unique.

During the long years when I thought myself the only one to possess this depraved and mysterious talent, it was normal to keep it hidden in my other world, where both my pleasures and the evil inside me had free reign. This was the world I would enter when, out of pure boredom, I pretended to be someone else and somewhere else. It was a very easy to escape into this other world I concealed from everyone. In my grandmother's sitting room, I'd pretend to be inside a submarine. I'd just had my first trip to the movies to see an adaptation of Jules Verne's *Twenty Thousand Leagues Under the Sea,* and as I sat watching it in the dusty Palace Cinema, what terrified me most were the film's silences. In its frantic, claustrophobic camerawork, its shadowy black-and-white submarine interiors, I could not help but recognize something of our house. I was too young to read the subtitles, but my imagination filled in the blanks. (Even later, when I could read a book perfectly well, what mattered most was not to "understand" it but to supplement the meaning with the right fantasies.)

"Don't swing your legs like that, you're making me dizzy," my grandmother used to say, when I was obviously immersed in one of my carefully staged daydreams.

I would stop swinging my legs, but in my daydream an airplane was still banking in and out of the smoke rising from the Gelincik cigarette she was raising to her lips, and soon I would enter the forest inhabited by the many rabbits, leaves, snakes, and lions I had previously identified among the geometric shapes on the carpets. Involving myself in an adventure from one of my comics, I'd mount a horse, start a fire, kill a few people. With one ear always alert for external sounds, I would hear the door of the elevator slam shut and, before returning my thoughts to half-naked redskins, note that İsmail the caretaker had gone up to our floor. I enjoyed setting houses on fire, spraying burning houses with bullets, escaping from burning houses through tunnels I had dug with my own hands, and slowly killing flies I had caught between the windowpane and the tulle curtains, which stank of cigarettes; when they fell to the perforated board over the radiator, the flies were gangsters who were finally paying the price for their crimes. Until the age of forty-five, it was my habit, whenever I was drifting in that sweet cloud between sleep and wakefulness, to cheer myself by imagining I was killing people. I would like to apologize to my close relatives—some, like my brother, very close indeed—as well as to the many politicians, literary luminaries, tradesmen, and mostly imaginary characters among my victims. Another frequent crime: I'd lavish affection on a cat, only to strike it cruelly in a moment of despair, from which I would emerge with a bout of laughter that made me so ashamed I would shower the poor cat with even more love than before. One afternoon twenty-five years later, when I was doing my military service, watching an entire company linger in the canteen after lunch for a chat and a smoke, I surveyed these 750 almost identical soldiers and imagined that their heads were separated from their bodies. As I contemplated their bloody esophagi through the cigarette smoke that bathed the cavernous canteen in a sweet transparent-blue haze, one of my soldier friends said, "Stop swinging your legs, son. I'm tired and I've had enough."

The only person who seemed at all aware of my secret fantasy world was my father.

I'd be thinking of my bear—whose only eye I'd snapped off in a moment of angry excitement and who was getting thinner and thinner as I pulled more and more stuffing out of its chest—or I'd be thinking of the finger-sized soccer player who kicked when you pressed a button in his head; it was my third soccer player—I'd broken the first two in bursts of excitement—and now I'd broken this one too, and I'd be wondering if my wounded toy was dying in his hiding place. Or else I'd be lost in fearful imaginings about the martens our maid Esma Hanım claimed to have seen on the roof of the house next door—she'd used the same voice she used when speaking of God—when suddenly I'd hear my father say, "What's going on in your head? Tell me and I'll give you twenty-five kurus."

Never sure whether to tell him the whole truth, change it a little, or tell an outright lie, I would fall silent; after a short while, he would smile and say, "It's too late now—you should have told me right away."

Had my father spent time in the other world too? It would be years before I discovered that my strange pastime was commonly known as *daydreaming*. So my father's question always induced panic; eager, as always, to avoid disturbing thoughts, I evaded his question and then put it out of my mind.

Keeping the second world secret made it easier for me to come and go. When I was sitting across from my grandmother, and a shaft of light came through her curtains—just like searchlights on the ships passing through the Bosphorus at night—I could, if I stared right into it and blinked, will myself to see a fleet of red spaceships floating past me. After that I could summon up the same armada whenever I liked, returning to the real world as someone else might leave a room and turn off the lights behind him (as throughout my childhood, people were always reminding me to do in the real world).

If I dreamed of changing places with the other Orhan in the other house, if I longed for a life beyond the museum's rooms, corridors, carpets (how I hated those carpets!) and beyond the company of positivist men who loved mathematics and crossword puzzles, if I felt hemmed in by this gloomy, cluttered house that rejected (though my family would deny it later) any suggestion of spirituality, love, art, literature, or even mythology, if I was from

time to time a refugee in the second world, it was not because I was unhappy. Far from it, especially in those years between the ages of four and six, when, as a bright well-behaved child I felt the love of nearly everyone I met, endlessly kissed and passed from lap to lap and offered treats no good boy could resist: the greengrocer's apple ("Don't eat it until it's washed," my mother would tell me), the raisins from the man in the coffee store ("Have them after lunch"), the sweets my aunt gave me when we met her in the street ("Say *thank you*").

If I had cause for complaint, it was my inability to see through walls. When looking out the window, I hated seeing nothing of the building next door, nothing of the street below, and only the narrowest strip of sky. At the smelly butcher shop across from us (I'd forget about the smell, only to remember it the moment I stepped into the cool street), it vexed me to be too short to see the butcher pick up one of his knives (each of them as big as my leg) to chop meat on the wooden block; I hated not being able to inspect counters, tabletops, or the insides of ice-cream freezers. When there was a small traffic accident in the street, drawing policemen on horseback, an adult would stand in front of me and I'd miss half the action. At the soccer matches to which my father took me from an early age, every time our team found itself in jeopardy, all the rows ahead of us would stand up, occluding my view of the decisive goals. But in truth, my eyes were never on the ball; they were on the cheese bread and cheese toasts and foil-covered chocolates my father bought for my brother and me. Worst of all was leaving the stadium, finding myself imprisoned by the legs of men jostling toward the exits, a dark airless forest of wrinkled trousers and muddy shoes. Apart from beautiful ladies like my mother, I cannot say I was very fond of adults in Istanbul, finding them in the main ugly, hairy, and coarse. They were too clumsy, too heavy, and too realistic. It could be they had once known something of a hidden second world, but they seemed to have lost their capacity for amazement and forgotten how to dream, which disability I took to coincide with the sprouting of objectionable hair on their knuckles and on their necks, in their noses, and in their ears. And so while I enjoyed their kind smiles and—even more—their presents, their incessant kisses meant enduring the abrasions of their beards and whiskers, the stink of their perfume, and their smoker's breath. I thought of men as part of some lower and more vulgar race and was thankful most of them belonged to the streets outside.

CHAPTER FOUR

The Destruction of the Pashas' Mansions: A Sad Tour of the Streets

The Pamuk Apartments were built at the edge of a large lot in Nişantaşı that had once been the garden of a pasha's mansion. The name itself, meaning "target stone," comes from the days of the reformist westernizing sultans of the late eighteenth and early nineteenth century (Selim III and Mahmud II), who placed stone tablets in the empty hills above the city in those areas where they practiced shooting and archery; the tablets marked the spot where an arrow landed or where an empty earthenware pot was shattered by a bullet; they usually carried a line or two describing the occasion. When the Ottoman sultans, fearing tuberculosis and desirous of western comforts (as well as a change of scene), abandoned Topkapı Palace for new palaces in Dolmabahçe and Yıldız, their viziers and princes began to build their own wooden mansions in the hills of nearby Nişantaşı. My first schools were housed in the Crown Prince Yusuf İzzeddin Pasha Mansion, and in the Grand Vizier Halil Rifat Pasha Mansion. Each would be burned and demolished while I was studying there, even as I played soccer in the gardens. Across the street from our home, another apartment building was built on the ruins of the Secretary of Ceremonies Faik Bey Mansion. In fact, the only stone mansion still standing in our neighborhood was a former home of grand viziers that had passed into the hands of the muncipality after the Ottoman Empire fell and the capital moved to Ankara. I remember going for my smallpox vaccination to another old pasha's mansion that had become the head-quarters of the district council. The rest—those mansions where Ottoman officials had once entertained foreign emissaries and those that belonged to the nineteenth-century Sultan Abdülhamit's daughters—I recall only as dilapidated brick shells with gaping windows and broken staircases darkened by bracken and untended fig trees; to remember them is to feel the deep sadness they evoked in me as a young child. By the late fifties, most of them had been burned down or demolished to make way for apartment buildings.

Through the back windows of our building on Teşvikiye Avenue, beyond the cypress and linden trees, you could see the remains of the mansion of Tunisian Hayrettin Pasha, a Circassian from the Caucasus who served as grand vizier for a short while during the Russian-Ottoman War. As a young boy (in the 1830s, a decade before Flaubert wrote that he wanted to "move to Istanbul and buy a slave"), he'd been brought to Istanbul and sold into slavery, eventually to find his way into the household of the Governor of Tunis, where he was raised speaking Arabic, before being taken to France for much of his later youth. When he returned to Tunis to join the army, he quickly rose through the ranks, serving in top posts at command headquarters, in the governor's office, the diplomatic corps, and the finance ministry. Finally, just as he was turning sixty, he retired to Paris, whereupon Abdülhamit (acting at the suggestion of another Tunisian, Sheikh Zafiri) summoned him to Istanbul. After engaging him as a financial adviser for a short time, he made him grand vizier. The pasha thus became one of the first in a long line of foreign-educated financial experts who, given the mandate to pull Turkey from a sea of debts, went beyond dreaming (like their counterparts in so many other poor countries) of national reform along western lines. As with many of his successors, people expected a great deal from this pasha, simply because he was more western than Ottoman or Turk. And for precisely the same reason—that he wasn't Turkish—he felt a deep shame. The gossip was that Tunisian Hayrettin Pasha would make notes in Arabic when returning home in his horse-drawn carriage from his meetings held in Turkish at the palace; later he would dictate these to his secretary in French. The

coup de grâce was a report of rumors that his Turkish was poor and
that his secret aim was to establish an Arabic-speaking nation; while
knowing them to be mostly baseless, the ever-suspicious Abdülhamit nevertheless gave these denunciations some credence and
removed the pasha as vizier. Because it would have been unseemly
for a fallen grand vizier to take refuge in France, the pasha was
forced to end his days in Istanbul, spending his summers at his
Bosphorus villa in Kuruçeşme and his winters as a half prisoner in
the mansion in whose garden we would later build our apartment
house. When he was not writing reports for Abdülhamit, he passed
the time composing his memoirs in French. These memoirs (translated into Turkish only eighty years later) prove their author to have
possessed a greater sense duty than of humor: He dedicated the
book to his sons, one of whom would later be executed for his
involvement in the attempted assassination of Grand Vizier Mahmut Şevket Pasha, by which time Abdülhamit had bought the mansion for his daughter Şadiye Sultan.

Watching the pashas' mansions burn to the ground, my family
maintained a stony equanimity—much as we had done in the face of
all those stories about crazy princes, opium addicts in the palace

harem, children locked in attics, treacherous sultans' daughters, and exiled or murdered pashas—and ultimately the decline and fall of the empire itself. As we in Nişantaşı saw it, the Republic had done away with the pashas, princes, and high officials, so the empty mansions they had left behind were only decrepit anomalies.

Still, the melancholy of this dying culture was all around us. Great as the desire to westernize and modernize may have been, the more desperate wish was probably to be rid of all the bitter memories of the fallen empire, rather as a spurned lover throws away his lost beloved's clothes, possessions, and photographs. But as nothing, western or local, came to fill the void, the great drive to westernize amounted mostly to the erasure of the past; the effect on culture was reductive and stunting, leading families like mine, otherwise glad of republican progress, to furnish their houses like museums. That which I would later know as pervasive melancholy and mystery, I felt in childhood as boredom and gloom, a deadening tedium I identified with the *"alaturka"* music to which my grandmother tapped her slippered feet. I escaped this state by cultivating dreams.

The only other escape was to go out with my mother. Because it was not yet the custom to take children to parks or gardens for their daily fresh air, the day I went out with my mother was an event. "Tomorrow I'm going out with my mother!" I'd boast to my aunt's son, who was three years my junior. After walking down the spiral staircase, we would pause before the little window facing the door through which the caretaker (when he was not in his basement apartment) could see everyone coming and going. I would inspect my clothes in the reflection, and my mother made sure all my buttons were buttoned; once outside I would exclaim in amazement, "The street!"

Sun, fresh air, light. Our house was so dark sometimes that stepping out was like opening the curtains too abruptly on a summer's day; the light would hurt my eyes. Holding my mother's hand, I would gaze in fascination at the displays in the shops: through the steamy window of the florist, at the cyclamens that looked like red wolves; in the window of the shoe shop, at the barely visible wires that suspended the high-heeled shoes in midair; and at the laundry (just as steamy as the florist's) where my father sent his shirts to be starched and ironed. But it was from the windows of the stationery store—in which I noticed the same school notebooks my brother used—that I learned an early lesson: Our habits and possessions were not unique, and there were other people outside our apartment who lived lives very similar to our own. My brother's primary school, which I, too, would attend a year later, was right next door to Teşvikiye Mosque, where everyone had their funerals. All my brother's excited talk at home about *my teacher, my teacher* had led me to imagine that—just as every child had his own nanny—every pupil had his own teacher. And so when I walked into that school the following year to find thirty-two children pressed into one classroom with a single teacher, my disappointment was profound. The discovery that in effect I counted for nothing in the outside world made it only harder to part each day from my mother and the comforts of home. When my mother entered the local branch of the Bank of Commerce, I would refuse, without explaining, to accompany her up the six steps to the cashier: wooden steps with gaps between them into which I had convinced myself I might fall and disappear forever. "Why won't you come in?" my mother would call down to me, as I pretended to be someone else. I'd imagine scenes in which my mother kept disappearing: Now I was in a palace, now at the foot of a well. . . . If we walked as far as Osmanbey or Harbiye past the

Mobil station on the corner, the winged horse on the sign covering the entire side of an apartment building would find its way into those dreams. There was an old Greek lady who darned stockings and sold belts and buttons; she also sold "eggs from the village," which she'd take out of a varnished chest one by one, like jewels. In her store was an aquarium where undulating red fish would open their small but frightening mouths trying to bite my finger pressed against the glass, swimming up with a stupid determination that never failed to amuse me. Next, there was a small tobacconist-cum-stationery-newspaper shop run by Yakup and Vasil, so small and crowded that most days we'd give up the moment we entered. There was a coffee shop called the "Arab shop" (just as Arabs in Latin America were often known as Turks, the handful of blacks in Istanbul were known as Arabs); its enormous belted coffee grinder would begin to thunder like the washing machine at home, and as I moved away from it the "Arab" would smile indulgently at my fear. When these shops went out of fashion and closed one by one to make way for a string of other, more modern enterprises, my brother and I would play a game—less inspired by nostalgia than to test our memories—that went like this: One of us would say, "The shop next to the Girls' Night School," and the other would list its later incarnations: "The Greek lady's pastry shop, a florist, a handbag store, a watch shop, a bookmaker, a gallery bookshop, and a pharmacy."

Before entering the cavelike shop where for fifty years a man named Alaaddin sold cigarettes, toys, newspapers, and stationery, I would, by design, ask my mother to buy me a whistle or a few marbles, a coloring book or a yo-yo. As soon as she put the present into her handbag, I'd be seized by an impatience to go home. But it wasn't only the glamour of the new toy.

"Let's walk as far as the park," my mother would say, but all at once sharp pains would travel up my legs to my chest, and I knew I could walk no farther. Years later, when my daughter was the same age and we went out for walks, she would complain of a remarkably similar affliction; when we took her to the doctor, he diagnosed ordinary fatigue and growing pains. Once fatigue had eaten into me, the streets and shopwindows that had been captivating only moments ago would slowly drain of color and I'd begin to see the whole city in black and white.

"Mummy, pick me up!"

"Let's walk as far as Maçka," my mother would say. "We'll go back on the tram."

The trams had been going up and down our street since 1914, connecting Maçka and Nişantaşı to Taksim Square, Tünel, the Galata Bridge, and all the other old, poor, historic neighborhoods that then seemed to belong to another country. When I went to bed in the early evenings, I'd be lulled to sleep by the melancholy music of the trams.

I loved their wooden interiors, the indigo-blue glass on the bolted door between the driver's "station" and the passenger area; I loved the crank that the driver would let me play with if we got on at the end of the line and had to wait to leave . . . until we could travel home again, the streets, the apartments, and even the trees in black and white.

CHAPTER FIVE

Black and White

Accustomed as I was to the semidarkness of our bleak museum house, I preferred being indoors. The street below, the avenues beyond, the city's poor neighborhoods seemed as dangerous as those in a black-and-white gangster film. And with this attraction to the shadow world, I have always preferred the winter to the summer in Istanbul. I love the early evenings when autumn is slipping into winter, when the leafless trees are trembling in the north wind and people in black coats and jackets are rushing home through the darkening streets. I love the overwhelming melancholy when I look at the walls of old apartment buildings and the dark

surfaces of neglected, unpainted, fallen-down wooden mansions; only in Istanbul have I seen this texture, this shading. When I watch the black-and-white crowds rushing through the darkening streets of a winter's evening, I feel a deep sense of fellowship, almost as if the night has cloaked our lives, our streets, our every belonging in a blanket of darkness, as if once we're safe in our houses, our bedrooms, our beds, we can return to dreams of our long-gone riches, our legendary past. And likewise, as I watch dusk descend like a poem in the pale light of the streetlamps to engulf these old neighborhoods, it comforts me to know that for the night at least we are safe; the shameful poverty of our city is cloaked from Western eyes.

A photograph by Ara Güler perfectly captures the lonely back streets of my childhood, where concrete apartment buildings stand beside old wooden houses, the streetlamps illuminate nothing, and the chiaroscuro of twilight—the thing that for me defines the city—has descended. (Though today concrete apartments have come to crowd out the old wooden houses, the feeling is the same.) What draws me to this photograph is not just the cobblestone streets and pavements, the iron grilles on the windows or the empty, ramshackle wooden houses—rather, it is the suggestion that, with

evening having just fallen, these two people dragging long shadows with them on their way home are actually pulling the blanket of night over the entire city.

In the 1950s and 1960s, like everyone, I loved watching the film crews all over the city—the minibuses with the logos of film companies on their sides; the two huge generator-powered lights; the prompters, who preferred to be known as *souffleurs* and who had to shout mightily over the generators' roar at those moments when the heavily made-up actresses and romantic male leads forgot their lines; the workers who jostled children and curious onlookers off the set. Forty years later, the Turkish film industry no longer exists (mostly due to the ineptitude of its directors, actors, and producers but also because it couldn't compete with Hollywood); they still show those old black-and-white films on television, and when I see the streets, the old gardens, the Bosphorus views, the broken-down mansions and apartments in black and white, I sometimes forget I am watching a film; stupefied by melancholy, I feel as if I am watching my own past.

Between the ages of fifteen and sixteen, when I imagined myself an impressionist artist of the Istanbul streets, it was my great joy to

paint the cobblestones one by one. Before the zealous district councils began to cover them mercilessly with asphalt, the city's taxi drivers complained bitterly about the damage the stone pavements did to their vehicles. They also carped about the interminable excavations of roads for sewer works, electricity, or general repairs. When a street was dug up, the cobblestones had to be removed one at a time, and the work draggged on forever—particularly if they found a Byzantine corridor underneath. When the repairs were done, I loved watching the workmen replacing the cobblestones one by one, with a bewitching skill and rhythm.

The wooden mansions of my childhood and the smaller, more modest wooden houses in the city's back streets were in a mesmerizing state of ruin. Poverty and neglect had ensured these houses were never painted, and the combination of age, dirt, and humidity slowly darkened the wood to give it that special color, that unique texture, so prevalent in the back neighborhoods that as a child I took the blackness to be original. Some houses had a brown undertone, and perhaps there were those in the poorest streets that had never known paint at all. But Western travelers in the eighteenth and mid-nineteenth centuries described the mansions of the rich as brightly painted, finding in them and the other faces of opulence a powerful and abundant beauty. As a child, I would sometimes imagine painting all these houses, but even then the loss of the city's black-and-white shroud was daunting. In summer, when these old wooden houses would dry out and turn a dark, chalky, tinderbox brown, you could imagine them catching fire at any moment; during the winter's long cold spells, the snow and the rain endowed these same houses with the mildewy hint of rotting wood. So it was too with the old wooden dervish lodges, forbidden by the Republic to be used as places of worship, now mostly abandoned and of interest only to street urchins, ghosts, and antiques hunters. They would awaken in me the same degrees of fear, worry, and curiosity; as I peered at them over half-broken walls, past the damp trees, and into the broken windows, a chill would pass through me.

Having always apprehended the city's soul in black and white, I am captivated by the line drawings of more discerning western travelers like Le Corbusier and by any book set in Istanbul with black-and-white illustrations. (My entire childhood, I waited in vain for the

cartoonist Hergé to set a Tin-Tin adventure in Istanbul; when the first Tin-Tin film was made here, a pirate publishing outfit issued a black-and-white comic book called *Tin-Tin in Istanbul,* the creation of a local cartoonist who mixed his own renderings of various frames from the film with frames from various other Tin-Tin adventures.) I am likewise fascinated by old newspapers; whenever I come across an account of a murder, a suicide, or a robbery gone wrong, I catch the whiff of a long-repressed childhood fear.

There are places—in Tepebaşı, Galata, Fatih, and Zeyrek, a few of the villages along the Bosphorus, the back streets of Üsküdar—where the black-and-white haze I've been trying to describe is still in evidence. On misty smoky mornings, on rainy windy nights, you can see it on the domes of mosques on which flocks of gulls make their homes; you can see it, too, in the clouds of exhaust, in the wreaths of soot rising from stovepipes, in the rusting trash cans, the parks and gardens left empty and untended on winter days, and the crowds scurrying home through the mud and the snow on winter evenings. These are the sad joys of black-and-white Istanbul: the crumbling fountains that haven't worked for centuries; the poor quarters with their forgotten mosques; the sudden crowds of schoolchildren in white-collared black smocks; the old and tired mud-covered trucks; the little grocery stores darkened by age, dust, and lack of custom; the dilapidated little neighborhood shops packed with despondent unemployed men; the crumbling city walls like so many upended cobblestone streets; the entrances to cinemas that begin, after a while, to look identical; the pudding shops; the newspaper hawkers on the pavement; the drunks that roam in the middle of the night; the pale streetlamps; the ferries going up and down the Bosphorus and the smoke rising from their chimneys; the city blanketed in snow.

It is impossible for me to remember my childhood without this blanket of snow. Some children can't wait for their summer holiday to begin, but I couldn't wait for it to snow—not because I would be going outside to play in it but because it made the city look new, not only by covering up the mud, the filth, the ruins, and the neglect, but by producing in every street and every view an element of surprise, a delicious air of impending disaster. It snowed on average between three and five days a year, with the accumulation staying on the ground for a week to ten days, but Istanbul was always caught unawares, greeting each snowfall as if it were the first: The back streets would close and then the main roads; queues would form outside the bakeries, just as they had in times of war and national disaster. What I loved most about the snow was its power to force people out of themselves to act as one; cut off from the world, we were stranded together. On snowy days, Istanbul felt like an outpost, but the contemplation of our common fate drew us closer to our fabulous past.

Once, freak arctic temperatures caused the Black Sea to freeze over from the Danube to the Bosphorus. This was an astounding occurrence for what is really a Mediterranean city, and people talked about it with childish joy for many years afterward.

To see the city in black and white is to see it through the tarnish of history: the patina of what is old and faded and no longer matters to the rest of the world. Even the greatest Ottoman architecture has a humble simplicity that suggests an end-of-empire gloom, a pained submission to the diminishing European gaze and to an

ancient poverty that must be endured like an incurable disease. It is resignation that nourishes Istanbul's inward-looking soul. To see the city in black and white, to see the haze that sits over it and breathe in the melancholy its inhabitants have embraced as their common fate, you need only to fly in from a rich western city and

head straight to the crowded streets; if it's winter, every man on the Galata Bridge will be wearing the same pale, drab, shadowy clothes. The *İstanbullus* of my era have shunned the vibrant reds, greens, and oranges of their rich, proud ancestors; to foreign visitors, it looks as if they have done so deliberately, to make a moral point. They have

not—but there is in their dense gloom a suggestion of modesty. This is how you dress in a black-and-white city, they seem to be saying; this is how you grieve for a city that has been in decline for a hundred and fifty years.

Then there are the packs of dogs, mentioned by every western traveler to pass through Istanbul during the nineteenth century,

from Lamartine and Gérard de Nerval to Mark Twain; they continue to bring drama to the city's streets. They all look alike, their coats all the same color for which no one has a name—a color somewhere between gray and charcoal that is no color at all. They are the bane of the city council. When the army stages a coup, it is

only a matter of time before a general mentions the dog menace; the state and the school system have launched campaign after campaign to drive dogs from the streets, but still they roam free. Fearsome as they are, united as they have been in their defiance of the state, I can't help pitying these mad, lost creatures still clinging to their old turf.

If we see our city in black and white, it's partly because we know it from the engravings left to us by western artists; the glorious colors of its past were never painted by local hands. There is no Ottoman painting that can easily accommodate our visual tastes. Nor is there a single piece of writing or work in today's world that can teach us how to take pleasure in Ottoman art or the classic Persian art that influenced it. Ottoman miniaturists took their inspiration from Persians. Like the Divan poets who praised and loved the city not as a real place but as a word, like the cartographer Nasuh the Polo Player, they saw the city as a map or as a procession passing in front of them. Even in their Books of Ceremonies, their attention was on the sultan's slaves, subjects, and magnificent possessions; the city was not a place where people lived but an official gallery, viewed through a lens of unvarying focus.

So when magazines or schoolbooks need an image of old Istanbul, they use the black-and-white engravings produced by western travelers and artists. My contemporaries tend to overlook the subtly colored gouaches of imperial Istanbul painted by Antoine-Ignace Melling, about whom I shall have more to say later; accepting of their fate and seeking convenience, they prefer to see their past in a more easily reproduced monochrome. For when they gaze into a colorless image, they see their melancholy confirmed.

There were very few tall buildings in the days of my childhood; as night fell over the city, it would erase the third dimension from the houses and the trees, the summer cinemas, balconies, and open windows, endowing the city's crooked buildings, twisting streets, and rolling hills with a dark elegance. I love this engraving from an 1839 travel book by Thomas Allom in which night has a metaphorical charge. In portraying darkness as a source of evil, it captures what some have called Istanbul's "moonlight culture." Like so many others who flock to the waterfront to enjoy the simple rituals of moonlit nights, the full moon that saves the city from total darkness, its play on the surface of the water, the weaker light of the half-moon, or (as here) the hint of moonlight behind the clouds—the

murderer has just turned off the lights so no one can see him commit his crime.

It was not just western travelers who used the language of the night to describe the city's impenetrable mysteries. If they knew anything at all about palace intrigues, it was because *İstanbullus* also loved to whisper about murdered harem girls whose bodies were smuggled out through the palace walls under cover of darkness and taken out into the Golden Horn to be thrown overboard.

The legendary Salacak murder (which happened in 1958, before I learned to read, but which caused such panic in my family—and, indeed, in every other family in the city—that I was acquainted with every detail) drew upon the same familiar elements; this terrifying story fed my black-and-white fantasies about nighttime, rowboats, and the waters of the Bosphorus and is the stuff of nightmare to this day. The villain, as first described to me by my parents, was a poor, young fisherman, but in time the city would build him up into a folk demon. Having agreed to take a woman and her children out on the Bosphorus in his rowboat, he decided to rape her and so threw the children into the sea. The newspapers dubbed him the "Salacak Monster" and my mother was so afraid another might be lurking among the fishermen who cast their nets near our summerhouse in Heybeliada that she stopped letting my brother and me go outside to play, even in our own garden. In my nightmares I could see the fisherman throwing the children into the waves and the children struggling to hold on to the boat by their fingernails; I could hear the mother's screams, as the ghostly shadow of the fisherman bashed them on the head with his oars. Even today, when I read about murders in Istanbul papers (something I do with peculiar pleasure), I still see these scenes in black and white.

CHAPTER SIX

Exploring the Bosphorus

After the Salacak murder, my brother and I never again went out in a rowboat with our mother. But the winter before, when my brother and I had whooping cough, there was a time when she took us out on the Bosphorus every day. My brother fell ill first and I followed ten days later. There were things I enjoyed about my illness: My mother treated me even more tenderly, saying all the sweet things I liked to hear and fetching me all my favorite toys. But there was one thing I found harder to bear than the illness itself, and that was being excluded from family meals, listening to the clink of knives, forks, and plates, hearing the laughter, without being close enough to make out what was being said.

After our fevers broke, Dr. Alber, the pediatrician (everything about this man scared us, from his bag to his mustache), instructed my mother to take us to the Bosphorus for fresh air once a day. The Turkish word for Bosphorus is the same as the word for *throat,* and after that winter I always associated the Bosphorus with fresh air. This may explain why I was not surprised to discover that the Bosphorus town of Tarabya—once a sleepy Greek fishing village, now a famous promenade lined with restaurants and hotels—was known as Therapia when the poet Cavafy lived there as a child a hundred years ago.

If the city speaks of defeat, destruction, deprivation, melancholy, and poverty, the Bosphorus sings of life, pleasure, and happiness. Istanbul draws its strength from the Bosphorus. But in earlier times, no one gave it much importance: They saw the Bosphorus as

a waterway, a beauty spot, and, for the last two hundred years, a fine location for summer palaces.

For centuries, it was just a string of Greek fishing villages, but from the eighteenth century, when Ottoman worthies began building their summer homes, mostly around Göksü, Küçüksu, Bebek, Kandilli, Rumelihisarı, and Kanlıca, there arose an Ottoman culture that looked toward Istanbul to the exclusion of the rest of the

world. The *yalıs*—splendid waterside mansions built by the great Ottoman families during the eighteenth and nineteenth centuries—came to be seen, in the twentieth, with the advent of the Republic and Turkish nationalism, as models of an obsolete identity and architecture. But these *yalıs* that we see photographed in *Memories of the Bosphorus*, reproduced in Melling's engravings, and echoed in the *yalıs* of Sedad Hakkı Eldem—these grand houses, with their narrow

high windows, spacious eaves, bay windows, and narrow chimneys, are mere shadows of this destroyed culture.

In the 1950s, the bus route from Taksim Square to Emirgân still passed through Nişantaşı. When we went by bus to the Bosphorus with my mother, we would board it just outside our house. If we went by tram, the last stop was Bebek, and after a long walk along the shore, we would meet up with the boatman, who was always waiting for us in the same place at the same time, and climb into his caïque. As we slipped among the rowboats, pleasure craft, and city-bound ferries, the mussel-encrusted barges and the lighthouses, leaving the still waters of Bebek Bay to meet the currents of the Bosphorus, rocking in the wake of passing ships, I would pray that these outings might last forever.

To be traveling through the middle of a city as great, historic, and forlorn as Istanbul, and yet to feel the freedom of the open sea—that is the thrill of a trip along the Bosphorus. Pushed along by its strong currents, invigorated by the sea air that bears no trace of the dirt, smoke, and noise of the crowded city that surrounds it, the traveler begins to feel that, in spite of everything, this is still a place in which he can enjoy solitude and find freedom. This water-way that passes through the center of the city is not to be confused with the canals of Amsterdam or Venice or the rivers that divide Paris and Rome in two: Strong currents run through the Bosphorus, its surface is always ruffled by wind and waves, and its waters are deep and dark. If you have the current behind you, if you are fol-lowing the itinerary of a city ferry, you will see apartment buildings and *yalıs,* old ladies watching you from balconies as they sip their tea, the pergolas of coffeehouses perched by landings, children in their underwear entering the sea just where the sewers empty into it and sunning themselves on the concrete, men fishing from the banks, people lazing on their yachts, schoolchildren emptying out of

school and walking along the shore, travelers gazing through bus windows out to the sea while stuck in traffic, cats sitting on wharfs waiting for fishermen, trees you hadn't realized were so tall, hidden villas and walled gardens you didn't even know existed, narrow alleyways rising up into the hills, tall apartment buildings looming

in the background, and slowly, in the distance, Istanbul in all its confusion—its mosques, poor quarters, bridges, minarets, towers, gardens, and ever-multiplying high-rises. To travel along the Bosphorus, be it in a ferry, a motor launch, or a rowboat, is to see the city house by house, neighborhood by neighborhood, and also from afar as a silhouette, an ever-mutating mirage.

What I enjoyed most about our family excursions to the Bosphorus was to see the traces everywhere of a sumptuous culture that had been influenced by the West without having lost its originality or vitality. To stand before the magnificent iron gates of a grand *yali* bereft of its paint, to notice the sturdiness of another *yali*'s moss-covered walls, to admire the shutters and fine woodwork of a third even more sumptuous *yali* and to contemplate the judas trees on the hills rising high above it, to pass gardens heavily shaded

by evergreens and centuries-old plane trees—even for a child, it was to know that a great civilization had stood here, and, from what they told me, people very much like us had once upon a time led a life extravagantly different from our own—leaving us who followed them feeling the poorer, weaker, and more provincial.

From the middle of the nineteenth century, as a string of military defeats was eroding the empire, the Old City was swamped by immigrants, and even the grandest imperial buildings began to show marks of poverty and ruin, it became fashionable for the pashas and dignitaries of the modern western-influenced bureaucracy to take refuge in the mansions they had built along the Bosphorus, where they set about creating a new culture that shut out the world. Western travelers could not penetrate this closed society; there were no paved roads. Even after ferries arrived in the mid-nineteenth century, the Bosphorus did not become part of the city proper—and the Ottomans ensconced in their Bosphorus mansions chose not to write about their lives, so we must rely on memoirs of their sons and grandsons.

The brightest of these memoirists is Abdülhak Şinasi Hisar (1887–1963), whose *Bosphorus Civilization* is studded with long sentences of a Proustian sensibility. Hisar, who grew up in a Rumeli Hisar *yalı,* spent part of his youth in Paris and was friends with the poet Yahya Kemal (1884–1958), with whom he studied political science; in *Bosphorus Moonscapes* and *Bosphorus Yalıs* he tried to re-create

the mysterious allure of his vanishing culture "by weaving and working it with all the care and attention of an old-time miniaturist."

He wrote of their daytime rituals and their nighttime idylls, when they would gather in caïques to gaze at the silver moonlight playing on the water and savor the music wafting across the sea from a distant rowboat. I cannot pick up his *Bosphorus Moonscapes* without a distinct sorrow at never having had the chance to witness its passions and its silences at first hand, and I enjoy seeing how this

writer's intense nostalgia almost blinds him to the dark and evil undercurrents of his lost paradise. On moonlit nights, when the rowboats gathered in a still patch of sea and the musicians fell silent, even A. Ş. Hisar felt them: "When there is not a breath of wind, the

waters sometimes shudder as if from inside and take on the finish of washed silk."

On the rowboat with my mother, it seemed to me that the colors of the Bosphorus hills were not reflections of an external light. The judas and plane trees, the wings of the gulls that would flap so rapidly past us, and the half-broken walls of the boathouses—all of them glowed with a dim light that seemed to come from within. Even on the hottest days, when poor children jump from the shore road into the sea, the sun here is not in total command of the landscape. On summer evenings, when the reddening sky merges with the dark mysteries of the Bosphorus, the water foams, dragging madly after the rowboats cutting through it. But right beside the foam there is a smoother part of sea whose colors do not change so much as undulate, like Monet's pool of water lilies.

In the mid-sixties, while studying at Robert Academy, I spent a great deal of time standing in the aisle of the crowded Besiktaş–Sariyer bus, looking over to the hills on the Asian shore and watching as the Bosphorus, glimmering like a mysterious sea, changed color with the sunrise. On misty spring evenings, when not a leaf in the city is rustling, on windless, noiseless summer nights, when a

man walking alone after midnight along the Bosphorus shore can hear only the sound of his own footsteps, a moment will arrive, as he is walking around Akıntı Burnu, the point just beyond Arnavutköy, or as he reaches the lighthouse at the foot of the Aşıyan Cemetery, when he hears the happy roar of the current and notices with apprehension the gleaming white foam that seems to have come from nowhere, and he cannot help but wonder, as A. Ş. Hisar once did and as I too have done, whether the Bosphorus has a soul.

To see the cypress trees, the dark woods in the valleys, the empty and neglected *yalıs,* and the old weathered ships with their rusty hues and mysterious cargoes, to see—as only those who have spent their lives on these shores can—the poetry of the Bosphorus ships and *yalıs,* to discard historical grievances and enjoy it as fully as a child, to long to know more about this world, to understand it—this is the awkward surrender to uncertainty that a fifty-year-old writer has come to know as pleasure. Whenever I find myself talking of the beauty and the poetry of the Bosphorus and Istanbul's dark streets, a voice inside me warns against exaggeration, a tendency perhaps motivated by a wish not to acknowledge the lack of beauty in my own life. If I see my city as beautiful and bewitching, then my life must be so too. A good many writers of earlier generations fell into

this habit when writing about Istanbul: Even as they extol the city's beauty, entrancing me with their stories, I am reminded they no longer live in the place they describe, preferring the modern comforts of western cities. From these predecessors I learned that the right to heap immoderate lyrical praise on Istanbul's beauties belongs only to those who no longer live there, and not without some guilt: for the writer who talks of the city's ruins and melancholy is never unaware of the ghostly light that shines down on his life. To be caught up in the beauties of the city and the Bosphorus is to be reminded of the difference between one's own wretched life and the happy triumphs of the past.

The boat trips with my mother always ended in the same way. After we'd been caught once or twice by its dangerous currents and rocked a few times by the wakes of passing ships, the boatman would drop us at the foot of the Aşiyan road, just before the Rumeli Hisar point, where the currents come right up to the shore. My mother would then walk us around the point, the narrowest stretch of the strait, and my brother and I would play for a while by the cannons that Mehmet the Conqueror used in his siege of the city, now displayed just outside the castle walls. Looking inside these huge old cylinders, where drunks and homeless people spent the night—they were filled with feces and broken glass, crushed tin cans, and cigarette butts—we could not help but feel that our "magnificent heritage" was, at least for those who lived here now, beyond comprehension.

When we reached the Rumeli Hisar ferry station, my mother would point out a cobblestone road and a stretch of pavement now occupied by a small coffeehouse. "There used to be a wooden *yalı* here," she'd say. "When I was a little girl, your grandfather used to bring us here for the summer." This summerhouse, which I imagined as old, derelict, and spooky, is always associated in my mind with the first story I heard about it: The owner, a pasha's daughter who lived on the ground floor, had been murdered by thieves under

mysterious circumstances around the time my mother spent her summers here in the mid-thirties. Seeing how struck I was by this dark tale, my mother would direct my attention to the ruins of the vanished villa's boathouse and switch to another story; with a sad smile she would recount the time our grandfather was so displeased with our grandmother's okra stew that in a fit of temper he threw the pot out the window into the deep fast-running waters of the Bosphorus.

There was another *yalı* in Istinye, just overlooking the boatyard, where a distant relation lived and where my mother would go during her estrangements from my father; but as I remember, it too later became derelict. In my childhood, these Bosphorus villas held no allure for the nouveau riche and the slowly growing bourgeoisie. The old mansions provided little protection against the north wind and the cold of winter; perched as they were on the edge of the water, they were difficult and expensive to heat. Because the rich of the republican era were not as powerful as the Ottoman pashas, and because they felt more western sitting in their apartments in the neighborhoods surrounding Taksim, viewing the Bosphorus from a

distance, the old Ottoman families now weakened and brought low—the pashas' children who had fallen into poverty, the relatives of people like A. Ş. Hisar—could find no takers for their old Bosphorus *yalis*. And so throughout my childhood and right up to the seventies, as the city expanded, most of the *yalis* and mansions were either tied up in inheritance disputes between the pashas' grandchildren and the crazy women from the sultan's harem who lived in them or they were divided up and rented out as apartments or even single rooms; the paint would flake off, cold and humidity would blacken the wood, or parties unknown would, perhaps in the hope of building a modern apartment, burn them to the ground.

By the late 1950s, a Sunday wasn't a Sunday without my father or my uncle taking us out for a morning excursion to the Bosphorus in our 1952 Dodge. The vestiges of the vanishing Ottoman culture, however mournful, did not cripple us; we belonged, after all, to the nouveau riche of the republican era, so the last traces of A. Ş. Hisar's "Bosphorus civilization" were in fact a reassurance. We were consoled, and even proud, to see a great civilization extended. We would always go to the Çınaraltı Café in Emirgan for "paper helva" and walk along the shore, either near Emirgan or Bebek, to watch the passing ships; somewhere along the road my mother would stop the car and buy a flowerpot or two large bluefish.

As I grew older, these outings with my parents and my brother began to bore and depress me. The little family quarrels, the rivalry with my older brother that turned every game into a fight, the discontents of a "nuclear family" wandering around in a car, hoping

for a brief escape from the prison of their apartment—all this came to poison my love for the Bosphorus, though I could not bring myself to stay behind at home. In later years, when I would see other noisy, unhappy, quarrelsome families in other cars on the Bosphorus road, out on the same Sunday excursions, what impressed me most was not the commonalities in our lives but the fact that, for many Istanbul families, the Bosphorus was their only solace.

Slowly they disappeared: the *yalıs* that were burned down one by one, the old fish traps my father used to point out to me, the fruit sellers who used to go from *yalı* to *yalı* in their caïques, the beaches along the Bosphorus where my mother would take us to swim, the pleasure of swimming in the Bosphorus. The ferry stations that had stood abandoned turned into fancy restaurants; the fishermen who would pull their boats up next to the ferry stations are gone. It is no longer possible to hire their boats for little tours. But for me, one thing remains the same: the place the Bosphorus holds in our collective heart. As in my childhood, we still see it as the font of our good health, the cure of our ills, the infinite source of goodness and goodwill that sustains the city and all those who dwell in it.

Life can't be all that bad, I'd think from time to time. Whatever happens, I can always take a walk along the Bosphorus.

CHAPTER SEVEN

Melling's Bosphorus Landscapes

O f all the western artists who painted the Bosphorus, it's Melling I find the most nuanced and convincing. His book *Voyage pittoresque de Constantinople et des rives du Bosphore*—even the title is poetry to me—was published in 1819; in 1969 my uncle Şevket Rado, a poet and publisher, brought out a half-sized facsimile edition, and because my heart was then ablaze with a passion for painting, he gave us a copy as a present. I would spend hours studying every corner of those paintings, finding in them what I thought to be Ottoman Istanbul in all its unspoiled glory. I derived this

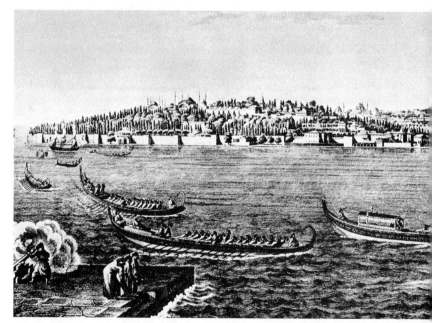

sweet illusion not from the gouaches, whose attention to detail is worthy of an architect or a mathematician, but from the engravings that were later made from them. At times when I was most desperate to believe in a glorious past—and those of us overly impressed by western art and literature do often succumb to this sort of Istanbul chauvinism—I found Melling's engravings consoling. But even as I allow myself to be transported, I am aware that part of what makes Melling's paintings so beautiful is the sad knowledge that what they depict no longer exists. Perhaps I look at these paintings precisely because they make me sad.

Born in 1763, Antoine-Ignace Melling was a true European: a German of French and Italian ancestry. After studying under his father, a sculptor in the palace of Grand Duke Karl Friedrich in Karslruhe, he went to Strasbourg to study painting, architecture, and mathematics with his uncle. At the age of nineteen, he set out for Istanbul, perhaps inspired by the Romantic Movement, which was slowly gathering momentum in Europe. He could hardly have guessed that he would remain in the city for eighteen years.

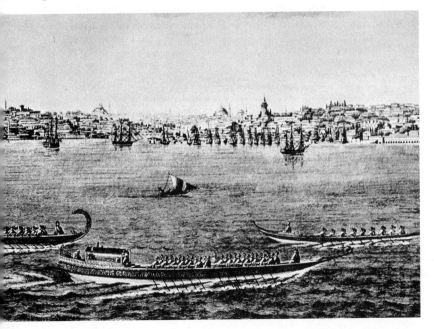

In the beginning, Melling worked as a tutor in the Pera vineyards, where a cosmopolitan society was growing up in the neighborhoods surrounding the embassies, and where we can see the first seeds of today's Beyoğlu. When Hatice Sultan, the sister of Selim III, was visiting the gardens of the Büyükdere home of Baron de Hubsch, the former Danish ambassador, she expressed her wish for a similar garden and he recommended young Melling.

The first thing Melling did for Hatice Sultan was to design a western-style maze garden with acacias and lilacs. Later he built a small ornate *köşk* for her palace in Defterdarburnu (on the European shore of the Bosphorus between two towns now known as Kuruçeşme and Ortaköy). This colonnaded neoclassical building no longer exists, so we know it only from Melling's own paintings; it did not just express a Bosphorus identity but set the standard for what the novelist Ahmet Hamdi Tanpınar (1901–1962) would later call a "hybrid style": a new Ottoman architecture that successfully combined motifs of western and traditional origin.

Melling then oversaw the construction and decoration of extensions to Beşiktaş Palace, Selim III's summer dwelling, using the same airy neoclassical style that suited the Bosphorus climate so well. At the same time, he was working for Hatice Sultan as what we

would today call an interior designer. He would buy flowerpots for her, oversee the sewing of pearls onto embroidered napkins, give Sunday tours of the palace to ambassadors' wives, and supervise the making of her mosquito nets.

We know all this from the letters the two exchanged. In these letters Melling and Hatice conducted a small intellectual experiment: One hundred and thirty years before Atatürk launched the Alphabet Revolution of 1928, they wrote Turkish using Latin characters. The Istanbul of their day was not given to memoir and novel writing, but thanks to these letters we can get a rough sense of how a sultan's daughter might speak:

> Master Melling, what day is the mosquito net coming? Please, tell me it's tomorrow. . . . Tell them to get to work at once. Let me see you soon. . . . A very strange engraving . . . the Istanbul picture is in transit, it didn't fade. . . . I don't like the chair, I don't want it. I want gilded chairs. . . . I don't want much silk, but use lots of silk thread. . . . I've looked at the picture for the silver chest, but I do hope you're not having it made like that, please use the old picture, and please, don't spoil it. . . . I'll give you the pearls and the stamp money on Martedi [Tuesday].

It is clear from these letters that Hatice Sultan had mastered not just the Latin alphabet but some Italian too. When she began her correspondence with Melling, she was not yet thirty years old. Her husband, Seyyid Ahmed Pasha, was the governor of Erzurum and so rarely in Istanbul. After news of Napoleon's Egyptian campaign reached the city, there was a great deal of anti-French sentiment in palace circles; it was around the same time that Melling married a Genoese girl, and as we can see from his plaintive letters to Hatice Sultan, he now fell mysteriously out of favor:

> Your Highness, on Saturday I, your humble servant, sent my manservant to collect my monthly salary [and] they told him it's been stopped. . . . After seeing so much kindness from Your Highness, I could not believe this order came from you. . . . This

gossip, it must be jealous gossip . . . it's because they see how much Your Highness loves her subjects. . . . Winter is coming, I am going to Beyoğlu, but how will I go? I don't have a single coin to my name. The landlord wants the rent, we need coal, wood, things for the kitchen, and my girl has smallpox, the doctor wants 50 kurus, and where will I find it? No matter how many times I plead, no matter how much I pay to travel by boat and by road, still I've not received a favorable response. . . . I entreat you, I've been left without a coin to my name. . . . Your Highness, I implore you not to abandon me.

After Hatice Sultan had failed to respond to his final entreaties, Melling prepared to return to Europe and began to think of other ways to make money. It seems to have occurred to him that he might profit from his close ties to the palace by turning the large detailed gouaches he had been painting for some time into a book of engravings. With the help of Pierre Rufin, the French chargé d'affaires in Istanbul and a renowned orientalist, he began to correspond with publishers in Paris. Although Melling returned to Paris in 1802, it would be seventeen years before the book was published (when he was fifty-six); he was able to work with the best engravers of his age, and from the very beginning there was a strong commitment to be as faithful to the original paintings as the form allowed.

When we look at the forty-eight engravings in this enormous book, what strikes us first is his precision. As we survey these landscapes from a lost world, enjoying the fine architectural detail and the skillful manipulation of perspective, our desire for versimilitude is fully satisfied. This is true even of the tableau set inside the harem—of all the engravings the most fantastical—which still partakes of a draftsman's precision as it explores the possibilities of "Gothic" perspective. Depicting the scene with a dignity and elegance far removed from the usual lurid western sexual fantasies of the harem, it has a seriousness that convinces even the Istanbul viewer. Melling balances the painting's almost academic air with the humanizing details he slips into the edges. On the ground floor of the harem, we see two women standing next to the far wall; they are

embracing lovingly, lips pressed to lips, but—unlike other western painters—Melling does not exaggerate these women or sentimentalize their intimacy by placing them at the painting's center.

In Melling's Istanbul landscapes it is almost as if there is no center. This effect, and his attention to detail, may be what draws me to the Istanbul he depicts. On a map placed at the end of his book, Melling shows where each of his forty-eight tableaux is located and

indicates the angle from which they are being viewed, thus suggesting an obsessive concern with point of view, but as with Chinese scrolls or some camerawork in Cinemascope, the point of view seems to be endlessly shifting. Because Melling never places human dramas at the center of his paintings, to see them is for me rather like driving along the Bosphorus when I was a child: one bay suddenly emerging from behind another, with every bend in the shore road bringing a view from a surprising new angle. And so it is, as I leaf through this book, that I begin to think of Istanbul as centerless and infinite and feel myself inside one of the tales I loved so much as a boy.

To look at Melling's Bosphorus views is not just to conjure up the Bosphorus as I first saw it: the slopes and valleys and hills that were then still bare, a purity almost impossible to recall for all the ugly construction that would crop up over the next forty years. As I leaf through his book, the very thought that this lost heaven has bequeathed to me even a few of the landscapes and houses I've known in my own lifetime produces a kind of rapture. Here, at the point where melancholy mixes with joy, is where I notice the little continuities discernible only to those very familiar with the Bosphorus. When the time comes to leave that lost heaven to reenter my

present life, the effect operates in the other direction too. Yes, I'll tell myself, just when you're leaving Tarabya Bay and the sea is no longer calm, suddenly the north wind ripping down from the Black Sea ruffles its surface, and on the crests of its hurried, nervous waves there are the same small, angry, impatient bubbles that Melling shows in his painting. Yes, in the evenings, the woods on the hills over Bebek recede into just this sort of darkness, and only someone like me or someone like Melling, someone who has lived here for at least ten years, would know this darkness for one that comes from within.

Cypress trees figure prominently in traditional Islamic gardens and Islamic paintings of heaven, and in Melling's paintings they serve much the same function as they do in Persian miniatures: standing sedately like so many dark stains, bringing the painting into poetic harmony. When Melling is painting the curves and curls of the Bosphorus pines, he refuses to go the way of other western artists, who exaggerated their branches to create dramatic tension or provide a frame. In this sense, Melling is like the miniaturists: Just as

he sees the trees from a distance, so too does he see his people, even at moments of heightened emotion. True, he is not very good at depicting human gestures, and, also true, his placement of boats and ships on the Bosphorus is sometimes clumsy (they look as if they're coming directly toward us). In spite of the great attention he paid to buildings and figures, he sometimes gets them childishly out of proportion, but it is in these very defects that we encounter Melling's poetry, and it is his poetic vision that makes him a painter who speaks to modern-day *İstanbullus*. When we notice that the many women in Hatice Sultan's palace and the sultan's harem have faces so similar they could be sisters, it's the naïve purity of Melling's vision that makes us smile and his affinity with the miniaturists that makes us proud.

Melling gives us a sense of the city's golden age with a fidelity to architectural, topographical, and everyday detail that other western artists, influenced by western ideas of presentation, never achieved.

In his map he indicates the point in Pera from which he painted Kızkulesi and Üsküdar—a point no more than forty paces from the study in Cihangir where I am writing these lines. When he painted Topkapı Palace, he was viewing it through the windows of a coffeehouse on the slopes of Tophane, and he painted his Istanbul skyline on the slopes of Eyüp. In these views we know and love intimately, he gives us a vision of heaven in which the Ottomans no longer think of the Bosphorus as a string of Greek fishing villages but as a place they have claimed for themselves. As architects respond to the pull of the West, they reflect a mood in which purity has been abandoned. It's because Melling gives us such precise images of a culture in transition that the Ottoman Empire before Selim III seems so very distant.

Marguerite Yourcenar once wrote of inspecting Piranesi's eighteenth-century engravings of Venice and Rome "with a magnifying glass in hand"; I like to do the same with the figures that

inhabit Melling's Istanbul landscapes. I might begin with the picture of Tophane Square and Tophane Fountain—which the artist visited frequently—subjecting it to obsessive scrutiny, down to the centimeter. I'll look at the watermelon seller on the left and observe with pleasure that today's watermelon sellers display their wares in just the same way. Thanks to Melling's attentiveness, we can see that Tophane Fountain was elevated above the street in Melling's time; today, long after the roads around it were paved with cobblestones and then covered with layer after layer of asphalt, the fountain sits in a pit. In every garden, on every street, we see mothers holding tightly to their children's hands (fifty years later, Théophile Gautier posited that Melling preferred painting women with children, find-

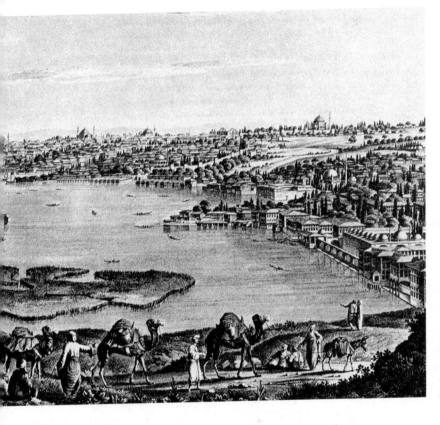

ing them less unsettling and more deserving of respect than women walking alone).

Melling's city, like ours, teems with peddlers hawking clothes and food who display their wares on three-legged tables. A youth is fishing from the old fishing station at Beşiktaş (and loving Melling as much as I do, I am not going to say that the sea at Beşiktaş is never quite so calm as he depicts it); beside this youth, only five paces away, are the two mysterious men who appear on the cover of a Turkish edition of *The White Castle;* on the hills of Kandilli is a man with a dancing bear and an assistant, shaking a tambourine; in the center of Sultanahmet Square (the Hippodrome, according to Melling), seemingly unmoved by the crowds and the monuments, in the manner of all true *İstanbullus,* there is a man walking slowly alongside his burdened donkey; sitting in the same picture, with his back to the crowd, is a man selling the sesame rolls we still call *simits,* and his three-legged table is the same as the three-legged tables some *simit* sellers still use today.

No matter how great the monument or how magnificent the view, Melling never lets them dominate his paintings. Although he loves perspective as much as Piranesi, Melling's paintings are never dramatic. (Not even when the boatmen of Tophane engage in a quarrel!) What crushes people in Piranesi's engravings is the dramatic violence of his architectural perpendiculars; these reduce his figures to freaks, beggars, cripples, and ragged grotesques. Melling's landscapes give us a sense of horizontal movement. Nothing jumps at the eye. By exploiting the endless possibilities of Istanbul's geography and architecture, he offers us a wondrous paradise and invites us to wander through it at our leisure.

By the time he left, Melling had spent half his life here, so it would be wrong to see his time in Istanbul as an education. These were the years when he found out what he was made of; it was here that he began to earn his living and, while earning his living, to produce his first works. Seeing the details and materials of Istanbul as its own inhabitants saw them, Melling was not interested in exoticizing or orientalizing his scenes in the manner of so many other celebrated painters and engravers, like William Henry Bartlett (*The Beauties of the Bosphorus,* 1835), Thomas Allom (*Constantinople and the Scenery of the Seven Churches of Asia Minor,* 1839), and Eugène Flandin (*L'Orient,* 1853), to name a few. Melling saw no need to fill his paintings with figures from *A Thousand and One Nights;* the Romantic Movement, now in full flower in the West, did not interest him at all; he never sought to add to the atmosphere by playing with light and shadow, mist and clouds, or to portray the city and its people as rounder, wavier, plumper, poorer, or more "arabesque" than they really were.

Melling's is an insider's eye. But because the *İstanbullus* of his time did not know how to paint themselves or their city—indeed, had no interest in doing so—the techniques he brought with him from the West still give these candid paintings a foreign air. Because he saw the city like an *İstanbullu* but painted it like a clear-eyed Westerner, Melling's Istanbul is not only a place graced by hills, mosques, and landmarks we can recognize, it is a place of sublime beauty.

CHAPTER EIGHT

My Mother, My Father, and Various Disappearances

My father often went to faraway places. We would not see him for months on end. Strangely, we hardly noticed his absence until he'd already been gone for some time. By then, we were already accustomed to it—rather in the way you might realize belatedly that a seldom-used bicycle has been lost or stolen or that a classmate who has not been to school for some time is not coming back. No one ever explained why our father wasn't with us, and neither did anyone tell us when to expect his return. It did not occur to us to press for information; because we lived in a big and crowded apartment building surrounded by uncles, aunts, my grandmother, cooks, and maids, it was easy to pass lightly over his absence without stopping to question it, and it was almost as easy to forget he wasn't there. Sometimes we would feel the sadness of the circumstance we'd not quite forgotten in the excessive warmth of our maid Esma Hanım's embrace, in the way my grandmother's cook, Bekir, read

too much into something we'd said, and in my Uncle Aydın's excessive bravado during a Sunday morning spin along the Bosphorus in his '52 Dodge.

Sometimes, too, I would sense, from the way my mother spent her mornings talking endlessly on the phone to my aunts, her friends, and her own mother, that something was wrong. My mother would be wearing her long cream-colored robe with the red carnations; as she sat with one leg crossed over the other, the robe would fall to the floor in a cascade of folds that caused me confusion; I could see her nightgown as well as her beautiful skin, and I could see her beautiful neck, and I'd want to climb onto her lap and nestle up to her, get closer to that beautiful triangle between her hair, her neck, and her breasts. As my mother told me herself years later, after a fierce mealtime argument with my father, I actually enjoyed the air of disaster that descended on our family and our house when she and my father quarreled.

While I waited for my mother to notice me, I would sit at her dressing table and fiddle with her perfume bottles, lipsticks, fingernail polish, colognes, rose water, and almond oils; I would rummage through the drawers and play with the assortment of tweezers, scissors, nail files, eyebrow pencils, brushes, combs, and various other sharp-pointed instruments; I'd look at the baby photographs of me and my brother that she had slid under the pane of glass atop the table. One showed me sitting in a high chair as she, dressed in the same robe, gave me a spoonful of baby food; we were both smiling the sort of smile you only saw in advertisements, and when I looked at this picture I would think what a shame it was no one could hear how happy my scream was.

When boredom loomed, I would cheer myself up with a game very similar to one I would later play in my novels. I would push the bottles and brushes toward the center of the dressing table, along with the locked silver box with the floral decorations that I had never once seen my mother open, and, bringing my own head forward so that I could see it in the central panel of the mirror triptych, I would push the two wings of the mirror inward or outward until the two side mirrors were reflecting each other and I could see thousands of Orhans shimmering in the deep, cold, glass-colored infinity. When I looked into the nearest reflections, the strangeness of the back of my head would shock me, as did my ears at first—they came to a rounded point at the back and one of them stuck out more than the other, just like my father's. Even more interesting was the back of my neck, which made me feel as if my body were a stranger I carried with me—the thought is still chilling. Caught between the three mirrors, the tens and hundreds of reflected Orhans changed every time I altered the panels' positions even slightly; although each new succession was different from all the others, I was proud to see how slavishly each link in the chain aped my every gesture. I would try out all sorts of gestures until I was sure they copied me perfectly. Sometimes I would look into the mirror's green eternity for the Orhan who was farthest away. Sometimes it seemed that a few of my faithful imitators did not move their hands or their heads at exactly the same moment as I did but rather a moment later. The most frightening time was when I was making faces—puffing up my cheeks, raising my eyebrows, sticking out my tongue, and singling out eight of the hundreds of Orhans in a corner—and then (not noticing I had moved my own hand) seeing what I thought to be another group of tiny and very distant renegades gesturing among themselves.

Losing myself inside my reflections came to be the Disappearing Game, and perhaps I played it to prepare myself for the thing I dreaded most. Although I did not know what my mother was saying on the phone, or where my father was, or when he would return, I knew for sure that one day my mother would disappear too.

And sometimes she did. But when *she* disappeared, they'd give us a reason: something like, "Your mother is ill and resting at Aunt Neriman's." I dealt with these explanations as I did with the mirror reflections: Knowing them to be illusions, I still accepted them, allowing myself to be fooled. A few days would pass before we'd be handed over to Bekir the cook or İsmail the caretaker. With them we'd take boats and buses all the way across Istanbul—to relatives on the Asian side of the city in Erenköy or to other relatives in the Bosphorus town of İstinye—to visit my mother. These were not

sad visits; they felt like adventures. Because I had my elder brother with me, I thought I could count on him to meet all dangers first. The houses and *yalis* we visited were all inhabited by near and distant relations of my mother; when these compassionate old aunts and scary hairy uncles had finished kissing us and pinching our cheeks, after they had shown us whatever strange thing in their house had attracted our attention—a German barometer that I once thought was shared by all the westernized houses of the city (a man and wife in Bavarian dress would leave and reenter their home according to the weather), or a clock with a cuckoo that would turn on its axis and retreat sharply into its cage every half hour, or a real canary warbling in response to its mechanical cousin—we would proceed to our mother's room.

Dazzled by the bright expanse of sea through the window and the beauty of the light (perhaps this is why I've always loved Matisse's south-facing window views), we would remember sadly that our mother had left us for this strange and beautiful place, but we were reassured by the familiar things we saw on her dressing table—the same tweezers and perfume bottles, the same hairbrush with its lacquered back half peeled away, and, wafting through the air, her incomparably sweet smell. I remember every detail: how she would take each of us on her lap in turn and embrace us warmly, how she would give my brother detailed instructions about what he was to say, how he was to behave, and where to find the things he was to bring her the next time we came—my mother was always fond of giving instructions. While she did all this, I'd look out the window, paying them no attention, until it was my turn to sit on her lap.

During one of my mother's disappearances, my father came back to the house one day with a nanny. She was short with very pale skin, far from beautiful, round, and always smiling. When she took charge of us she said, with an air of wisdom she seemed proud to possess, that we were to behave just as she did; unlike the nannies we'd seen in other families, she was Turkish. This disappointed us and we never warmed to her. The nannies we knew were mostly Germans with Protestant souls, and this one held no authority for us; when we fought, she'd say, "Nice and quiet, please, nice and quiet," and when we imitated her in front of my father, he laughed, and before long this nanny disappeared too.

Years later, during my father's other disappearances, when my brother and I were in a fight to the death and my mother really lost her temper, she would say something like "I'm leaving!" or "I'm going to throw myself out the window!" (once going so far as to put one of her beautiful legs over the windowsill)—all to no avail. But whenever she said, "And then your father will marry that other woman!" the candidate for new mother I'd imagine was not one of the women whose names she would sometimes blurt out in a moment of anger but that pale, round, well-meaning, and bewildered nanny.

Because these dramas all took place on the same small stage, and because (I would later imagine this was the case for all real families) we almost always talked about the same things and ate the same things, even arguments could be deadly dull (routine being the source of all happiness, its guarantee, and its death!), and so I came to welcome these sudden disappearances as a form of release from the terrible curse of boredom; like my mother's mirrors, they were fun, perplexing poisonous flowers that opened my way into another universe. Because they took me into a dark place that made me remember myself and restored me to a solitude I had tried to forget, I wasted few tears on them.

Most of the quarrels would begin over a meal. In later years, however, it became more convenient to begin the quarrel in my father's 1959 Opel, because it was harder for combatants to extract themselves from a fast-moving car than it was for them to leave the table. Sometimes, if we set out on a car journey we'd been planning for days, or if we were just out on one of our drives along the Bosphorus, a quarrel would break out within minutes of leaving the house. My brother and I would then make a bet. Would it be after the first bridge or after the first petrol station that my father would brake suddenly, make a U-turn, and (like an ill-tempered captain returning his cargo to its place of origin) drop us off at home before taking himself and his car somewhere else?

There was one row from the early years that had a deeper effect on us, perhaps owing to a certain poetic grandeur. One evening, during supper in our summer home in Heybeliada, my mother and father both left the table (I liked it when this happened, because it meant I could eat the way I wanted to and not the way my mother made me). For a while my brother and I sat staring at our plates as we listened to our mother and father shouting at each other on the top floor, and then, almost by instinct, we went upstairs to join them. (Just as, almost by instinct, I find myself opening this parenthesis, suggesting that I have no desire, none at all, to recall this incident.) When my mother saw us trying to join the scuffle, she pushed us into the next room and shut the door. The room was dark, but there was a strong light shining directly in through the Art Nouveau designs on the frosted glass of the two large French doors. My brother and I watched through the illuminated glass as our mother and father's shadows approached each other and pulled apart, moved forward again to touch each other, shouting as they blended into a single shadow. From time to time this shadow play would become so violent that the curtains (the frosted glass) would tremble—just as they did when we went to the Karagöz shadow theater—and everything was black and white.

CHAPTER NINE

Another House: Cihangir

Sometimes my parents would disappear together. So it was in the winter of 1957, when my brother was sent two floors up to live for a while with my aunt and uncle. As for me, another aunt came to Nişantaşı one evening and took me off to her home in Cihangir. She did everything she could to make sure I was not upset. The moment we were in the car (a '56 Chevrolet, very popular in Istanbul throughout the sixties), she said, "I've asked Çetin to bring you some yogurt this evening," and I remember having no interest in yogurt but much interest in the fact that they had a chauffeur. When we reached their big apartment building (my grandfather had built it, and I would later live in one of its apartments) and discovered that it had no lifts or heating and that the apartments were very small, I was badly disappointed. To make things worse, the next day as I was glumly trying to accustom myself to my new house, I had another nasty surprise: After I'd been bedded down in my pajamas like a nice pampered child for my afternoon nap, I called out to the maid of the house just as I did at home—"Emine Hanım, come and pick me up, get me dressed!"—only to get a sharp reprimand in return. This may be why, for the rest of my stay, I tried to act older than my age and put on a few airs. One evening, when I was eating supper with my aunt, my uncle Şevket Rado (the poet and publisher of the Melling facsimile edition), and my twelve-year-old cousin Mehmet, with my unnerving double in the kitsch reproduction staring down from the white frame on the wall, I happened to mention in passing that Adnan Menderes, the prime minister, was my

uncle. My comment was not received in the respectful way I had hoped; when everyone at the table began to giggle, I felt deeply wronged, because I really did believe that the prime minister was my uncle.

But I believed this only in one enciphering corner of my mind. Both my Uncle Özhan and Prime Minister Adnan had five-letter names ending in the same two letters; the prime minister had just been to the United States, where my uncle had been living for years; I saw both their pictures many times every day (the prime minister's in the papers, and my uncle's all over my grandmother's sitting room), and in some of those pictures they looked very much alike—so it is not so outlandish that the illusion took root. In later life, my awareness of this mental mechanism failed to save me from many other specious beliefs, opinions, prejudices, and aesthetic preferences. For instance, I have in all honesty believed that two people with similar names must have similar characters; that an unfamiliar word—be it Turkish or foreign—must be semantically similar to a word spelled like it; that the soul of a dimpled woman must carry something of the soul of another dimpled woman I knew before; that all fat people are the same; that all poor people belong to a fraternity about which I know nothing; that there must be a link between peas and Brazil—not just because Brazil is *Brezilya* in Turkish and the word for pea is *bezelye* but also because the Brazilian flag has, it seems, an enormous pea on it. I've seen many Americans do the same thing when they assume a link between Turkey the country and turkey the bird. My uncle and the prime minister are linked in my mind to this day; once the connection has been made, nothing can sever it, so when I think of a distant relation I once saw eating eggs with spinach at a restaurant (one of the great pleasures of childhood was running into relatives and acquaintances wherever I went in the city), a part of me is convinced that this relative is still in that same restaurant, eating spinach with eggs, half a century later.

My talent for prettifying my life with soothing illusions served me well in this house, where I was not taken seriously and did not feel I belonged. I soon embarked on some bold new experiments. Every morning, after my cousin had left for the German lycée, I would open up one of his huge, thick, handsome books (it was a Brockhaus edition, I think) and, sitting myself down at a table, I would copy out its lines. Because I knew no German, much less how to read, I did this without comprehension, drawing, as it were, the prose I saw before me. I drew an exact picture of every line and every sentence. After I had finished a word containing one of the more difficult Gothic letters (a *g* or a *k*), I would do as the Safevi miniaturists did after drawing thousands of leaves of a great plane tree one by one: I would rest my eyes by looking out through the gaps between the apartments, the empty lots, and the streets leading down to the sea, and gaze at the ships passing up and down the Bosphorus.

It was in Cihangir (where we too would move as our fortunes dwindled) that I first learned Istanbul was not an anonymous multitude of walled-in lives—a jungle of apartments where no one knew who was dead or who was celebrating what—but an archipelago of neighborhoods in which everyone knew one another. When I looked out the window, I didn't see just the Bosphorus and the ships moving slowly down the familiar channels, I also saw the gardens between the houses, old mansions that had not yet been pulled down, and children playing between their crumbling walls. As with so many houses that look out on the Bosphorus, there was, just in front of the building, a steep and winding cobblestone alley that went all the way down to the sea. On snowy evenings I would stand

with my aunt and my cousin and watch from afar with the rest of the neighborhood as noisy, happy children slid down this alley on sleds, chairs, and planks of wood.

The center of the Turkish film industry—which put out seven hundred films a year in those days and was ranked second largest in the world, after India—was in Beyoğlu, on Yeşilçam Street, only ten minutes away, and because many of the actors lived in Cihangir, the neighborhood was full of the "uncles" and tired, heavily made-up "aunties" who played the same character in every film they did. So when children recognized actors they knew only from their hackneyed film personae (for example, Vahi Öz, who always played the fat old card shark who seduced innocent young housemaids), they'd heckle them and chase them down the street. At the top of the steep alley, on rainy days, cars would skid on the wet cobblestones, and trucks had to struggle to get to the top; on sunny days, a minibus would appear from nowhere, and actors, lighting men, and "film crews" would pile out; after shooting a love scene in ten minutes

flat, they would disappear again. It was only years later, when I happened to see one of these black-and-white films on television, that I realized the true subject was not the love affair raging in the foreground but the Bosphorus glittering in the distance.

While I was looking at the Bosphorus through the gaps between the apartment buildings of Cihangir, I learned something else about neighborhood life: There must always be a center (usually a shop) where all the gossip is gathered, interpreted, and assessed. In Cihangir this center was the grocery store on the ground floor of our apartment building. The grocer was Greek (like most of the other families living in the apartments above him); if you wanted to buy anything from Ligor, you'd lower a basket from your floor and then shout down your order. Years later, when we moved into the same building, my mother, who found it unbecoming to shout down to the grocer every time she wanted bread or eggs, preferred to write her order down on paper and send it down in a basket much more stylish than those used by our neighbors. (When my aunt's naughty son opened the window, it was usually to spit onto the roof

of a car that was struggling up to the top of the alley, or throw a nail, or a firecracker he had skillfully attached to a string. Even today, whenever I am at a high window that looks out onto a street, I can't help wondering how it would feel to spit down on passersby.)

Şevket Rado, my aunt's husband, spent his early life trying and failing to be a poet; he would later become a journalist and editor, and at the time of my stay he was editing *Hayat* (Life), then Turkey's most popular weekly magazine. But at the age of five I had no interest in this or in the fact that my uncle was a friend and colleague of many of the poets and writers who would come to influence my own ideas about Istanbul. His circle of friends included Yahya Kemal, Ahmet Hamdi Tanpınar, and Kemalettin Tuğcu, the author of melodramatic Dickensian children's stories that painted a thrilling and textured picture of the street life in the city's poor neighborhoods. Rather, what excited me then were the hundreds of children's books that my uncle published and gave to me as presents after I had learned to read (*The Abridged 1001 Nights*, *The Falcon Brother* series, *The Encyclopedia of Discoveries and Inventions*).

Once a week my aunt would take me back to Nişantaşı to see my brother, who would tell me how happy he was in the Pamuk Apartments: how he'd eaten anchovies for breakfast; how they'd laughed and played together in the evenings and done all the other family things I missed so much—playing soccer with my uncle, going out to the Bosphorus on Sunday in my uncle's Dodge, listening to sports hour on the radio and to our favorite radio plays. All this he'd relate in detail, exaggerating wherever possible. Then Şevket would say, "Don't go; from now on you should stay here."

When the time came to return to Cihangir, it was very hard to leave my brother and even to say goodbye to the sad locked door of our apartment. One time I tried to fend off the moment of departure by clinging to the radiator in the hall, crying all the louder when they tried to pry off my hands; though it shamed me to do so, I hung on for a very long time—I felt like one of my comic book heroes, clinging to a lonely branch at the edge of a sheer cliff.

Was I attached to the house, perhaps? Fifty years later, I am indeed back in the same building. But it's not the rooms of a house that matter to me or the beauty of the things inside it. Then as now, home served as a center for the world in my mind—as an escape, in both the positive and negative sense of the word. Instead of learning to face my troubles squarely—awareness of my parents' quarrels, my father's bankruptcies, my family's never-ending property squabbles, our dwindling fortune—I amused myself with mental games in which I changed the focus, deceived myself, forgot what had been troubling me altogether, or wrapped myself in a mysterious haze.

We might call this confused, hazy state melancholy, or perhaps we should call it by its Turkish name, *hüzün,* which denotes a melancholy that is communal rather than private. Offering no clarity, veiling reality instead, *hüzün* brings us comfort, softening the view like the condensation on a window when a teakettle has been spouting steam on a winter's day. Steamed-up windows make me feel *hüzün,* and I still love getting up and walking over to those windows to trace words on them with my finger. As I shape words and figures on the steamy window, the *hüzün* inside me dissipates and I can relax; after I have done all my writing and drawing, I can erase it all with the back of my hand and look outside.

But the view itself can bring its own *hüzün.* It is time to come to a better understanding of this feeling that the city of Istanbul carries as its fate.

CHAPTER TEN

Hüzün

H*üzün,* the Turkish word for *melancholy,* has an Arabic root; when it appears in the Koran (as *huzn* in two verses and *hazen* in three others) it means much the same thing as the contemporary Turkish word. The Prophet Muhammad referred to the year in which he lost both his wife Hatice and his uncle, Ebu Talip, as *Senettul huzn, the year of melancholy;* this confirms that the word is meant to convey a feeling of deep spiritual loss. But if *hüzün* begins its life as a word for loss and the spiritual agony and grief attending it, my own readings indicate a small philosophical fault line developing over the next few centuries of Islamic history. With time, we see the emergence of two very different *hüzün*s, each evoking a distinct philosophical tradition.

According to the first tradition, we experience the thing called *hüzün* when we have invested too much in worldly pleasures and material gain; the implication is, "If you hadn't involved yourself so deeply in this transitory world, if you were a good and true Muslim, you wouldn't care so much about your worldly losses." The second tradition, which rises out of Sufi mysticism, offers a more positive and compassionate understanding of the word and of the place of loss and grief in life. To the Sufis, *hüzün* is the spiritual anguish we feel because we cannot be close enough to Allah, because we cannot do enough for Allah in this world. A true Sufi follower would take no interest in worldly concerns like death, let alone goods or possessions; he suffers from grief, emptiness, and inadequacy because he can never be close enough to Allah, because his apprehension of

Allah is not deep enough. Moreover, it is the absence, not the presence, of *hüzün* that causes him distress. It is the failure to experience *hüzün* that leads him to feel it; he suffers because he has not suffered enough, and it is by following this logic to its conclusion that Islamic culture has come to hold *hüzün* in high esteem. If *hüzün* has been central to Istanbul culture, poetry, and everyday life over the past two centuries, if it dominates our music, it must be at least partly because we see it as an honor. But to understand what *hüzün* has come to mean over the past century, to convey its enduring power, it is not enough to speak of the honor that Sufi tradition has brought to the word. To convey the spiritual importance of *hüzün* in the music of Istanbul over the last hundred years; to understand why *hüzün* dominates not just the mood of modern Turkish poetry but its symbolism, and why, like the great symbols of Divan poetry, it has suffered from overuse and even abuse; to understand the central importance of *hüzün* as a cultural concept conveying worldly failure, listlessness, and spiritual suffering, it is not enough to grasp the history of the word and the honor we attach to it. If I am to convey the intensity of the *hüzün* that Istanbul caused me to feel as a child, I must describe the history of the city following the destruction of the Ottoman Empire and—even more important—the way this history is reflected in the city's "beautiful" landscapes and its people. The *hüzün* of Istanbul is not just the mood evoked by its music and its poetry, it is a way of looking at life that implicates us all, not only a spiritual state but a state of mind that is ultimately as life-affirming as it is negating.

To explore the ambiguities of the word, we must return to the thinkers who see *hüzün* not as a poetic concept or a state of grace but as an illness. According to El Kindi, *hüzün* was associated not just with the loss or death of a loved one but also with other spiritual afflictions, like anger, love, rancor, and groundless fear. The philosopher-doctor Ibn Sina saw *hüzün* in the same broad terms, and this was why he suggested that the proper way of diagnosing a youth in the grip of a helpless passion was to ask the boy for the girl's name while taking his pulse. The approach outlined by these classic Islamic thinkers is similar to the one proposed in *The Anatomy of Melancholy,* Robert Burton's enigmatic but entertaining tome of the early seventeenth century. (At some 1,500 pages, it makes Ibn Sina's great work, *Fi'l Huzn,* seem like a pamphlet.) Like Ibn Sina, Burton takes an encyclopedic view of the "black pain," listing fear of death, love, defeat, evil deeds, and any number of drinks and foods as its possible causes, and his list of cures ranges just as broadly. Combining medical science with philosophy, he advises his readers to seek relief in reason, work, resignation, virtue, discipline, and fasting—another interesting instance of common ground underlying these two texts that rise out of such very different cultural traditions.

So *hüzün* stems from the same "black passion" as melancholy, whose etymology refers to a basis in humors first conceived in Aristotle's day (*melaina kole*—black bile) and gives us the coloration normally associated with this feeling and the all-occluding pain it implies. But here we come to the essential difference between the two words. Burton, who was proud to be afflicted, believed that melancholy paved the way to a happy solitude; because it strengthened his imaginative powers, it was, from time to time, to be joyfully affirmed. It did not matter if melancholy was the result of solitude or its cause; in both instances, Burton saw solitude as the heart, the very essence, of melancholy. By contrast, while El Kindi saw *hüzün* both as a mystical state (engendered by the frustration of our common aim to be at one with Allah) and as an illness, solitude was not a desirable or even admissible condition. The central preoccupation, as with all classic Islamic thinkers, was the *cemaat,* or community of believers. He judged *hüzün* by the values of the *cemaat* and suggested remedies that return us to it; essentially, he saw *hüzün* as an experience at odds with the communal purpose.

My starting point was the emotion that a child might feel while looking through a steamy window. Now we begin to understand *hüzün* not as the melancholy of a solitary person but the black mood shared by millions of people together. What I am trying to explain is the *hüzün* of an entire city: of Istanbul.

Before I try to paint this feeling that is unique to Istanbul and that binds its people together, let us remember that the primary aim

of a landscape painter is to awaken in the viewer the same feelings that the landscape evoked in the artist himself. This idea had an especially wide currency in the mid-nineteenth century among the Romantics. When Baudelaire identified the thing in the paintings of Eugène Delacroix that affected him most as their air of melancholy, he was using the word in a wholly positive way, as praise, like the Romantics and the Decadents who followed them. It was six years

after Baudelaire set down his thoughts on Delacroix (in 1846) that his friend, the author and critic Théophile Gautier, paid a visit to Istanbul. Gautier's writings on the city would later imprint themselves deeply on Istanbul writers like Yahya Kemal and Tanpınar; it is therefore worth noting that when Gautier described some of the city's views as melancholy in the extreme, he too meant it as praise.

But what I am trying to describe now is not the melancholy of Istanbul but the *hüzün* in which we see ourselves reflected, the *hüzün* we absorb with pride and share as a community. To feel this *hüzün* is to see the scenes, evoke the memories, in which the city itself becomes the very illustration, the very essence, of *hüzün*. I am speaking of the evenings when the sun sets early, of the fathers under the streetlamps in the back streets returning home carrying plastic bags. Of the old Bosphorus ferries moored to deserted stations in the middle of winter, where sleepy sailors scrub the decks, pail in hand and one eye on the black-and-white television in the distance; of the old booksellers who lurch from one financial crisis to the next and then wait shivering all day for a customer to appear; of the barbers who complain that men don't shave as much after an economic crisis; of the children who play ball between the cars on cobblestoned streets; of the covered women who stand at remote bus stops clutching plastic shopping bags and speak to no one as they wait for the bus that never arrives; of the empty boathouses of the old Bosphorus villas; of the teahouses packed to the rafters with unemployed men; of the patient pimps striding up and down the city's greatest square on summer evenings in search of one last drunken tourist; of the broken seesaws in empty parks; of ship horns booming through the fog; of the wooden buildings whose every board creaked even when they were pashas' mansions, all the more now that they have become municipal headquarters; of the women peeking through their curtains as they wait for husbands who never manage to come home in the evening; of the old men selling thin religious treatises, prayer beads, and pilgrimage oils in the courtyards of mosques; of the tens of thousands of identical apartment house entrances, their facades discolored by dirt, rust, soot, and dust; of the crowds rushing to catch ferries on winter

evenings; of the city walls, ruins since the end of the Byzantine Empire; of the markets that empty in the evenings; of the dervish lodges, the *tekkes,* that have crumbled; of the seagulls perched on rusty barges caked with moss and mussels, unflinching under the pelting rain; of the tiny ribbons of smoke rising from the single chimney of a hundred-year-old mansion on the coldest day of the year; of the crowds of men fishing from the sides of the Galata

Bridge; of the cold reading rooms of libraries; of the street photographers; of the smell of exhaled breath in the movie theaters, once glittering affairs with gilded ceilings, now porn cinemas frequented by shamefaced men; of the avenues where you never see a woman alone after sunset; of the crowds gathering around the doors of the state-controlled brothels on one of those hot blustery days when the wind is coming from the south; of the young girls who queue at the doors of establishments selling cut-rate meat; of the holy messages spelled out in lights between the minarets of mosques on holidays that are missing letters where the bulbs have burned out; of the walls covered with frayed and blackened posters; of the tired old *dolmuşes*, fifties Chevrolets that would be museum pieces in any western city but serve here as shared taxis, huffing and puffing up the city's narrow alleys and dirty thoroughfares; of the buses packed with passengers; of the mosques whose lead plates and rain gutters are forever being stolen; of the city cemeteries, which seem like gateways to a second world, and of their cypress trees; of the dim lights that you see of an evening on the boats crossing from

Kadıköy to Karaköy; of the little children in the streets who try to sell the same packet of tissues to every passerby; of the clock towers no one ever notices; of the history books in which children read about the victories of the Ottoman Empire and of the beatings these same children receive at home; of the days when everyone has to stay home so the electoral roll can be compiled or the census can be taken; of the days when a sudden curfew is announced to facilitate the search for terrorists and everyone sits at home fearfully awaiting "the officials"; of the readers' letters, squeezed into a corner of the paper and read by no one, announcing that the dome of the neighborhood mosque, having stood for some 375 years, has begun to cave in and asking why the state has not done something; of the underpasses in the most crowded intersections; of the overpasses in which every step is broken in a different way; of the girls who read Big Sister Güzin's column in *Freedom,* Turkey's most popular newspaper; of the beggars who accost you in the least likely places and those who stand in the same spot uttering the same

appeal day after day; of the powerful whiffs of urine that hit you on crowded avenues, ships, passageways, and underpasses; of the man who has been selling postcards in the same spot for the past forty years; of the reddish-orange glint in the windows of Üsküdar at sunset; of the earliest hours of the morning, when everyone is asleep except for the fishermen heading out to sea; of that corner of Gülhane Park that calls itself a zoo but houses only two goats and

three bored cats, languishing in cages; of the third-rate singers
doing their best to imitate American vocalists and Turkish pop stars
in cheap nightclubs, and of first-rate singers too; of the bored high
school students in never-ending English classes where after six
years no one has learned to say anything but "yes" and "no"; of the

immigrants waiting on the Galata docks; of the fruits and vegeta-
bles, garbage and plastic bags and wastepaper, empty sacks, boxes,
and chests strewn across abandoned street markets on a winter
evening; of beautiful covered women timidly bargaining in the
street markets; of young mothers struggling down streets with their
three children; of all the ships in the sea sounding their horns at the
same time as the city comes to a halt to salute the memory of
Atatürk at 9:05 on the morning of November tenth; of a cobblestone staircase with so much asphalt poured over it that its steps
have disappeared; of marble ruins that were for centuries glorious
street fountains but now stand dry, their faucets stolen; of the apartment buildings in the side streets where during my childhood
middle-class families—of doctors, lawyers, teachers, and their wives
and children—would sit in their apartments listening to the radio in
the evenings, and where today the same apartments are packed with
knitting and button machines and young girls working all night long

for the lowest wages in the city to meet urgent orders; of the view of the Golden Horn, looking toward Eyüp from the Galata Bridge; of the *simit* vendors on the pier who gaze at the view as they wait for customers; of everything being broken, worn out, past its prime; of

the storks flying south from the Balkans and northern and western Europe as autumn nears, gazing down over the entire city as they waft over the Bosphorus and the islands of the Sea of Marmara; of the crowds of men smoking cigarettes after the national soccer matches, which during my childhood never failed to end in abject defeat: I speak of them all.

It is by seeing *hüzün*, by paying our respects to its manifestations in the city's streets and views and people, that we at last come to sense it everywhere. On cold winter mornings, when the sun suddenly falls on the Bosphorus and that faint vapor begins to rise from the surface, the *hüzün* is so dense you can almost touch it, almost see it spread like a film over its people and its landscapes.

So there is a great metaphysical distance between *hüzün* and the melancholy of Burton's solitary individual; there is, however, an affinity between *hüzün* and another form of melancholy, described by Claude Lévi-Strauss in *Tristes Tropiques*. Lévi-Strauss's tropical

cities bear little resemblance to Istanbul, which lies on the 41st parallel and where the climate is gentler, the terrain more familiar, the
poverty not so harsh; but the fragility of people's lives in Istanbul,
the way they treat one another and the distance they feel from the
centers of the West, make Istanbul a city that newly arrived Westerners are at a loss to understand, and out of this loss they attribute
to it a "mysterious air," thus identifying *hüzün* with the *tristesse* of
Lévi-Strauss.

Tristesse is not a pain that affects a solitary individual; *hüzün* and
tristesse both suggest a communal feeling, an atmosphere and a culture shared by millions. But the words and the feelings they describe
are not identical, and if we are to pinpoint the difference it is not
enough to say that Istanbul is much richer than Delhi or São Paolo.
(If you go to the poor neighborhoods, the cities and the forms
poverty takes are in fact all too similar.) The difference lies in the
fact that in Istanbul the remains of a glorious past civilization are
everywhere visible. No matter how ill-kept, no matter how neglected or hemmed in they are by concrete monstrosities, the great
mosques and other monuments of the city, as well as the lesser
detritus of empire in every side street and corner—the little arches,
fountains, and neighborhood mosques—inflict heartache on all
who live among them.

These are nothing like the remains of great empires to be seen in
western cities, preserved like museums of history and proudly displayed. The people of Istanbul simply carry on with their lives amid
the ruins. Many western writers and travelers find this charming.
But for the city's more sensitive and attuned residents, these ruins
are reminders that the present city is so poor and confused that it
can never again dream of rising to its former heights of wealth,
power, and culture. It is no more possible to take pride in these neglected dwellings, which dirt, dust, and mud have blended into their
surroundings, than it is to rejoice in the beautiful old wooden
houses that as a child I watched burn down one by one.

While traveling through Switzerland, Dostoyevsky struggled to
understand the inordinate pride Genevans took in their city. "They
gaze at even the simplest objects, like street poles, as if they were the

most splendid and glorious things on earth," wrote the West-hating chauvinist in one letter. So proud were the Genevans of their historic city that, even when asked the simplest directions, they'd say things like "Walk straight down this street, sir, past that elegant, magnificent bronze fountain." If an Istanbul resident were to do likewise, he might find himself uttering such instructions as are found in the story *Bedia and the Beautiful Eleni* by the great writer Ahmet Rasim (1865–1932): "Go past Ibrahim Pasha's *hamam*. Walk a little farther. On your right, looking out over the ruin you've just passed [the bath], you'll see a dilapidated house." Today's *İstanbullu* would be uneasy about everything the foreigner might see in those miserable streets.

A more confident resident might prefer to use the city's grocery stores and coffeehouses as his landmarks, now common practice, as these count among the greatest treasures of modern Istanbul. But

the fastest flight from the *hüzün* of the ruins is to ignore all historical monuments and pay no attention to the names of buildings or their architectural particularities. For many Istanbul residents, poverty and ignorance have served them well to this end. History becomes a word with no meaning; they take stones from the city walls and add them to modern materials to make new buildings, or they go about restoring old buildings with concrete. But it catches up with them: By neglecting the past and severing their connection with it, the *hüzün* they feel in their mean and hollow efforts is all the greater. *Hüzün* rises out of the pain they feel for everything that has been lost, but it is also what compels them to invent new defeats and new ways to express their impoverishment.

The *tristesse* that Lévi-Strauss describes is what a Westerner might feel as he surveys those vast poverty-stricken cities of the tropics, as he contemplates the huddled masses and their wretched lives. But he does not see the city through their eyes. *Tristesse* implies a guilt-ridden Westerner who seeks to assuage his pain by refusing to let cliché and prejudice color his impressions. *Hüzün,* on the other hand, is not a feeling that belongs to the outside observer. To varying degrees, classical Ottoman music, Turkish popular music, especially the *arabesque* that became popular during the 1980s, are all expressions of this emotion, which we feel as something between physical pain and grief. And Westerners coming to the city often fail to notice it. Even Gérard de Nerval (whose own melancholy would eventually drive him to suicide) spoke of being greatly refreshed by the city's colors, its street life, its violence, and its rituals; he reported hearing women laughing in its cemeteries. Perhaps it is because he visited Istanbul before the city went into mourning, when the Ottoman Empire was still in its glory, or perhaps it was his need to escape his own melancholy that inspired him to decorate the many pages of *Voyage en Orient* with the bright eastern fantasies.

Istanbul does not carry its *hüzün* as "an illness for which there is a cure" or "an unbidden pain from which we need to be delivered": It carries its *hüzün* by choice. And so it finds its way back to the melancholy of Burton, who held that "All other pleasures are empty. / None are as sweet as melancholy"; echoing its self-denigrating wit, it dares to boast of its importance in Istanbul life. Likewise, the *hüzün* in Turkish poetry after the foundation of the Republic, as it too expresses the same grief that no one can or would wish to escape, an ache that finally saves our souls and also gives them depth. For the poet, *hüzün* is the smoky window between him and the world. The screen he projects over life is painful because life itself is painful. So it is, also, for the residents of Istanbul as they resign themselves to poverty and depression. Imbued still with the honor accorded it in Sufi literature, *hüzün* gives their resignation an air of dignity, but it also explains their choice to embrace failure, indecision, defeat, and poverty so philosophically and with such pride, suggesting that *hüzün* is not the outcome of life's worries and great losses but their principal cause. So it was for the heroes of the Turkish films of my childhood and youth, and also for many of my real-life heroes during the same period: They all gave the impression that because of this *hüzün* they'd been carrying around in their hearts since birth they could not appear desirous in the face of money, success, or the women they loved. *Hüzün* does not just paralyze the inhabitants of Istanbul; it also gives them poetic license to be paralyzed.

No such feeling operates in heroes like Balzac's Rastignac, who in his furious ambition comes to convey, even glorify, the spirit of the modern city. The *hüzün* of Istanbul suggests nothing of an individual standing against society; on the contrary, it suggests an erosion of the will to stand against the values and mores of the community and encourages us to be content with little, honoring the virtues of harmony, uniformity, humility. *Hüzün* teaches endurance in times of poverty and deprivation; it also encourages us to read life and the history of the city in reverse. It allows the people of Istanbul to think of defeat and poverty not as a historical end point but as an honorable beginning, fixed long before they were born. So the honor we derive from it can be rather misleading. But it does suggest that Istanbul does not bear its *hüzün* as an incurable illness that has spread throughout the city, as an immutable poverty to be endured like grief, or even as an awkward and perplexing failure to be viewed and judged in black and white; it bears its *hüzün* with honor.

As early as 1580, Montaigne argued that there was no honor in the emotion he called *tristesse*. (He used this word even though he knew himself to be a melancholic; years later, Flaubert, likewise diagnosed, would do the same.) Montaigne saw *tristesse* as the enemy of self-reliant rationalism and individualism. *Tristesse*, in his view, did

not deserve to be set in capital letters alongside the great virtues, Wisdom, Virtue, and Conscience; he approved of the Italian association of *tristezza* with all manner of madness and injury, the source of countless evils.

Montaigne's own sorrow was as solitary as mourning, eating away at the mind of a man who lives alone with his books. But the *hüzün* of Istanbul is something the entire city feels together and affirms as one. Just like the heroes of Tanpınar's *Peace*, the greatest novel ever written about Istanbul: Because of the *hüzün* they derive from the city's history, they are broken and condemned to defeat. It is *hüzün* which ordains that no love will end peacefully. Just as in the old black-and-white films—even in the most affecting and authentic love stories—if the setting is Istanbul, it is clear from the start that the *hüzün* the boy has carried with him since birth will lead the story into melodrama.

In these black-and-white films, as in works of "high art" like Tanpınar's *Peace,* the moment of identification is always the same. It is when the heroes have withdrawn into themselves, when they have failed to show enough determination or enterprise, submitting instead to the conditions imposed on them by history and society, that we embrace them, and at that same moment so does the whole city. No matter how picturesque, how famous the scenery in the drama unfolding on the city's black-and-white streets, it too will shimmer with *hüzün.* Sometimes, when I am changing channels on television and happen upon one of these films at some random point in the middle, a curious thought occurs to me. When I see the hero walking along the cobblestones of a poor neighborhood, gazing up at the lights in the windows of a wooden house and thinking

of his beloved, who is of course about to marry someone else, or when the hero answers a rich and powerful factory owner with humble pride and, resolving to accept life as it is, turns to gaze at a black-and-white Bosphorus, it seems to me that *hüzün* does not come from the hero's broken, painful story or from his failure to win the hand of the woman he loves; rather, it is almost as if the *hüzün* that infuses the city's sights and streets and famous views has seeped into the hero's heart to break his will. It then seems that to know the hero's story and share his melancholy I need only to look at the view. For the heroes of these popular films, as for the heroes of Tanpınar's *Peace*, there are only two ways to face the impasse: Either they go for a walk along the Bosphorus or they head off into the back streets of the city to gaze at its ruins.

The hero's only resort is the communal resort. But for those Istanbul writers and poets who are excited by western culture and wish to engage with the contemporary world, the matter is more complex still. Along with the sense of community that *hüzün* brings, they also aspire to the rationalism of Montaigne and to the emotional solitude of Thoreau. In the early years of the twentieth century, some drew upon all these influences to create an image of Istanbul that is, it must be said, still part of the city and so part of my story too. I wrote this book in constant—and sometimes fierce—dialogue with four lonely authors who (after voracious reading, long hesitant discussion, and meandering walks strewn with coincidences) gave modern Istanbul its melancholy.

CHAPTER ELEVEN

Four Lonely Melancholic Writers

I knew little of these writers as a child. The one I knew best was the great fat poet, Yahya Kemal: I'd read a few of his poems, which were famous through the country. I knew another, the popular historian Reşat Ekrem Koçu, from the history supplements in newspapers—I'd been very interested in the illustrations of Ottoman torture techniques that accompanied his articles. By the time I was ten, I knew all their names because their books were in my father's library. But they still had no influence on my developing ideas about Istanbul. When I was born, all four were in good health and living within a half-hour walk of where I lived. By the time I was ten, all but one were dead and I'd never seen any of them in person.

In later years, when I was reinventing the Istanbul of my childhood with the black-and-white pictures in my mind, elements of these writers' Istanbul blended together, and it became impossible to think about the city, even my own city, without thinking of them all. For a time, when I was thirty-five and dreaming of writing a great novel about Istanbul along the lines of *Ulysses,* I used to enjoy imagining these four writers wandering about the same streets that I wandered as a child. I knew, for example, that the fat poet often ate at Abdullah Efendi Restaurant in Beyoğlu, where during a certain period my grandmother also went to eat once a week, only to return home on each occasion with petulant complaints about the food. I liked to imagine the celebrated poet eating his midday meal as Koçu the historian, searching for material for his *Istanbul Encyclopedia,*

passed in front of the window. The historian journalist was known to have a soft spot for beautiful youths, so I would imagine a lovely young paper boy selling him a newspaper in which Tanpınar the novelist had an article. I would imagine that, at the very same moment, the white-gloved Bosphorus memoirist Abdülhak Şinasi Hisar, a slight man who seldom left home and was obsessed with cleanliness, was engaged in a quarrel with an offal dealer who had failed to wrap the livers Hisar had bought for his cat in a clean newspaper. I imagined all four of my heroes standing on the same corner at the exact same time, walking down the same alleyways in the same rainstorms, their paths occasionally crossing.

I would open up the famous insurance maps that the Croatian Pervitich did of the Beyoğlu-Taksim-Cihangir-Galata area so that I could see every street, every building that my heroes would have passed, and when my memory failed me I would dream up the details of every florist, coffeehouse, pudding shop, and *meyhane* they might have frequented. I'd conjure up the food smells in the shops; the rough talk, smoke, and alcohol fumes in the *meyhanes;* the lines of the newspapers in the coffeehouses, read and reread and crumpled, and the posters on the walls; the street vendors; the crawling letters of news headlines once visible at the top of a big apartment house (now demolished) on the edge of Taksim Square—these would be my heroes' shared points of reference. Whenever I think of these writers together, I am reminded that what gives a city its special character is not just its topography or its buildings but rather the

sum total of every chance encounter, every memory, letter, color, and image jostling in its inhabitants' crowded memories after they have been living, like me, on the same streets for fifty years. That's when I daydream that I too might have had chance encounters with these four melancholic writers at some point during my childhood.

I would have crossed paths with the novelist Tanpınar, the writer with whom I feel the closest bond, during my earlest excursions to Taksim with my mother. We often went to the French Hachette Bookstore in Tünel, and so did he. As it happened, the novelist (whose nickname was "Down at Heel") lived right across the street from this bookstore, in a little room at the Narmanlı Buildings. Just after I was born, while the Pamuk Apartments were still under construction, we lived in the Ongan Apartments in Ayazpaşa, which was just across the street from the Park Hotel, where Tanpınar's mentor and former teacher, Yahya Kemal, would spend his final years. Would the novelist Tanpınar not have been paying regular evening visits to Yahya Kemal in the Park Hotel while I was living across the street? I could also have crossed paths with them later, after we moved to Nişantaşı, because my mother often went to the Park Hotel Patisserie to buy cakes. Abdülhak Şinasi Hisar, whose Bosphorus memoirs I've mentioned, often came to Beyoğlu to shop and dine, as did the popular historian Koçu. I might have crossed paths with them too.

I am not unaware of acting like a starstruck fan who takes details from the lives and films of his favorite stars and uses them to imagine coincidences and chance encounters. But it is these four heroes, whom I will discuss from time to time in this book, whose poems, novels, stories, articles, memoirs, and encyclopedias opened my eyes to the soul of the city in which I live. For these four melancholic writers drew their strength from the tensions between the past and the present, or between what Westerners like to call East and West; they are the ones who taught me how to reconcile my love for modern art and western literature with the culture of the city in which I live.

All these writers were, at one point in their lives, dazzled by the brilliance of western (and particularly French) art and literature. The poet Yahya Kemal spent nine years in Paris, and it was from the poetry of Verlaine and Mallarmé that he drew the idea of "pure poetry" that he would adapt to his own purposes later on, when he went in search of a "nationalist" poetics. Tanpınar, who looked up to Yahya Kemal almost as a father, was an admirer of the same poets and of Valéry too. And A. Ş. Hisar, in common with Yahya Kemal and Tanpınar, held André Gide in the highest esteem. It was from Théophile Gautier, another author greatly admired by Yahya Kemal, that Tanpınar learned how to put a landscape into words.

The great and sometimes almost childish esteem in which these writers held French literature in particular and western culture in general during their youths informed their modern—western—approach to their own work. They wanted to write like Frenchmen, of this there is no doubt. But in a corner of their minds they also knew that, if they wrote exactly like Westerners, they would not be as original as the western writers they so admired. For one lesson

they'd taken from French culture and French ideas about modern literature was that great writing is original, authentic, and truthful. They were vexed by contradictions they felt between these two injunctions—to be western and yet, at the same time, to be authentic—and this unease can be heard even in their earliest works.

Something else they learned from writers like Gautier and Mallarmé, which helped them in their efforts to achieve truth and originality, was the concept of art for art's sake or "pure poetry." Other poets and novelists of their generation were reading different French authors with the same dazzlement, but the lesson they derived was not the value of authenticity but the value of work that was useful and instructive. This too was perilous, as it propelled writers either along a path into didactic literature or into the rough-and-tumble of politics. But while this latter group of writers were playing around with ideals gleaned from Hugo and Zola, writers like Yahya Kemal, Tanpınar, and Abdülhak Şinasi Hisar were asking themselves how to profit from the ideas of Verlaine, Mallarmé, and Proust. Their principal constraint in this pursuit was domestic politics—during their youths they had witnessed the fall of the Ottoman Empire, followed by the days when Turkey seemed doomed to become a colony of the West, and then came the Republic and the age of nationalism.

From the aesthetics they had acquired in France, they knew enough to realize that in Turkey they would never achieve a voice as strong and authentic as Mallarmé's or Proust's. But after long deliberation they found an important and authentic subject: the decline and fall of the great empire into which they were born. Their deep understanding of Ottoman civilization and its irreversible decline helped them avoid the traps of watered-down nostalgia, simple historic pride, or the virulent nationalism and communitarianism to which so many of their contemporaries succumbed, and it became the basis for the beginnings of a poetics of the past. The Istanbul in which they lived was a city littered with the ruins of the great fall, but it was *their* city. If they gave themselves to melancholic poems about loss and destruction, they would, they discovered, find a voice all their own.

In "The Philosophy of Composition," Edgar Allan Poe, reasoning along the same cold-blooded lines as Coleridge, wrote that his main concern while composing "The Raven" was to create a "melancholic tone." "I asked myself—of all melancholy topics, what, according to the universal understanding of mankind, is the most melancholy? Death was the obvious reply." As he went on to explain, with the practicality of an engineer, this was why he chose to place a very beautiful dead girl at the heart of the poem.

The four writers who crossed my path so many times in my imaginary childhood never consciously followed Poe's logic, but they did believe that they could find their own authentic voice only if they looked to their city's past and wrote of the melancholy it inspired. When they recalled the splendor of old Istanbul, when their eyes lit on a dead beauty lying by the wayside, when they wrote about the ruins that surrounded them, they gave the past a poetic grandeur. As it happened, this eclectic vision, which I'll call "the melancholy of the ruins," made them seem nationalist in a way that suited the oppressive state, while also saving them from the full force of the authoritarian decrees that befell their contemporaries with an equal interest in history. What allows us to enjoy Nabokov's memoirs without becoming depressed at the flawlessness of his rich aristocratic family is that he makes it clear we are listening to a writer speaking a different language, from a different age: We are always aware that this age has long since vanished, never to return. The time and memory games so suited to the Bergsonian fashions of the era could evoke the fleeting illusion that, as an aesthetic pleasure at least, the past was still alive; by applying these same techniques, our four melancholic writers conjured old Istanbul out of its ruins.

Indeed, they present this illusion as a game, a game that merges pain and death with beauty. But their starting point is that the beauties of the past are lost forever.

When Abdülhak Şinasi Hisar mourns for the thing he calls "Bosphorus civilization," he sometimes stops short and (almost as if the thought has just occurred to him) remarks that "all civilizations are as transitory as the people now in cemeteries. And just as we must die, so too must we accept that there is no return to a civilization whose time has come and gone." What unites these four writers is the poetry they made of this knowledge and the melancholy attending to it.

In the period just after the First World War, Yahya Kemal and Tanpınar went in search of an image of melancholic "Ottoman-Turkish" Istanbul. When, lacking Turkish precedents, they followed the footsteps of western travelers, wandering around the ruins of the city's poor neighborhoods, the population of Istanbul was hardly half a million. By the end of the 1950s, when I was starting school, it had roughly doubled. By 2000, it had grown to ten million. If we put the Old City, Pera, and the Bosphorus to one side, today's Istanbul is ten times bigger than the city these writers knew.

Still, the image most residents have of their city depends very much on the images these writers created. For no competing image of Istanbul has risen, not from the native-born and not from the newcomers of the past fifty years, the immigrants who live beyond the Bosphorus, the Old City, and the historic neighborhoods. You often hear people complaining that "there are ten-year-old children in those areas who've never seen the Bosphorus," and studies have shown that those living in the city's vast new suburbs don't feel themselves to be *İstanbullus*. Caught as the city is between traditional and western culture, inhabited as it is by an ultra-rich minority and an impoverished majority, overrun as it is by wave after wave of immigrants, divided as it has always been along the lines of its many ethnic groups, Istanbul is a place where, for the past 150 years, no one has been able to feel completely at home.

Our four melancholic writers have been attacked for fretting too much about the Ottomans and the past during the first four decades of the Republic when, according to these same critics, they ought to have been constructing westward-looking utopias. For this they have been branded "reactionary."

In fact, their aim was to draw inspiration from both traditions at once—the two great cultures that journalists coarsely refer to as East and West. They could share in the communal spirit of the city by embracing its melancholy, and at the same time they sought to express this communal melancholy, this *hüzün*—to bring out the poetry in their city—by seeing Istanbul through the eyes of a Westerner. To act contrary to the dictates of society and the state, to be "eastern" when asked to be "western" and "western" when they were expected to be "eastern"—these might have been instinctive gestures but they opened up a space that gave them the protective solitude they so craved.

The memoirist Abdülhak Şinasi Hisar, the poet Yahya Kemal, the novelist Ahmet Hamdi Tanpınar, and the journalist-historian Reşat Ekrem Koçu—all four melancholic writers lived and died alone, never marrying. With the exception of Yahya Kemal, they died without achieving their dreams. Not only did they leave behind unfinished books, but the books they did publish during their lifetimes never reached the readers these men had sought. As for Yahya Kemal, Istanbul's greatest and most influential poet, throughout his life he refused to publish any book at all.

CHAPTER TWELVE

My Grandmother

If anyone asked, my grandmother would say she was in favor of Atatürk's westernizing project, but in fact—and in this she was like everyone else in the city—neither the East nor the West interested her. She seldom left the house, after all. Like most people who live comfortably in a city, she had no interest in its monuments, history, or "beauties"—this despite the fact that she'd studied to be a history teacher. After becoming engaged to my grandfather, and before marrying him, she did something rather brave in Istanbul in 1917—she went out with him to a restaurant. Because they were sitting opposite each other at a table, and because they were served drinks, I like to imagine they were in a restaurant café in Pera; and when my grandfather asked her what she'd like to drink (meaning tea or lemonade), she, thinking he was offering her something stronger, answered him harshly.

"I'll have you know, sir, that I never touch alcohol."

Forty years later, if she got a bit merry on the glass of beer she allowed herself at our family dinners on New Year's Day, someone would always repeat this story, and she would let out a large embarrassed laugh. If it was an ordinary day and she was sitting in her usual chair in her sitting room, she would laugh for a while and then shed a few tears about the early death of that "exceptional" man, whom I knew only from a collection of photographs. As she cried, I would try to imagine my grandparents sauntering through the city streets, but it was hard to imagine this woman, a round, relaxed matron from a Renoir painting, as a tall thin nervous woman in a Modigliani tableau.

After my grandfather had made a large fortune and died of leukemia, my grandmother became the boss of our large family. That was the word her cook and lifelong friend Bekir used with light sarcasm, whenever he tired of her never-ending commands and

complaints: "Whatever you say, boss!" But my grandmother's authority did not extend beyond the house she patrolled with a large set of keys. When my father and my uncle lost the factory they had inherited at a very young age from my grandfather, when they entered into large construction projects and made rash investments that ended in failure, forcing her to sell off the family assets one by one, my grandmother would just shed a few more tears and then tell them to be a bit more careful next time.

She would pass her mornings in bed, under thick heavy quilts, propped up against a pile of huge down pillows. Every morning, Bekir would serve her soft-boiled eggs, olives, goat cheese, and toasted bread on a huge tray he would place carefully on a pillow he had arranged on the quilt (it would have spoiled the ambiance to put an old newspaper between the flower-embroidered pillow and the silver tray, as practicality would have dictated); my grandmother would linger over her breakfast, reading the paper and receiving her first guests of the day. (It was from her that I learned the joy of drinking sweet tea with a piece of hard goat cheese in my mouth.) My uncle, who could not go to work without first embracing his mother, paid his visit early every morning. After my aunt had sent him off to work, she too would arrive, clutching her handbag. For a short period before beginning school, when it had been decided that it was time I learned to read, I did as my brother had done; every morning I would arrive with a notebook in hand, prop myself up on my grandmother's quilt, and try to learn from her the mystery of the alphabet. As I would discover when I began school, it bored me to learn things from someone else, and when I saw a blank piece of paper, my first impulse was not to write something but to blacken the page with drawings.

Right in the middle of these reading and writing lessons, Bekir would come in and ask, using the same words, "What are we going to serve these people today?"

He treated this question with enormous gravity, as if he were charged with running the kitchen of a large hospital or army barracks. My grandmother and her cook would discuss who was coming from which apartment for lunch and supper and what they should cook for them, and then my grandmother would take out her great almanac, which was full of mysterious information and pictures of clocks; they would look for inspiration at the "menu of the day" as I watched a crow flying between the branches of the cypress tree in the back garden.

Despite his heavy workload, Bekir never lost his sense of humor and had nicknames for everyone in the household, from my grandmother to her youngest grandchild. Mine was "Crow." Years later, he told me it was because I was always watching the crows on the roof next door, and also because I was very thin. My older brother was much attached to his teddy bear and wouldn't go anywhere without it, so to Bekir he was "Nurse." One cousin who had very narrow eyes was "Japan," another who was very stubborn was "Goat." A cousin born prematurely was called "Six-month." For years, he called us by these names, his gentle mockery softened by compassion.

In my grandmother's room—as in my mother's room—there was a dressing table with a winged mirror; I would have liked to open its panels and lose myself in the reflections, but this mirror I was not allowed to touch. My grandmother, who spent half the day in bed and never made herself up, had positioned the table in such a way that she could see all the way down the long corridor, past the service entrance and the vestibule, and right across the sitting room to the windows that looked out to the street, thus allowing her to supervise everything happening in the house—the comings and goings, the conversations in corners, and the quarreling grandchildren beyond—without getting out of bed. Because the house was always so dark, the reflection of a particular maneuver was often too faint to see, so my grandmother would have to shout to ask what was going on—for example, next to the inlaid table in her sitting room—and Bekir would rush in to report who was doing what.

When she wasn't reading the paper or (from time to time) embroidering flowers on pillowcases, my grandmother spent her afternoons smoking cigarettes with other Nişantaşı ladies, mostly of her age, and playing bezique. I remember their playing poker on occasion too. Among the real poker chips, which she kept in a soft blood-red velvet pouch, were old perforated Ottoman coins with serrated edges inscribed with imperial monograms, and I liked to take these into the corner and play with them.

One of the ladies at the game table was from the sultan's harem; after the fall of the empire, when the Ottoman family—I can't bring myself to use the word *dynasty*—was forced to leave Istanbul and they closed the harem, this lady came out of it and married one of my grandfather's colleagues. My brother and I used to make fun of her overly polite way of speaking: despite her being grandmother's friend, the two would address each other as "madam," while still falling happily upon the oily crescent rolls and cheese toasts that Bekir brought them from the oven. Both were fat, but because they lived at a time and in a culture in which this was not stigmatized, they were at ease about it. If—as happened once every forty years—my fat grandmother had to go outside or was invited out, the preparations would go on for days; until the last step, when my grandmother would shout for Kamer Hanım, the janitor's wife, to come up and pull with all her strength on the strings of her corset. I would watch with my hair on end as the corseting progressed behind the screen—with much pushing and pulling and cries of "Easy, girl, easy!" I was bewitched, too, by the manicurist who would have paid her a visit some days earlier; this woman would sit there for hours with bowls of soapy water and many strange instruments assembled all around her; I would stand transfixed as she painted my revered grandmother's toenails firehouse red, and the sight of her placing cotton balls between my grandmother's plump toes evoked in me a strange combination of fascination and revulsion.

Twenty years later, when we were living in other houses in other parts of Istanbul, I would often go to visit my grandmother in the Pamuk Apartments, and if I arrived in the morning I would find her in the same bed, surrounded by the same bags, newspapers, pillows, and shadows. The smell in the room—a mixture of soap, cologne, dust, and wood—never varied either. My grandmother always kept with her a slim leather-bound notebook in which she wrote something every day. This notebook, in which she recorded bills, memories, meals, expenses, plans, and meteorological developments, had the strange and special air of a protocol book. Perhaps because she'd studied history, she liked to follow "official etiquette" on occasion, but there was always a note of sarcasm in her voice when she did; her interest in protocol and Ottoman etiquette had another result—every one of her grandsons was named after a victorious sultan. Every time I saw her, I kissed her hand; then she would give me some money, which I would shamefacedly (but also gladly) slip into my pocket, and after I had told her what my mother, father, and brother were up to, my grandmother would sometimes read me what she'd written in her notebook.

"My grandson Orhan came to visit. He's very intelligent, very sweet. He's studying architecture at university. I gave him ten liras. With God's will, one day he'll be very successful and the Pamuk family name will once again be spoken with respect, as it was when his grandfather was alive."

After reading this, she would peer at me through the glasses that made her cataracts look even more disconcerting and give me a strange mocking smile, leading me to wonder, as I tried to smile in the same way, whether she was laughing at herself or because she knew by now that life was nonsense.

CHAPTER THIRTEEN

The Joy and Monotony of School

The first thing I learned at school was that some people are idiots; the second thing I learned was that some are even worse. I was still too young to grasp that people of breeding were meant to affect innocence of this fundamental distinction, and that the same courtesy applied to any disparity that might rise out of religious, racial, sexual, class, financial, and (most recently) cultural difference. So in my innocence I would raise my hand every time the teacher asked a question, just to make it clear I knew the answer.

After some months of this, the teacher and my classmates must have been vaguely aware I was a good student, but still I felt the compulsion to raise my hand. By now the teacher seldom called on me, preferring to give other children a chance to speak too. Still, my hand shot up without my even willing it, whether or not I knew the answer. If I was putting on airs, like someone who, even in ordinary clothes, sports a gaudy piece of jewelry, it's also true that I admired my teacher and was desperate to cooperate.

Another thing I was happy to discover at school was the teacher's "authority." At home, in the crowded and disordered Pamuk Apartments, things were never clear; at our crowded table, everyone talked at the same time. Our domestic routines, our love for one another, our conversations, meals, and radio hours—these were never debated; they just happened. My father held little obvious authority at home, and he was often absent. He never scolded my brother or me, never even raised his eyebrows in disapproval. In later years, he would introduce us to his friends as "my two younger brothers," and we felt he had earned the right to say so. My mother was the only authority I recognized at home. But she was hardly a distant or alien tyrant: Her power came from my desire to be loved by her. And so I was fascinated by the power my teacher wielded over her twenty-five pupils.

Perhaps I identified my teacher with my mother, for I had an insatiable desire for her approval. "Join your arms together like this and sit down quietly," she would say, and I would press my arms against my chest and sit patiently all through the lesson. But gradually the novelty wore off; soon it was no longer exciting to have every answer or solve an arithmetic problem ahead of everyone else or earn the highest mark, and time began to flow with painful slowness or stop flowing altogether.

Turning away from the fat half-witted girl who was writing on the blackboard, who gave everyone—teachers, janitors, and her classmates—the same vapid, trusting smile, my eyes would float to the window, to the upper branches of the chestnut tree that I could just see rising up between the apartment buildings. A crow would land on a branch. Because I was viewing it from below, I could see the little cloud floating behind it; as the cloud moved it kept changing shape: first a fox's nose, then a head, then a dog. I didn't want it to stop looking like a dog, but as it continued its journey it changed into one of the four-legged silver sugar bowls from my grand-mother's always-locked display case, and I'd long to be at home. Once I'd conjured up the reassuring silence of the shadows of home, my father would step out from them, as if from a dream, and off we'd go on a family outing to the Bosphorus. Just then, a window in the apartment building opposite the school would open, and a maid would shake her duster and gaze absentmindedly at the street, which I could not see from where I was sitting. What was going on down there? I'd wonder. I'd hear a horse cart rolling over the cobblestones, and a rasping voice would cry out, *"Eskiciiiiii!,"* and the maid would watch the junk dealer make his way down the street before pulling her head back inside and shutting the window behind her. Then, right next to that window, moving as fast as the first cloud but going in the opposite direction, I'd see a second cloud. But now my attention was called back to the classroom, and seeing all the other raised hands, I would eagerly raise my hand too: Long before I had worked out from my classmates' responses what the teacher had asked us, I was foggily confident I had the answer.

It was exciting, though sometimes painful, to get to know my classmates as individuals and to find out how different they were from me. There was a sad boy who, whenever he was asked to read out loud in Turkish class, would skip every other line; the poor boy's mistake was as involuntary as the laughter it would elicit from the class. In first grade, there was a girl who kept her red hair in a pony-tail and sat next to me for a time. Although her schoolbag was a slovenly jumble of half-eaten apples, *simits,* sesame seeds, pencils, and hair bands, she always smelled of dried lavender, and that attracted me. I was also drawn to her gift for speaking so openly about the little taboos of daily life, and if I didn't see her on the weekend, I missed her, though there was another girl so tiny and delicate that I was utterly entranced by her as well. Why did that boy keep on telling lies, even knowing no one was going to believe him? How could that girl be so indiscreet about the goings-on in her house? And could this other girl be shedding real tears as she read that poem about Atatürk?

Just as I was in the habit of looking at the fronts of cars and seeing noses, so too I liked to scrutinize my classmates, looking for the creatures they resembled. The boy with the pointed nose was a fox, and the big one next to him was, as everyone said, a bear, and the one with the thick hair was a hedgehog. . . . I remember a Jewish girl named Mari telling us all about Passover; there were days when no one in her grandmother's house was allowed to touch the light switches. Another girl reported that one evening, when she was in her room, she turned around so fast she glimpsed the shadow of an angel—a fearsome story that stayed with me. There was a girl with very long legs who wore very long socks and always looked as if she was about to cry; her father was a government minister, and when he died in a plane crash from which Prime Minister Menderes emerged without a scratch, I was sure she'd been crying because she knew in advance what was going to happen. Lots of children had problems with their teeth; a few wore braces. On the top floor of the building that housed the lycée dormitory and the gymnasium, just next to the infirmary, there was rumored to be a dentist, and when teachers got angry they would often threaten to send naughty children there. For lesser infractions, pupils were made to stand in the corner between the blackboard and the door with their backs to the class, sometimes on one leg, but because we were all so curious to see how long someone could stand on one leg that the lessons suffered, this particular punishment was rare.

In his memoirs, *Falaka* and *Nights,* Ahmet Rasim wrote at length about his school days a century ago, when teachers in Ottoman schools held rods so long they could hit their pupils without even rising from their seats; our teachers encouraged us to read these books, perhaps to show us how lucky we were to have been spared the pre-Republican, pre-Atatürk era of the *falaka.* But even in wealthy Nişantaşı, in the well-endowed Işık Lycée School, the old teachers left over from the Ottoman period found in some "modern" technical innovations new tools for oppressing the weak and defenseless: Our French-made rulers, and especially the thin hard strips of mica inserted into their sides, could, in their practiced hands, be as effective as the *falaka* and the rod.

In spite of myself, I almost rejoiced whenever someone else was disciplined for being lazy, uncivilized, stupid, or insolent. I was happy to see it applied to one gregarious girl who came to school in a chauffeur-driven car; a teacher's pet, she was always standing up before us to do a croaky rendition of "Jingle Bells" in English, but this earned her no clemency when she was found guilty of doing sloppy homework. There were always a few who hadn't done their homework but pretended they had, acting as if it was somewhere in their notebook if only they could find it. They'd cry out, "I can't find it right now, teacher!" just to delay the inevitable for a few seconds, but it only added to the violence with which the teacher smacked them or pulled their ear.

When we'd moved on from the sweet and motherly women teachers of our early years to the angry old embittered men who taught us religion, music, and gymnastics in the upper grades, these rituals of humiliation became more elaborate, and there were times when the lessons were so boring that I was glad for the few minutes of entertainment the punishments provided.

There was a girl I admired from a distance, perhaps because she was tidy and attractive or perhaps because she was fragile—when she was being punished and I saw tears gather in her eyes and her face went bright red, I'd long to come to her rescue. When the fat blond boy, my tormentor at recess, got caught for talking and then got beaten for being caught, I'd watch with cold-blooded joy. There was one child who was, I'd decided, a hopeless imbecile—no matter how severe the punishment meted out to him, this boy would resist it. Some teachers seemed to call pupils to the blackboard not so much to test their knowledge as to prove their ignorance, and some of the ignorant seemed to enjoy being humiliated. Other teachers would go mad when they saw a notebook that had been covered with paper of the wrong color, still others would go for long stretches taking offense at nothing, only to hit a child for whispering. Some pupils, even when giving correct answers to simple questions, would look like rabbits caught in a car's headlights; some—and I appreciated these the most—would, if they didn't know the answer, tell the teacher anything else they knew, gormlessly hoping that this might save them.

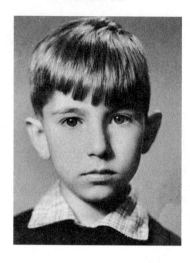

I'd watch these scenes—first a scolding, then an angry shower of books and notebooks, while the rest of the class sat in frozen silence—thankful I was not one of those hapless pupils marked for humiliation. I shared my good fortune with about a third of the class. If this had been a school for children of all backgrounds, the line that set the lucky ones apart might have been more distinct, but this was a private school and all the pupils came from wealthy families. In the playground during recess, we enjoyed a childish fellowship that made the line disappear, but whenever I watched the beating and humiliation, I, like the awesome figure seated at the teacher's desk, would ask myself why it was that some children could be so lazy, dishonorable, weak-willed, insensitive, or brainless. There were no answers to my dark moral probings in the comic books I'd begun reading; *their* evil characters were always drawn with crooked mouths. Finding nothing, either, in the shadowy depths of my own childish heart, I'd let the question fade away. I came to understand that the place they called school had no part in answering life's most profound questions; rather, its main function was to prepare us for "real life" in all its political brutality. And so, until I reached lycée, I preferred to raise my hand and remain safely on the right side of the line.

That said, the main thing I learned at school was that it was not enough to accept the facts of life without question; you had to be dazzled by their beauty too. In the first years of school, teachers would seize on any excuse to interrupt class to teach us a song. While I mouthed the words to these French and English ditties, I didn't understand them and I didn't like them, though I did like watching my classmates. (We sang them in Turkish, and the words would be something like, "Father Watchman, Father Watchman, today's a holiday, so blow your whistle.") A short plump boy who only half an hour earlier had been in tears for having once again left his notebook at home would now be singing gleefully, his mouth open as wide as could be. The girl who was always pushing her long hair behind her ears would do it less anxiously in the middle of the song. The fat brute who beat me up at playtime, and even his sly evil mentor beside him, who knew all about the secret line and made sure to keep himself on the right side of it—even they would be beaming like angels as they lost themselves in the clouds of music. In the middle of the song, the neat girl would turn to check that her pencil boxes and notebooks were still in order. The clever hard-working girl who, if I asked her to be my partner when we lined up two by two at the end of recess to return to class, would silently give me her hand—even she was singing her heart out, and the fat, stingy boy who would always wrap his arm around his paper—as if he were nursing a baby so no one could see it—had spread his arms out wide. Even the hopeless halfwit who hardly ever made it through a day without a beating joined in the singing of his own free will. When I noticed that the redheaded girl with the ponytail had noticed this too, we'd look into each other's eyes and smile as we sang. I didn't know the song, but when we got to the *la-la-la* part, I would join in, singing my loudest, and as I looked out the window, I would conjure up the future. In just a little while, the bell would ring and the whole class would erupt; I would skip outside with my bag to find our janitor waiting; I would take his huge hand, and as he walked my brother and me home, I would think that when we got there I'd be too tired even to remember everyone in this classroom, but even so my pace would quicken when I remembered I'd soon be seeing my mother.

CHAPTER FOURTEEN

Esaelp Gnittips On

From the moment I learned how to read, the imaginary world inside my head was adorned with constellations of letters. They did not convey meaning or even tell a story; they just made sounds. Every word I saw—whether the name of a company on an ashtray or a poster, a news headline, an advertisement, a sign over a shop or a restaurant or on the side of a truck—and no matter where the word was—on a piece of wrapping paper, a traffic sign, the packet of cinnamon on the supper table, the tin of oil in the kitchen, the bar of soap in the bathroom, my grandmother's cigarettes, her medicine bottles—I read them automatically. Sometimes I repeated the words out loud; it didn't matter that I had no idea what they meant. It was as if a machine had set itself up between

the visual and cognitive parts of my brain to translate letters into syllables and sounds. Like a radio in a coffeehouse so noisy that no one can hear it, my machine sometimes operated without my even being aware of it.

Walking home from school, even if I was very tired, my eyes would find words and the machine in my head would say, FOR THE SECURITY OF YOUR MONEY AND YOUR FUTURE. İETT REQUEST BUS STOP. APİKOĞLU'S REAL TURKISH SAUSAGES. PAMUK APT.

Once at home, my eyes would go to the headlines on my grand-mother's paper: DEATH OR PARTITION IN CYPRUS. FIRST BALLET SCHOOL IN TURKEY. AMERICAN NARROWLY ESCAPES LYNCHING AFTER KISSING TURKISH GIRL IN STREET. HULA HOOP BAN IN CITY STREETS.

Sometimes the letters arranged themselves in such strange ways that I was taken back to the magical days when I was first learning the alphabet. The decree on some of the cement pavements around the Governor's Mansion in Nişantaşı, three minutes away from our house, was one of them. When I was walking with my mother and my brother from Nişantaşı toward Taksim or Beyoğlu, we'd play a sort of hopscotch on the empty pavement squares between the let-ters and read them in the order we saw them:

ESAELP GNITTIPS ON

This mysterious decree would incite me to defy it and spit on the ground at once, but because the police were stationed two steps away in front of the Governor's Mansion, I'd just stare at it uneasily instead. Now I began to fear that spit would suddenly climb out of my throat and land on the ground without my even willing it. But as I knew, spitting was mostly a habit of grown-ups of the same stock as those brainless, weak-willed, insolent children who were always being punished by my teacher. Yes, we would sometimes see people spitting on the streets, or hawking up phlegm because they had no tissues, but this didn't happen often enough to merit a decree of this severity, even outside the Governor's Mansion. Later on, when I read about the Chinese spitting pots and discovered how common-place spitting was in other parts of the world, I asked myself why they'd gone to such lengths to discourage spitting in Istanbul, where it had never been popular. (Still, whenever anyone mentions the French writer Boris Vian, it's not his best work that springs to mind but a terrible book he wrote called *I Shall Spit on Your Graves*.)

Perhaps the real reason the cautions on the pavements of Nişantaşı are engraved in my memory is that the automatic reading machine had installed itself in my head at about the same time that my mother had begun, with renewed energy, to instruct us in the do's and don't's of life outside; in other words, when we were among strangers. She would advise us, for example, not to buy food from the dirty vendors on quiet streets, and never to order *köftes* in restaurants because they always used the worst, oiliest, toughest meat. Such warnings got mixed up with various announcements that my reading machine had imprinted in my head: WE KEEP ALL OUR MEAT IN THE REFRIGERATOR. Another day, my mother cautioned us yet again to keep our distance from strangers in the street. The machine in my head said UNDER EIGHTEENS NOT ADMITTED. On the backs of trams, there was a sign that said HANGING FROM THE RAILS IS DANGEROUS AND FORBIDDEN, which was exactly what my mother thought too; seeing her words in an official announcement did not confuse me, because she'd also explained that people like us would never even think of hanging on the back of a tram just

to travel for nothing. The same applied to the sign on the back of the city ferries: IT IS DANGEROUS AND FORBIDDEN TO APPROACH THE PROPELLERS. When my mother's admonitions about littering took on an official voice, an unofficial graffiti written in uneven letters about THE MOTHER OF THE LITTERER caused me some confusion. When I was told to kiss my mother's and my grandmother's hands but never anyone else's, I would remember the words on anchovy tins: PREPARED WITHOUT BEING TOUCHED BY A SINGLE HAND. DON'T PICK THE FLOWERS or DON'T TOUCH—both these signs echoed my mother's own commands instilled in the streets, and there may have been a connection between these injunctions and her prohibition against pointing. But how was I to understand signs that said DON'T DRINK WATER FROM THE POOL when I'd never seen a drop of water in said pool or DON'T WALK ON THE GRASS in parks that were nothing but mud and dirt?

To understand the "civilizing mission" that these signs embodied and that turned the city into a jungle of announcements, threats, and reproaches, we must take a look at the city's newspaper columnists and the "city correspondents" who were their forefathers.

CHAPTER FIFTEEN

Ahmet Rasim and
Other City Columnists

Early one morning in the late 1880s—not long after Abdül-hamıt II began his thirty years of Absolute Rule—a twenty-five-year-old journalist was sitting at his desk in the offices of *Happiness,* a small newspaper in Babıali, when "all of a sudden" the door flew open and a tall man in a red fez wearing "some sort of military jacket" with sleeves made from red broadcloth marched into the room. Spotting the young journalist, he shouted, "Come here!" The young journalist rose fearfully to his feet. "Put on your fez! Get moving!"

The journalist followed the man in the military jacket into the horse-drawn carriage waiting at the door, and off they went. They crossed the Galata Bridge in silence. It was only halfway through the journey that the sweet-faced young journalist found the courage to ask where they were going.

"To the sultan's chief secretary! They told me to fetch you at once!"

After he had been waiting at the palace for some time, an irate gray-bearded man beckoned the young journalist to his table. "Come here!" this man cried. He had a copy of *Happiness* open before him. Pointing at it furiously, he asked, "What is this supposed to mean?"

When the young journalist did not grasp what the problem was, the man began to shout.

"Traitor! Ingrate! We should throw your head into a mortar and pummel it into paste!"

Although cowering in fear, the journalist noticed that the offending piece was a poem by a dead poet; its refrain was "Will spring never come, will spring never come?" Hoping to explain, he said, "Sir—"

"He still won't shut up!... Go stand outside!" said the sultan's chief secretary. After he had stood trembling outside for fifteen minutes, he was ushered inside again. But every time the young man tried to open his mouth to explain that he was not the author of the poem, he met with a new tirade.

"Impertinents! Dogs! Bastards! Shameless wretches! Damn them! They'll hang!"

When the young journalist understood that he wouldn't be allowed to speak, he gathered up all his courage, took his seal out of his pocket, and placed it on the table. When the sultan's chief secretary read the name on the seal, he immediately saw there'd been a mistake.

"What is your name?"

"Ahmet Rasim."

Relating this incident forty years later in a memoir entitled "Author, Poet, Writer," Ahmet Rasim recalled that when the sultan's chief secretary realized his officer had brought him the wrong man, he changed his tune. "Why don't you sit down, my son," he said. "You don't mind my calling you that, do you?" Pulling open a drawer, he beckoned for young Ahmet to approach and, handing him five liras, he said, "Let's leave it at that. Don't mention this to anyone." With that, he sent him off.

Rasim told of this encounter with his usual exuberance and good humor, adorning his story with the everyday details that became his hallmark.

His love of life, his wit, and the joy he took in his craft—these things made Ahmet Rasim one of Istanbul's great writers. He was able to balance the postimperial melancholy that engulfed Tanpınar the novelist, Yahya Kemal the poet, and Abdülhak Şinasi Hisar the memoirist with his limitless energy, optimism, and high spirits. Like all writers who love Istanbul, he was interested in its history and wrote books about it too, but because he was careful to keep his melancholy in check, he never yearned for a "lost golden age." Rather than see Istanbul's past as a sacred treasure chest, rather than dredge history for the authentic voice that might allow him to produce a western-style masterpiece, he preferred, like most others in the city, to confine himself to the present: Istanbul was an amusing place to live, and that was all there was to it.

Like most of his readers, he had no great interest in the East-West question or the "Drive to change our civilization." For him, westernization was something that had created a slew of new poseurs with new affectations he was happy to ridicule. His own youthful literary affectations—he'd written novels and poems but failed in each endeavor—had made him both suspicious and bitingly funny about anything that hinted at artifice or pretense. When he mocked the various ways in which Istanbul poets with pretensions read their poems—imitating the Parnassians and the Decadents and going so far as to stop people in the street for impromptu performances—and also mocked the genius of his fellow literati in directing any conversation straight to the matter of their own careers, you can feel at once the distance he put between himself and the westernizing elite, most of whom were, like him, based in the publishing district of Babıali.

But it was as a newspaper columnist—or, to use the French word in currency at the time, a *feuilletoniste*—that Ahmet Rasim found his own voice. Except for the odd fit of pique and the occasional affectation it inspired, politics did not interest him; after all, state oppression and state censorship made politics a tricky and sometimes impossible subject. (He loved explaining how the censoring of his own columns was sometimes so severe that there was nothing left to publish but a blank space.) Instead, he made the city his subject. ("If political prohibitions and narrowness mean you can't find anything to talk about, talk instead about the city council and city life, because people always love to read about it!" This advice from our Istanbul columnist is more than a hundred years old.)

So it is that Ahmet Rasim spent fifty years writing about the goings-on in Istanbul, from the various species of drunks to the street vendors in the city's poor neighborhoods, from grocers to

jugglers, from the beauties of the towns along the Bosphorus to its
rowdy taverns and *meyhanes,* from daily news to trading news, from
amusement parks to meadows and public gardens, the market days
and the particular charms of each season, including, in winter, the
joys of snowball fights and sledding, as well as developments in
publishing, local gossip, and restaurant menus. He had a penchant
for lists and classification systems and a good eye for people's habits
and idiosyncrasies. The elation that a botanist might feel at the variety of plants in a forest, Rasim felt about the many and varied manifestations of the westernizing impulse, immigration, and historical
coincidence, all of which gave him something compellingly new
and strange to write about every day. He advised young writers to
"always take a notebook" when wandering around the city.

The best of the columns that Ahmet Rasim dashed off between
1895 and 1903 are collected in a volume entitled *City Correspondence.*
He never referred to himself as a city correspondent except deri-
sively; in complaining about the city council, making observations
about daily life, and taking the city's pulse, he was borrowing a practice developed in the 1860s in France. In 1867, Namık Kemal,
whose name would become one of the most important in the modern Turkish canon and who admired Victor Hugo not only for his
drama and poetry but also for his romantic combativeness, wrote a
series of letters in the newspaper *Tasvir-i Efkar* about everyday life
in Istanbul during Ramadan. His letters, or "city columns" as they
were called, set the tone for those who would follow by taking on
the confidential, intimate, complicit tone of an ordinary letter. And
so, by addressing, all *İstanbullus* as relations, friends, and lovers, they
succeeded in turning the city from a string of villages into an imagined whole.

One such journalist was Insightful Ali Efendi, so known for
being the publisher of a newspaper called *Insight* (he published the
paper under the auspices of the palace, so when the paper was shut
down for carelessly publishing a piece later deemed undesirable, he
was known for a while as Insightless Ali Efendi). He made determined and relentless forays into everyday life, as often to advise his

readers as to scold them, and though quite humorless, he is rightly remembered as one of the most meticulous Istanbul letter writers of his day, if not the wittiest.

As the first chroniclers of the city's daily life, these columnists captured Istanbul's colors, smells, and sounds in amusing anecdotes and humorous reflections, and they also helped establish the ettiquette for Istanbul's streets, parks, gardens, shops, ships, bridges, squares, and tramways. Because it was imprudent to criticize the sultan, the state, the police, the military, the religious leaders, or even the more powerful councillors, the literary elite had only one possible target for their scorn, and that was the helpless, faceless crowds, the little people who went about the streets minding their own business and struggling to make ends meet. Everything we know about those unfortunate *İstanbullus* not quite so educated as columnists and newspaper readers—what they've done in the streets for the past 130 years, what they've eaten and said, what noises they've made—we know thanks to the often irate, sometimes compassionate, ever censorious columnists who made it their business to write about them.

Forty-five years after having learned to read, I find that whenever my eyes light on a newspaper column, whether it hectors me to return to tradition or to redouble my efforts to be western, I immediately think of my mother, saying, "Don't point."

CHAPTER SIXTEEN

Don't Walk down the Street with Your Mouth Open

I now present a random sampling of some of the most amusing pieces of advice, warnings, pearls of wisdom, and invective I've culled from the hundreds of thousands of pages written by Istanbul columnists of various persuasions over the past 130 years.

Our horse-drawn buses may be inspired by the French omnibus, but because our roads are so bad, they must mince like partridges from stone to stone all the way from Beyazıt to Edirnekapı [1894].

We're tired of seeing every square in the city flooded every time it rains. Whoever is supposed to fix this, should fix it soon [1946].

First the rents and taxes went up, and then, thanks to the immigrants, the city was flooded with razor sellers, *simit* sellers, stuffed mussel sellers, tissue sellers, slipper sellers, knife-and-fork sellers, sundries sellers, toy sellers, water sellers, and soft-drink sellers, and as if that weren't enough, the pudding sellers, sweet sellers, and *döner* kebab sellers have now invaded our ferries [1949].

It has been suggested that, to beautify the city, all horse-drawn carriage drivers should wear the same outfit; how chic it would be if this idea were to become a reality [1897].

One of the achievements of martial law has been to ensure that *dolmuşes* [shared taxis] stop only at their designated stops. Just remember the anarchy of the old days [1971].

The city council was right to decide that sherbet-makers could no longer use any coloring or fruits not sanctioned by the city council [1927].

When you see a beautiful woman in the street, don't look at her hatefully as if you're about to kill her and don't exhibit excessive longing either; just give her a little smile, avert your eyes, and walk on [1974].

Taking our inspiration from an article on the proper way to walk in a city that appeared recently in the celebrated Parisian magazine *Matin,* we too should make our feelings clear to people who have yet to learn how to conduct themselves on the streets of Istanbul and tell them, "Don't walk down the street with your mouth open" [1924].

It is our hope that both drivers and passengers will make full use of the new taxi meters installed by the military authorities, and that our city will never again see the sorts of haggling, arguments, and trips to the police station that plagued our city twenty years ago, when the last taxi meters were installed and our city's drivers took to saying, "Brother, give us as much as you can" [1983].

When dried chickpea and gum sellers allow children to pay them with pieces of lead instead of money, not only does it encourage them to steal, it also encourages them to pilfer stones from all Istanbul's fountains, cut off their taps, and remove the lead from the domes of all its *türbes* [tombs] and mosques [1929].

The loudspeakers on potato, tomato, and propane gas trucks and the ugly voices of the men selling these products have turned the city into a living hell [1992].

We had a drive to remove stray dogs from our streets. If it had been conducted in a more leisurely manner—instead of a fast one- or two-day sweep—if they'd all been rounded up and sent to the terrible island of Hayırsızada, if all the packs of dogs had been dispersed, we would have cleared the city of dogs for good. . . . But now it's still impossible to walk down the street without hearing *Grrrr!* [1911].

Porters still unjustly test the endurance of their packhorses by making them carry heavy loads and beating the poor animals in the middle of the city [1875].

Our eagerness to be the first off a boat or indeed any vehicle is so great that we are unable to deter those who jump off the Haydarpaşa ferry before it's even landed, no matter how many times we shout, "The first one off is a donkey" [1910].

Simply because they give the poor a livelihood, we are seeing horse carts entering the most exceptional corners of our city and—without Istanbul's lifting a finger—ruining views to which they have no right [1956].

Now that some newspapers have begun to increase their circulation by running lotteries for the Turkish Flying Fund, we have noticed unseemly queues and crowds gathering around their offices on the days they do the draw [1928].

The Golden Horn is no longer the Golden Horn; it's become a dirty pool surrounded by factories, workshops, and slaughterhouses; chemicals from those factories, tar from those workshops, the outflows of ships, and also sewage pollute its waters [1968].

Your city correspondent has received many complaints about our city's night watchmen, who, instead of patrolling our markets and neighborhoods, prefer to spend their time dozing in coffeehouses; in many of our neighborhoods, the sound of the watchman's club is rarely heard [1879].

The celebrated French author Victor Hugo was in the habit of riding from one side of Paris to the other on the top of a horse-drawn omnibus, just to see what his fellow citizens were doing. Yesterday we did the same, and we were able to establish that a large number of Istanbul residents take little notice of what they're doing when they're walking down the street and are forever bumping into each other and throwing tickets, ice-cream wrappers, and corn husks on the ground; everywhere there are pedestrians walking in the roads and cars mounting the pavements, and—not from poverty but from laziness and ignorance—everyone in the city is very badly dressed [1952].

It is only by giving up on our old way of comporting ourselves in the streets and in the city's public places, and only by complying with traffic regulations as they do in the West, that we can hope to deliver ourselves from the traffic chaos. But if you asked how many people in this city even know what the traffic regulations are—well, that's a different matter altogether [1949].

Like all the clocks that adorn our city's public spaces, the two great clocks on either side of the bridge at Karaköy don't tell the time so much as guess it; by suggesting that a ferry still tied to the

pier has long since departed, and at other times suggesting that a
long-departed ferry is still tied to the pier, they torture the residents
of Istanbul with hope [1929].

The rainy season has come, and the umbrellas of the city, God
bless them, are out in force. But tell me, how many of us are able to
hold an open umbrella without poking people in the eye, bumping
into other umbrellas like dodgem cars at Lunapark, and wandering
all over the pavement like brainless bums just because the umbrella
has impeded our vision [1953].

What a shame it is that the sex cinemas, the crowds, the buses,
and the exhaust fumes have made it impossible to go to Beyoğlu
anymore [1981].

Whenever a contagious disease breaks out in any part of the city,
our council throws lime here and there, but piles of filth are everywhere [1910].

The city council was to have followed its crackdown on dogs and
donkeys with a drive to remove all beggars and vagrants from our
streets. Not only did it soon become clear that this was not to hap-

pen, but packs of false witnesses began to flaunt their vagrancy in gangs [1914].

Yesterday it snowed, and did anyone in the city board a tram from the front or indeed show any respect to their elders? It is with regret that we note how quickly the city forgets the polite rules of society that so few of our inhabitants knew in the first place [1927].

After I made it my business to find out how much money people have been squandering on these frivolous and insanely ostentatious fireworks displays we've seen in every corner of Istanbul every night this summer, I had to ask myself if the people celebrating at those weddings might not have been happier—bearing in mind that we are now a city of ten million people—if the money had been spent on educating the children of the poor. Am I right or wrong [1997]?

Especially in recent years, our watered-down pseudo-Frankish "modern" buildings—so heartily hated by all the most vigorous and

large-hearted Frankish artists—have been chewing like moths into
Istanbul's greatest beauty spots. Before long, places like Yüksekkaldırım and Beyoğlu will have nothing to show for themselves
but great heaps of ugly buildings. We can't explain this just by saying
we're poor and weak and suffer from fires—it's also our obsession
with urban renewal [1922].

CHAPTER SEVENTEEN

The Pleasures of Painting

Not long after I started school, I discovered a pleasure in drawing and painting. Perhaps *discover* is the wrong word; it implies that there was something, like the New World, waiting to be found. If there was a secret love of or talent for painting lurking inside me, I was not aware of it by the time I started school. It would be more accurate to say that I painted because I found it blissful. The invention of my talent came afterward; at the start there was no such thing.

Perhaps I did have talent, but that was not the point. I simply found painting made me happy. That was the important part.

One evening many years later, I asked my father how they had come to recognize my gift for art. "You did a drawing of a tree," he told me, "and then you put a crow on one of the branches. Your mother and I looked at each other. Because the crow was perched on the branch just the way a real crow would be."

Although it did not really answer the question and may not have been strictly true, I loved this story and was more than happy to believe it. Most probably my crow was not unusually accomplished for a seven-year-old boy. What is clear is that my father, always the optimist and always much too sure of himself, had a talent for believing from the bottom of his heart that anything his sons did was extraordinary. This outlook was infectious, so I too came to think of myself as unusually artistic.

The sweet praise I would enjoy when I drew a picture gave me to imagine that I'd been given a machine that compelled people to love, kiss, and adore me. So whenever I got bored, I'd turn it on and churn out a few pictures. They kept buying me paper, pencils, and pens, and I kept drawing, and when it came to showing my pictures off, my first choice was my father. He always gave me the sort of response I sought: first looking at the drawing with an amazement and admiration that never failed to take my breath away and then interpreting it. "Look how beautifully you caught the way this fisherman is standing. It's because he's in a bad mood that the sea is so dark. That must be his son standing next to him. The birds and the fish look like they're waiting too. How clever of you."

I would run right inside and draw another picture. The boy beside the fisherman was supposed to be his friend, and I'd made him a bit too small. But by then I knew how to accept praise: When I showed the picture to my mother, I'd say, "Look what I did. A fisherman and his son."

"That's lovely, darling," my mother would say. "But what about your homework?"

One day after I'd done a drawing at school, everyone crowded around me to see it. The teacher with the crooked teeth even hung it on the wall. I felt like a conjurer pulling rabbits and pigeons from my sleeves—all I had to do was draw these marvels, show them off, and rake in the praise.

By now I was becoming skilled enough to claim a talent. I paid careful attention to the simple line drawings in my schoolbooks and comic books and newspaper cartoons, noting just how they drew a house, a tree, a standing man. I did not sketch from life: I drew the pictures I had seen elsewhere and memorized. The pictures I could hold in my mind long enough to reproduce had to be simple. Oil paintings and photographs were too complicated and I had no interest in them. I liked coloring books, and going with my mother to Alaaddin's to buy new ones, but not to color them in: Rather, I'd study the pictures so I could draw them myself. And once I'd drawn a house, a tree, or a street it would stay in my mind.

I would draw a tree, a lonely tree, all by itself. I would do the branches and the leaves as quickly as I could. Then the mountains you could see between the branches. Behind them I'd draw one or two larger mountains. And then—inspired by the Japanese paintings I'd seen—I'd put a higher, even more dramatic mountain behind the first. By now my hand had a mind of its own. My clouds and birds looked just like ones I'd seen in other drawings. And when I finished off a drawing, I'd come to the best part: On the summit of the highest mountain in the background, I'd draw a snowcap.

Gazing proudly at my creation, I would move my head from right to left, peering closely at some detail before standing back to take it all in. Yes, here was a thing of beauty and I had made it. No, it wasn't perfect, but still, I'd drawn it and it was beautiful. It had been a pleasure to create it, and now it was a pleasure to stand back from it and pretend I was someone else, admiring my picture through the window.

But sometimes, looking at my drawing through someone else's eyes, I'd notice a defect. Or else I'd be seized with a desire to prolong the joy I'd felt while drawing it. The fastest way of doing this was to add another cloud, a few more birds, a leaf.

In later years, there were times when I thought I'd ruined my drawings with these further touches. But there is no denying they could return me to the initial euphoria of creation, so I couldn't stop myself.

What sort of pleasure did I take in drawing? Here your fifty-year-old memoirist must put a little distance between himself and the child he once was:

1. I took pleasure in drawing because it allowed me to create instant miracles that everyone around me appreciated. Even before I was done, I was looking forward to the praise and love my drawing would elicit. As this expectation deepened, it became part of the act of creation and part of its joy.
2. After a time, my hand had become as skilled as my eyes. So if I was drawing a very fine tree, it felt as if my hand were moving without my directing it. As I watched the pencil race across the page, I would look on in amazement, as if the drawing were the proof of another presence, as if someone else had taken up residence in my body. As I marveled at his work, aspiring to become his equal, another part of my brain was busy inspecting the

curves of the branches, the placement of the mountains, the composition as a whole, reflecting that I had created this scene on a blank piece of paper. My mind was at the tip of my pen, acting before I could think; at the same time it could survey what I had already done. This second line of perception, this ability to analyze my progress, was the pleasure this small artist felt when he looked at the discovery of his courage and his freedom. To step outside myself, to know the second person who had taken up residence inside me, was to retrace the dividing line that appeared as my pencil slipped across the paper, like a boy sledding in the snow.

3. This division between my mind and my hand, the sense that my hand was acting of its own accord, had something in common with the sensation of escaping into my dreamworld when my head stood still. But—unlike the chimeras of my strange dreamworld—I made no effort to hide my drawings. Instead, I showed them to everyone, anticipating praise and taking pleasure in it. To draw was to find a second world whose existence was not cause for embarrassment.

4. The things I drew, no matter how imaginary the house, the tree, the cloud, had a basis in material reality. If I drew a house, I felt as if it were my house. I felt I owned everything I drew. To explore this world, to live inside the trees and scenes I drew, to depict a world so real I could show other people, was an escape from the boredom of the present moment.

5. I loved the smell and the look of paper, pencils, sketchbooks, paints, and other art materials. I loved to caress the blank drawing paper. I liked keeping my drawings, I liked their *thingness,* their material presence.

6. By discovering all these little pleasures, I dared, with the help of all the praise I garnered, to believe myself different, even special. I didn't like bragging, but I did want it known. The world I created through drawing, like the second world I hid in my head, enriched my life; even better, it gave me a legitimate escape from the dusty, shadowy world of everyday life. Not only did my family accept this new habit of mine, they accepted my right to it.

CHAPTER EIGHTEEN

Reşat Ekrem Koçu's Collection of Facts and Curiosities: The *Istanbul Encyclopedia*

In my grandmother's sitting room there was a bookcase; behind its bolted, rarely opened glass doors, gathering dust with the *Life Encyclopedia,* a row of yellowing girls' novels, and my American uncle's medical books, was a book as long and as wide as a newspaper that I discovered not long after I learned to read. Its title was *From Osman Gazi to Atatürk: A Panorama of Six Hundred Years of Ottoman History,* and I loved both its choice of subjects and its abundant and mysterious illustrations. In the days when our apartment was on the same floor as the laundry, or whenever I was too ill to go to school, or if I happened to be skipping school for no good reason, I'd go up to my grandmother's apartment, sit down at my uncle's writing table, and read. I read every line of this book many times over; in later years, when we were living in rented apartments, I'd take it out to read whenever I went to visit my grandmother.

I especially enjoyed the hand-drawn black-and-white pictures portraying Ottoman history: In my school textbooks this history was a long string of wars, victories, defeats, and treaties, a story narrated in a proud nationalist tone, but in *From Osman Gazi to Atatürk* it was a series of curiosities, strange events, and stranger people: a shocking, hair-raising, terrifying, sometimes even revolting picture gallery. In this sense the book was like one of those processions in

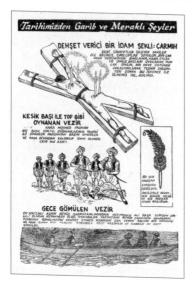

an Ottoman Book of Ceremonies, in which the guilds would march past the sultan, performing a sequence of strange acts. It was like entering one of the miniatures that illustrated these secret books and sitting next to the sultan as he looked out over Sultanahmet Square from the windows of what is now known as Ibrahim Pasha Palace, to survey the empire's riches, colors, and spectacles, its many and varied artisans, each in the clothes of his trade. We like to tell ourselves that, after the Republic was founded and Turkey became a western nation, we severed our Ottoman roots and became a "more logical and scientific" people. Perhaps this is why it was so thrilling to sit at a modern window gazing at the oddities, foreignness, and sudden humanity of the Ottoman ancestors we were meant to have left behind.

So it was that I came to read about the acrobat who crossed the Golden Horn on a tightrope drawn between the masts of two ships to celebrate the circumcision of Sultan Ahmet III's son, Prince Mustafa, and studied the black-and-white illustration of this feat. And so I discovered that because "our fathers" thought it unseemly to bury ordinary people in the same cemetery as men who killed people for a living, a special cemetery was created just for executioners in Karyağdi Bayırı in Eyüp. I read that in the time of Osman II, in 1621, there was a winter so harsh that all the Golden Horn and part of the Bosphorus froze over; as with so many illustrations in this book, it never occurred to me that the picture showing boats attached to sleds and ships caught in the ice might reflect the power of the artist's imagination more than historical reality; I never tired of looking at them. Also entrancing were the illustrations of two famous mad people of Istanbul from the time of Abdülhamıt II. The first, a man, was in the habit of walking the streets naked, though the genteel artist depicted him covering himself in shame; and the other was a woman named Madame Upola who wore whatever she could find. According to the author, whenever the madman and the madwoman ran into each other they'd launch into violent combat, on account of which they were forbidden to cross the bridge. (*The* bridge: In those days there weren't any bridges over the Bosphorus and there was only one over the Golden Horn, the Galata Bridge; built between Karaköy and Eminönü in 1845, it would be rebuilt three times by the end of the twentieth century, but the original, made of wood, was simply called "the bridge.") Just then my eyes would light on a picture of a man with a basket on his back, bound by rope to a tree, and I'd read on to find out that a hundred years ago, after an itinerant bread seller tied his horse and wares to a tree so he could play cards in the coffeehouse, a city official named Hüseyin Bey tied the bread seller himself to the tree to punish him for tormenting an innocent animal.

How true were these stories, so many of which are attributed to "contemporary newspapers"? We are told, for example, that in the fifteenth century, Kara Mehmet Pasha lost his head trying to put down a rebellion, and perhaps it is true that the sight of his severed head persuaded his men to end the rebellion, and perhaps, like many who find themselves in such situations, they expressed their anger at the vizier by throwing his head around. But did the men really do as they did in the illustration and play soccer with the pasha's head? I never dwelt long on such questions, preferring to move on to Ester Kira, the sixteenth-century "tax collector" who was said also to be Safiye Sultan's bribe collector; killed during another rebellion, she was cut into pieces and a bit of her was nailed to the doors of each of those who had bribed her. I examined the drawing of a hand nailed to a door with some trepidation.

Koçu—one of the four melancholic writers I described earlier—gave his greatest attention to the strange and terrifying details of another subject that also thrilled the travelers from the West: the methods of Istanbul's torturers and executioners. One place in Eminönü was especially constructed for what was known as the Hook. Wearing nothing but the suit in which he emerged from his mother's womb, the condemned was winched up with pulleys, skewered with the sharp hook, and, as the cord was released, left to drop.

There was also a Janissary, who, having fallen in love with an imam's wife, kidnapped her, chopped off all her hair, and took her around the city dressed as a boy; when he was caught they broke his arms and legs, stuffed him into the barrel of a cannon stoked with oily rags and gunpowder, and blew him into the sky.

A FORM OF EXECUTION GUARANTEED TO CAUSE TERROR! is how the encylopedia heading described another gruesome punishment. It involved tying the condemned, naked and facedown, to a cross and, by the light of the candles that had been bored into his shoulders and buttocks, parading him around the city as a lesson to all. My reaction to the naked criminal was not without a sexual frisson, and there was some pleasure in thinking of the history of Istanbul as a gallery of death, torture, and horror, illustrated in shadowy black and white.

In the beginning, Reşat Ekrem Koçu wasn't planning to write a book. It was only in 1954 that the four-page *Cumhuriyet* supplements containing "Strange and Curious Facts from Our History" were bound together in a collection. Behind these strange stories, oddities, and historical and encyclopedic minutiae was Koçu's own strange and tragic story. His labor of love—which he'd begun ten years earlier, in 1944, and which poverty had forced him to abandon in 1951 on page 1000, in volume 4, while still on the letter *B*—was the *Istanbul Encyclopedia.*

Seven years later, Koçu began work on a second *Istanbul Encyclopedia,* which he rightly and proudly claimed to be "the world's first encyclopedia about a single city," starting again with the letter A. Being now fifty-two years old, he was afraid of leaving his monumental labor unfinished yet again, so he resolved to scale it down to a mere fifteen volumes and also to make the entries more "popular."

Also, now more self-confident, he saw no reason why he shouldn't explore his personal interests in his encyclopedia. He brought out the first volume in 1958; by 1973 he was on the eleventh—but still only on the letter G—when he was forced, as he had feared, to abandon the effort. Nevertheless, this second *Encyclopedia*'s strange and colorful entries about twentieth-century Istanbul are an unrivaled guide to the city's soul, for the texture of the prose is the texture of the city itself. To understand why this is so, one must have a sense of Reşat Ekrem Koçu himself.

Koçu was one of those *hüzün*-drenched souls who helped create an image of a twentieth-century Istanbul as a half-finished city afflicted with melancholy. *Hüzün* defines his life, gives his work its hidden logic, and sets him on the lonely course that can only be his final defeat, but—as with other writers working in a similar vein— he did see it as central and certainly did not give it much thought.

Indeed, Reşat Ekrem Koçu, far from seeing his melancholy as proceeding from his history, his family, or his city, regarded his *hüzün* as innate. As for the attendant withdrawal from life and the conviction that life entailed accepting defeat from the start—he did not think of these as Istanbul's legacy. On the contrary, Istanbul was his consolation.

Reşat Ekrem Koçu was born in 1905 to a family of teachers and civil servants. His mother was the daughter of a pasha; his father had long worked as a journalist. All through his childhood, Koçu witnessed the wars, defeats, and waves of immigration that ended the Ottoman Empire and condemned Istanbul to a poverty from which it would not emerge for decades. He would return to these subjects often in his later books and articles, just as he would return to the city's last great fires, the firemen, the street fights, the neighborhood life, and the *meyhanes* he saw in his youth. He mentions a Bosphorus *yalı* in which he lived as a child and which later burned down. When Reşat Ekrem was twenty years old, his father rented an old Ottoman villa in Göztepe. Here Koçu the younger lived the traditional life of the Istanbul wooden *köşk,* remaining long enough to see his extended family dispersed. As with so many families of this sort, gradual impoverishment and family feuds forced Koçu's family to sell the wooden *köşk,* after which Koçu remained in Göztepe, though separated from his family and living in various concrete apartments. Perhaps no choice more clearly manifests Koçu's melancholy backward-looking soul than his decision—at a time when the empire had fallen, the ideology of the Turkish Republic was ascendant, and westward-looking Istanbul had begun to reject, suppress, deride, and suspect anything to do with its Ottoman past—to study history in Istanbul and, after graduating, to become an assistant to his beloved teacher, the historian Ahmet Refik.

Born in 1880 and twenty-five years Koçu's senior, Ahmet Refik was the author of a series entitled *Ottoman Life in Past Centuries;* it was published (as Koçu's encyclopedia would be) fascicle by fascicle, slowly gaining in popularity and finally making him Istanbul's first modern popular historian. When he was not teaching at the university, he was combing through the dust and dirt of the disordered Ottoman archives (then known as the "paper treasury") for handwritten accounts of Ottoman chroniclers; he scavenged whatever he could, and because—like Koçu—he had a knack for lively prose (he loved lyrics and wrote poetry in his spare time), his newspaper articles were widely read and later collected into books. To combine history with literature, to take the strange riches from the archives and turn them into newspaper and magazine articles, to be forever roaming from bookshop to bookshop, to make history something that could be ingested with ease, and to spend long evenings with friends in *meyhanes,* drinking and conversing—these were some of the passions Koçu inherited from his mentor. Sadly, their association was short-lived, for Ahmet Refik was removed from his university post in 1933 during the Istanbul University (Darülfünun) reforms. His sympathies had been known to lie with the Freedom and Entente Party, which had opposed Atatürk, but it was more his passionate interest in Ottoman history and culture that cost him his eminent post (my maternal grandfather was likewise dismissed from the law faculty during the same period). When his mentor lost his job, so too did Reşat Ekrem Koçu.

Koçu was distressed to witness his mentor's decline after his fall from favor with Atatürk and the state. Penniless, anonymous, and ignored, he had to sell off his library bit by bit to pay for medicines, and after struggling for five years he died in poverty. At the time, most of the ninety books he had written during his lifetime were out of print. (The same would be true for Koçu forty years later.)

After Ahmet Refik's death, in an article mourning the fact that his mentor had seen himself forgotten in his own lifetime, Koçu gave himself over to a childish lyricism: "In my idle childhood years, I was like the lead on a fisherman's hook, slipping in and out of the water from the pier opposite our Bosphorus *yalı* like a scaly fish."

He recalled first reading Ahmet Refik as a happy eleven-year-old, before the city made him as melancholy as Ottoman history. But it was not just the libertine poverty-stricken city that fed Reşat Ekrem Koçu's gloom; it was his own struggle to survive in the city as a homosexual in the first half of the twentieth century.

So it is all the more remarkable to see him expressing his sexual desires in his racy, violent popular novels and, even more daringly, in his *Istanbul Encyclopedia*. Indeed, Reşat Ekrem Koçu was far more courageous in this regard than any contemporary. From his first encyclopedic fascicles, and more emphatically with every new volume, he never missed an opportunity to praise the beauty of boys and young men. Here is Mirialem Ahmed Ağa, one of the boys taken in for education by Süleyman the Magnificent ("a fresh-faced youth, a human dragon with arms as thick as the branches of a plane tree") and Cafer the Barber, mentioned by the sixteenth-century poet Evliya Çelebi, who praised the beauty of tradesmen in "Şehringiz" ("a young blood famous for his beauty"). There is an entry on "Yetim Ahmed, the handsome junk dealer": "He was a barefoot boy whose baggy trousers had been patched in forty places and whose skin could be seen through the rips in his shirt, but to judge him by his appearance, he was a sip of water, the beauty stood on his brow and his forehead like a sultan's privilege, his hair was a riot of curls, his dark skin glinted with gold overtones, his gaze coy, his tongue flirtatious, his build tall, slender, and strong." Despite Koçu's breathless prose, he, like the Divan poets, took care that his loyal illustrators drew each of these imaginary barefoot heroes within the conventions of polite society and the law. But the tension between convention and reality is there all the same. In an entry titled "Janissary recruit," he boasts of how, when beardless youths first joined up, "swaggering Janissary toughs" would take them

under their wing. In an entry called "handsome young blade," he observes that "the beauty of which Divan Poetry most often sings is male beauty." The object of adoration was "always a young fresh-faced youth"—and he lovingly recounts the etymology of this term. In the early volumes, beautiful youths are carefully insinuated among the historic, cultural, and social facts they illustrate, but in later volumes Koçu needs no pretext for praising beautiful boys—for their beautiful legs—or commenting on their disfigurement. Under "Sailor Dobrilovitch" we read of a "remarkably handsome" young Croat, a sailor with the Hayriye Company, whose legs on December 18, 1864, as his ship was approaching Kabataş, got caught between the ship and the pier (a deep fear shared by everyone in the city). His leg, along with the boot he was wearing, dropped into the sea; all the Croat said was, "I've lost my boot."

In the first volumes, his beautiful youths, young boys, and handsome barefoot men from the Ottoman past were, if not wholly real, at least partly inspired by the "city books" (*şehringiz*), popular legends, and the treasures he found in the city's forgotten libraries; these included manuscripts, collected poems, books of fortune, "secret" books, and, especially rich in possibility, the nineteenth-century newspaper archives (indeed, it was in one of these he discovered the handsome young Croat sailor).

As Koçu grew older and came to realize with sadness and fury that he would be unable to limit his encyclopedia to fifteen volumes and that it was doomed to remain unfinished, he no longer felt obliged to confine himself to the beautiful boys of recorded history. He began to find excuses to insinuate entries on the many and varied youths he had, under various pretexts, met in the streets, *meyhanes,* coffeehouses, *gazinos* (open-air cafés), and bridges of the city, not to mention the newspaper boys, in each of whom he had a special interest, and even the spruce beauties who sold rosettes for the Turkish Flying Fund. So for example, in the encyclopedia's tenth year, in the ninth volume, published when Koçu was sixty-three years old, he includes on page 4767 an entry on "a skilled child acrobat between the ages of 14 and 15 encountered between 1955 and 1956." Koçu recalls seeing him one evening at And, a summer cinema in Göztepe, the neighborhood where he spent most of his life: "Wearing white shoes, white trousers, a flannel undershirt with a star and crescent on its front, and when displaying his skills, stripped down to tiny white shorts, with his clean and darling face, his gentlemanly air, manner, and politeness, he showed himself at once to be on an equal footing with his western peers." The author goes on to describe how, when the program was over, though he was saddened to see the boy doing the rounds with a collection tray, he was happy to see that the child was not too grasping or ingratiating. Koçu goes on to recount that the boy acrobat gave some in the audience his card, and that the fifty-year-old author and this boy later became acquainted. Despite the author's having written many letters to the child and his family, relations between the two were broken off sometime during the twelve years between their first meeting at the cinema and the writing of the encyclopedia entry; he goes on to lament never having received answers to his letters and is unable to say what became of the child.

During the 1960s, when Koçu's work was still coming out fascicle by fascicle, his patient readers did not regard the *Istanbul Encyclopedia* as a single factual reference to the city but read it more as a

magazine that mixed the strange and exotic with everyday life in the city. I remember visiting houses where people kept the fascicles with their weekly magazines. Still, Koçu was hardly a household name. The city of his melancholy encyclopedia was at odds with the mores of 1960s Istanbul, and there weren't many readers who could tolerate, let alone appreciate, his sexual tastes. But fifty years on, his first

Istanbul Encyclopedia and the first volumes of his second have a loyal following, particularly among writers and academics who, eager to understand Istanbul's rapid westernization and the burning, demolition, and erasure of its past, have pronounced the earlier volumes "serious" and "scientific." For my part, it is when I leaf through the later volumes, produced by a much reduced team of writers and giving ample space to Koçu's personal obsessions, that my mind takes flight, flitting happily between the present and the past.

I'm left feeling that Koçu's sadness is less the result of the fall of the Ottoman Empire and the decline of Istanbul than of his own shadowy childhood in those *yalıs* and *köşks*. We might see our encyclopedist as a typical collector who, after a personal trauma, withdrew from the world to live among objects. But Koçu lacked the materialism of a classic collector; his interest was not in objects but strange facts. Just as so many western collectors have no idea whether their collections will end up in a museum or dispersed, he had no grand plan when the compulsion first overtook him; he began collecting out of an attraction to any fact that told him something new about the city.

It was only after he realized that his collection might have no bounds that he hit on the idea of an encyclopedia, and from then on he remained aware of the "thingness" of his collection. When Professor Semavi Eyice, the historian of Byzantine and Ottoman art who'd known Koçu since 1944 and had written entries for the encyclopedia since its inception, wrote about Koçu after his death, he described his large library piled high with "material" he kept in envelopes—newspaper clippings, collections of pictures and photographs, dossiers, and notes (now lost) compiled from his long years of reading the nineteenth-century newspapers.

When Koçu realized he would not live to finish the encyclopedia, he told Semavi Eyice that he was going to take his entire collection, a lifetime of scavenging, and burn it in his garden. Only a true collector would consider such a gesture, which calls to mind the novelist Bruce Chatwin, who for part of his life worked at Sotheby's and whose hero, Utz, destroys his own porcelain collection in a moment of rage. Koçu did not, in the end, let anger get the better of him, but if he had, it would have made little difference; production of the *Istanbul Encyclopedia* steadily slowed and stopped altogether in 1973. Two years earlier, his rich partner had criticized him for cluttering the work with long and unnecessary passages following his own predilections; Koçu had quarreled with him and then removed his entire collection—typescripts, newspaper clippings, and photographs—from his Babıali office to his apartment in Göztepe. Unable to synthesize the sad story of the past into a text or to enshrine it in a museum, Koçu spent his last years in an apartment piled high with mountains of paper. After his sister died, the wooden *köşk* his father had built was sold, but Koçu did not leave

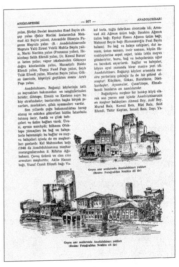

his old neighborhood. Koçu met Mehmet, the companion of his final years, just as he had met so many of the children he described in his encyclopedia; Mehmet was a homeless boy whom he took under his wing and brought up like a son; in later life, Mehmet founded a publishing house.

Forty or so "friends"—most of them historians like Semavi Eyice or literary figures—contributed to the *Istanbul Encyclopedia* for thirty years without ever receiving a single payment. Some, like Sermet Muhtar Alus (who wrote memoirs and humorous novels of nineteenth-century Istanbul—its characters, its mansions, and the mischief perpetrated by its pashas) and Osman Nuri Ergin (who wrote a detailed municipal history and published a famous guide to the city in 1934), belonged to an older generation that was dying off as Koçu's first volumes were coming out. As for those from the younger generation, in time they would distance themselves from Koçu "because of his caprices" (as Eyice put it). And so the rituals of the endeavor—the long conversations in the office and the longer evenings in a neighboring *meyhane*—became less frequent.

Between 1950 and 1970, Koçu liked to begin his evenings in conversation with friends at the encyclopedia offices, retiring later to a *meyhane* in Sirkeci. There were never any women with them: This celebrated band of writers lived in an unapologetically male world that might be deemed the last representation of Divan literature and Ottoman male culture. With its familiar female stereotypes, its zest for romance, its association of sex with sin, filth, trickery, deception, perversion, degradation, weakness, disaster, guilt, and fear, this traditional male culture manifests itself on every page of the encyclopedia; during its thirty-year span, only one or two women ever wrote an entry. Eventually the all-male *meyhane* evenings became such an important part of the writing-publishing ritual as to merit their own entry: in "*meyhane* nights," he claims that he and his literary contemporaries were following a fine tradition and went on to name the Ottoman poets who had likewise been unable to accomplish until they had first been to a *meyhane*. Once again, he rhapsodizes about the beautiful boys who fetched them their cups of wine; after his pen traces the delights of their clothes, and their sashes, the delicacy of their features, and their general elegance, Koçu goes on to declare that the greatest writer of the chroniclers of *meyhane* nights is Ahmet Rasim. His elegant but decorous love of Istanbul and his flair for living tableaux made him as great an influence on Reşat Ekrem Koçu as his mentor, Ahmet Refik.

In both the *Istanbul Encyclopedia* and the serials he "based on real documents" for the newspapers, Koçu took Ahmet Rasim's racy stories of old Istanbul and made them shimmer with evil, intrigue, and romance. (The two best examples are "what happened in Istanbul when people sought love" and "the old *meyhanes* of Istanbul, their exotic dancing boys and male women.") Taking advantage of the loose Turkish copyright laws, he quoted liberally from his master—sometimes too liberally but always in good faith.

The forty years between the birth of Rasim (1865) and Koçu (1905) saw the first newspapers published in the city, the long westernizing reign of Abdülhamıt and its political oppression, the opening of the universities, the protests and publications of the Young Turks, the admiration of the West in literary circles, the first Turkish novels, the great waves of immigration, and many greater fires; what separates Istanbul's two most eccentric writers even more than the flux of history are their views on western poetics. Having in his youth written western-inspired novels and poems, and accepting failure at an early age, Rasim came to see excessive western influence as an affectation, a "blind imitation"; it was, he said, like selling snails in a Muslim neighborhood. Moreover, he found western ideas about originality, literary immortality, and the cult worship of the artist as excessively "foreign" and adopted, instead, a more humble philosophy worthy of a dervish: He wrote for newspapers to earn his living and because he enjoyed it. Inspired as he was by the endless liveliness of Istanbul, he saw no need to suffer for his "art" or, indeed, to create "art" that might last. He simply wrote his columns as they came to him.

Koçu, by contrast, was utterly unable to free himself from western forms: Obsessed with western classification systems, he viewed science and literature with the same western eyes. And so it was difficult for him to reconcile his favorite subjects—the oddities, the obsessions, and the weirdness of life in the margins—with his western ideals. Living in Istanbul, he knew little about the literature of romantic perversion then thriving on the margins of the West. But even if he had known of it, he issued from an Ottoman tradition that expected its literati to operate not on the margins, not in the perverted underground, but out in the open, to engage in instructive dialogue with society's centers of culture and power. Koçu's first dream had been to be a university professor; after his expulsion, his next dream was to publish a major encyclopedia. His overriding desire, one senses, was to establish some authority over his "strange imaginings" and give them scientific legitimacy.

Ottoman writers who shared his taste for the city's liminal world had no need for such concealment. In the *şerengiz* that was so popular in the seventeenth and eighteenth centuries, these writers were able to extol the city in all its guises while also extolling the virtues of that city's beautiful young boys. In fact, these poetic city books freely juxtaposed verses about boys with verses about the city's beauties and monuments. A random perusal of any prominent Ottoman writer—say, the works of the seventeenth-century traveler Evliya Çelebi—is enough to understand how literary convention allowed poets to praise the city's boys in the same terms one might use to extol its mosques, its weather, or its waterways. But finding himself in the oppressing, centralizing, homogenizing grip that the westernizing movement brought with it, this "old-fashioned" Istanbul writer was left with very few ways in which to express his "socially unacceptable" tastes and obsessions. And so he took refuge in the encyclopedia business.

There is still something rather quaint about his understanding of encyclopedias. Somewhere in *From Osman Gazi to Atatürk,* which he wrote after abandoning the first *Istanbul Encyclopedia,* Koçu alluded to *Acaibu-l Mahlukat,* a medieval book of "wondrous creatures" by Kazvinli Zekeriya, describing it as a "sort of encyclopedia." This, says Koçu, with a kind of nationalistic pride, is proof that, even before the Ottomans fell under western influence, they were writing and using encyclopedialike books; this touching comment shows that he saw an encyclopedia as little more than a haphazard collection of facts in alphabetical order. Nor does it seem to have occurred to him that there is a difference between facts and stories, that there needs to be a hierarchical logic that gives some things more importance than others and casts light on the essence and the processes of civilization—put another way, some entries should be short and others long, and still other entries—ipso facto—omitted altogether. It did not occur to him that he served history; he thought history served him. In this sense, Koçu resembles the "powerless historian" in Nietzsche's *Use and Abuse of History*—homing in on historic details to change the history of his city into the history of himself.

He was powerless because—like those pure collectors who rate things according to subjective value, not market value—he was sentimentally attached to the stories he spent so many years digging out of newspapers, libraries, and Ottoman documents. A happy collector (usually this is a "western" gentleman) is someone who—regardless of the origins of his quest—is able to bring order to his assembled objects, to classify them in such a way that the relationship between different objects is clear and the logic of his system transparent. But in Koçu's Istanbul there was not a museum comprising a single collection (now there are several). Koçu's *Istanbul Encyclopedia* is not so much a museum as one of those cabinets of curiosities that were so popular among European princes and artists between the sixteenth and eighteenth centuries. To turn the pages of the *Istanbul Encyclopedia* is to look into the windows of one of those cabinets and see its seashells, animal bones, and mineral samples with an awe tempered just slightly by a smile.

Book lovers of my generation greet any mention of the *Istanbul Encyclopedia* with the same affectionate smile. Because there is half a century between us, because we like to think of ourselves as more "western" and "modern," there is a certain curling of the lip when we utter the word *encyclopedia*. But there is also compassion and understanding for the innocent optimism of a man who thought he could take a form that took centuries to develop in Europe and, in his own haphazard fashion, master it in one fell swoop. Behind that gentle condescension is the secret pride we take in seeing a book from an Istanbul writer caught between modernity and Ottoman culture, one that refuses to classify or in any way discipline the anarchic strangeness. Especially a book in twelve huge volumes, all of them out of print!

From time to time I meet someone who for one reason or another has been obliged to read all twelve volumes: an art historian friend of mine who's researching Istanbul's demolished Sufi *tekkes,* another friend who's trying to learn more about Istanbul's little-

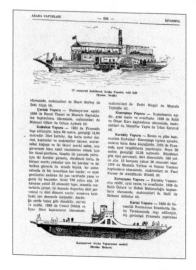 

known *hamams*. After we have exchanged knowing smiles, we are overcome by a deep urge to compare notes. I ask my researcher friend if he's read that in the old *hamams,* in front of the doors to the male sections there were a number of junk peddlers who washed the perforated shoes and mended clothes. My friend will throw me back a question of his own: In the same volume, in the entry entitled "Eyyubsultan Turbe plums," how does it explain why a certain sort of Istanbul plum is known as a Turbe? And who is Sailor Ferhad? (Answer: the brave seaman who on a summer's day in 1958 saved the life of a seventeen-year-old youth who'd fallen off an island ferry into the sea.) Now we turn to speak about Arnavud Cafer, the Beyoğlu gangster who in 1961 killed his godless rival's bodyguard (as described in the "Dolapdere Murder" entry), or about "the domino players' coffeehouse," where enthusiasts of this game, mostly from the city's Greek, Jewish, and Armenian minorities, once gathered to play. This brings the conversation to my family in Nişantaşı, because we played dominoes too. As I recall the old toy, tobacco, and sundries stores of Nişantaşı and Beyoğlu that once sold domino sets, we begin to lose ourselves in memories and then nostalgia. Or I'll talk about the "Underpants Man" entry, which describes the aesthetically circumcised procurer who wandered from city to city with his five daughters, who were, like their father, much loved by businessmen coming to Istanbul from Anatolia, or the "Imperial Hotel," so loved by western tourists in the mid-nineteenth century, or "shops," in which he describes at length how and for what reason the shops of Istanbul change their names.

Once my friends and I feel the old melancholy settling over us, we begin to realize there is more to it than that. The real subject is Koçu's failure to explain Istanbul using western "scientific" methods of classification. He failed in part because Istanbul is so unmanageably varied, so anarchic, so very much stranger than western cities; its disorder resists classification. But this otherness we complain about begins, after we have talked for a while, to look like a virtue, and we remember why it is we treasure Koçu's encyclopedia: because it allows us to indulge in a certain chauvinism.

Without falling into the strange habit of praising Istanbul's strangeness, we acknowledge that we love Koçu *because* he "failed." The reason why the *Istanbul Encyclopedia* could not succeed—and it is the downfall of all four melancholy writers—was the authors' ultimate inability to be western. To see the city with new eyes, these writers had to cleanse themselves of their traditional identities. To be western, they set out on an irreversible journey to that twilit place between East and West. As with our three other melancholics, Koçu's most beautiful and profound pages are the ones that remain between worlds, and (again, like the others) the price he paid for his originality was loneliness.

In the years after Koçu's death, in the mid-seventies, every time I went to the Covered Bazaar I would stop at the Sahaflar Second-hand Book Market next to the Beyazıt Mosque and find the final unbound fascicles and volumes that Koçu published at his own expense in his final years, sitting among the rows of yellowed, faded, mildewed, cheap old books. These volumes, which I began to read in my grandmother's library, were by now being sold at the price of waste paper, but still the booksellers I knew said they found no takers.

CHAPTER NINETEEN

Conquest or Decline?
The Turkification of Constantinople

Like most Istanbul Turks, I had little interest in Byzantium as a child. I associated the word with spooky, bearded, black-robed Greek Orthodox priests, with the aqueducts that still ran through the city, with Hagia Sophia and the red-brick walls of old churches. To me, these were remnants of an age so distant that there was little need to know about it. Even the Ottomans who conquered Byzantium seemed very far away. People like me were, after all, the first generation of the "new civilization" that had replaced them. But as strange as Reşat Ekrem Koçu had made the Ottomans sound, at least they had names we could recognize. As for the Byzantines, they had vanished into thin air soon after the conquest, or so I'd been led to believe. No one had told me that it was their grandchildren's grandchildren's grandchildren who now ran the shoe stores, patisseries, and haberdashery shops of Beyoğlu.

One of the great pleasures of my childhood was to go to Beyoğlu with my mother and wander in and out of its Greek shops. They were family enterprises. If we went into a draper's and my mother asked to look at damask for curtains or velvet for cushion covers, the background sound was of mothers, fathers, and daughters chattering to one another in rapid-fire Greek. Later, back home, I liked to imitate their strange language and the excited gestures of the girls at the counter when addressing their parents. From the household reaction to my imitations, I was made to understand that

the Greeks, like the city's poor and the denizens of its shantytowns, were not quite "respectable." I thought this must have something to do with the fact that Mehmet the Conqueror had taken the city away from them. The 500th anniversary of the Conquest of Istanbul—the "great miracle," as it is sometimes called—took place in 1953, a year after my birth, but it was not a miracle I found particularly interesting, apart from the stamp series they issued to commemorate it. One stamp showed the ships emerging from the night, another featured Bellini's portrait of Mehmet the Conqueror, and a third displayed the towers of Rumelihisarı, so it could be said that the series as a whole was a procession of all the sacred images associated with the conquest.

You can often tell whether you're standing in the East or in the West, just by the way people refer to certain historical events. For Westerners, May 29, 1453, is the Fall of Constantinople, while for Easterners it's the Conquest of Istanbul. Years later, when my wife was studying at Columbia University, she used the word *conquest* in an exam and her American professor accused her of nationalism. In fact, she'd used the word only because she was taught to use it as a Turkish lycée student; because her mother was of Russian extraction, it could be said that her sympathies were more with the Orthodox Christians. Or perhaps she saw it neither as a *fall* nor a *conquest* and felt more like an unlucky hostage caught between two worlds that offered no choice but to be Muslim or Christian.

It was westernization and Turkish nationalism that prompted Istanbul to begin celebrating the conquest. At the beginning of the twentieth century, only half the city's population was Muslim, and most of the non-Muslim inhabitants were descendents of Byzantine Greeks. When I was a child, the view among the city's more vocal nationalists was that anyone who so much as used the name Constantinople was an undesirable alien with irredentist dreams of the day when the Greeks, who had been the city's first masters would return to chase away the Turks, who had occupied it for five hundred years—or, at the very least, turn us into second-class citizens. It was the nationalists, then, who insisted on the word *conquest*. By contrast, many Ottomans were content to call their city Constantinople.

Even in my own time, Turks committed to the idea of a westernized republic were wary of making too much of the conquest. Neither President Celal Bayar nor Prime Minister Adnan Menderes attended the 500th anniversary ceremony in 1953; although it had been many years in the planning, it was decided at the last moment that to do so might offend the Greeks and Turkey's western allies. The Cold War had just begun, and Turkey, a member of NATO, did not wish to remind the world about the conquest. It was, however, three years later that the Turkish state deliberately provoked what you might call "conquest fever" by allowing mobs to rampage through the city, plundering the property of Greeks and other minorities. A number of churches were destroyed during the riots and a number of priests were murdered, so there are many echoes of the cruelties western historians describe in accounts of the "fall" of Constantinople. In fact, both the Turkish and the Greek states have been guilty of treating their respective minorities as hostages to geopolitics, and that is why more Greeks have left Istanbul over the past fifty years than in the fifty years following 1453.

In 1955 the British left Cyprus, and as Greece was preparing to take over the entire island, an agent of the Turkish secret service threw a bomb into the house where Atatürk was born in the Greek city of Salonika. After Istanbul's newspapers had spread the news in a special edition exaggerating the incident, mobs hostile to the city's non-Muslim inhabitants gathered in Taksim Square, and after they had burned, destroyed, and plundered all those shops my mother and I had visited in Beyoğlu, they spent the rest of the night doing the same in other parts of the city.

The bands of rioters were most violent and caused greatest terror in neighborhoods like Ortaköy, Balıklı, Samatya, and Fener, where the concentration of Greeks was greatest; not only did they sack and burn little Greek groceries and dairy shops, they broke into houses to rape Greek and Armenian women. So it is not unreasonable to say that the rioters were as merciless as the soldiers who sacked the city after it fell to Mehmet the Conqueror. It later emerged that the organizers of this riot—whose terror raged for two days and made the city more hellish than the worst orientalist nightmares—had the state's support and had pillaged the city with its blessing.

So for that entire night, every non-Muslim who dared walk the streets of the city risked being lynched; the next morning the shops of Beyoğlu stood in ruins, their windows smashed, their doors kicked in, their wares either plundered or gleefully destroyed. Strewn everywhere were clothes, carpets, bolts of cloth, overturned refrigerators, radios, and washing machines; the streets were piled

high with broken porcelain sets, toys (the best toy stores were all in Beyoğlu), kitchenware, and fragments of the aquariums and chandeliers that were so fashionable at the time. Here and there, amid the bicycles, overturned and burned cars, hacked-up pianos, and broken mannequins gazing up at the sky from the cloth-covered streets, were the tanks that had come too late to quell the riots.

Because my family told long stories about these riots for years afterward, the details are as vivid as if I had seen them with my own eyes. While the Christian families were cleaning up their shops and homes, mine was recalling how my uncle and my grandmother had raced from one window to the next, watching with rising panic as the angry mobs roamed up and down our streets, smashing shop windows and cursing the Greeks, the Christians, the rich. From time to time a group would gather outside our apartment, but it just so happened that my brother had developed a fancy for the little Turkish flags they'd just begun to sell at Alaaddin's shop, perhaps in the hope of capitalizing on the heightened nationalist sentiment then sweeping the country; he'd hung one in my uncle's Dodge, and that, we think, is why the angry mobs passed without overturning it and even spared the windows.

CHAPTER TWENTY

Religion

Until I was ten, I had a very clear image of God; ravaged with age and draped in white scarves, God had the featureless guise of a highly respectable woman. Although She resembled a human being, She had more in common with the phantoms that populated my dreams: not at all like someone I might run into on the street. Because when She appeared before my eyes, She was upside down and turned slightly to one side. The phantoms of my imaginary world faded bashfully into the background as soon as I noticed them, but then so did She; after the sort of elegant rolling shot of the surrounding world that you see in some films and television commercials, Her image would sharpen and She would begin to ascend, fading as She rose to Her rightful place in the clouds. The folds of Her white head scarf were as sharp and elaborate as the ones I'd seen on statues and in the illustrations in history books, and they covered Her body entirely; I couldn't even see Her arms or legs. Whenever this specter appeared before me, I felt a powerful, sublime, and exalted presence but surprisingly little fear. I don't remember ever asking for Her help or guidance. I was only too aware that She was not interested in people like me: She cared only for the poor.

Thus the people in my apartment building interested in this phantom were the maids and the cooks. Although I was faintly aware that, in theory at least, God's love extended beyond them to everyone under our roof, I also knew that people like us were lucky enough not to need it. God was there for those in pain, to offer comfort to those who were so poor they could not educate their children, to care for the beggars in the street who were forever invoking Her name, and to aid pure-hearted innocents in times of trouble. This is why, if my mother heard of a blizzard that had closed the roads to remote villages or of an earthquake that had left the poor homeless, she would say, "May God help them!" It seemed not so much a petition as an expression of the fleeting guilt that well-to-do people like us felt at such times; it helped us get over the emptiness of knowing we were doing nothing about the situation.

As creatures of logic, we were reasonably certain that the soft and elderly presence hiding its brilliance behind an abundance of white scarves would be disinclined to listen to us. After all, we did nothing for Her. Whereas the cooks and maids in our apartment, and all the other poor people around us, had to work very hard, seize every opportunity, to get in touch with Her; they even fasted for an entire month every year. Whenever she wasn't serving us, our Esma Hanım rushed back to her tiny room to spread out her rug and pray; every time she felt happy, sad, glad, fearful, or angry, she'd remember God; whenever she opened or closed the door or did anything for the first time or the last time, she'd invoke Her name and then whisper a few other things under her breath.

Except for those moments when we were made to remember Her mysterious bond with the poor, God did not trouble us unduly. You could almost say it was a relief to know they depended on someone else to save them, that there was another power that could help bear their burdens. But the comfort of this thought was sometimes dissolved by the fear that one day the poor might use their special relationship with God against us.

I remember the disquiet I felt on the few occasions when—more out of curiosity than boredom—I'd watch our elderly maid praying. Seen through the half-open door, our Esma Hanım looked a lot like the God of my imagination. Turned slightly sideways on her prayer rug, she would slowly bend over to press her forehead against it; she would rise only to bend over again, and now, as she prostrated herself, she looked as if she were begging, accepting her lowly place in the world; without quite knowing why, I'd feel anxious and vaguely angry. She only prayed when she had no pressing duties and no one else was at home, and the silence, broken intermittently by whispered prayers, made me nervous. My eyes would light on a fly crawling up the windowpane. The fly would fall on its back, and the buzzing of its half-transparent wings as it struggled to right itself would mix with Esma Hanım's prayers and whispers, and suddenly, when I could bear this no longer, I would tug at the poor woman's scarf.

That it would upset her when I interfered was something I knew from experience. As the old woman used all her willpower to ignore my intrusion and finish her prayers, it seemed that what she was doing was somehow false, nothing more than a game (because now she was only pretending to pray). But still I was impressed by her determination to immerse herself in prayer and took it as a chal-

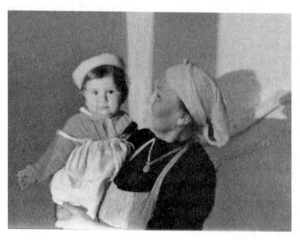

lenge. When God came between me and this woman—who was always so loving to me, taking me on her lap and telling people who stopped in the street to admire me that I was her "grandson"—I felt as uneasy as anyone else in the family about the devotion of deeply religious people. My fear, which I shared with everyone in the Turkish secular bourgeoisie, was not of God but of the fury of those who believed in Her too much.

Sometimes, when Esma Hanım was praying, the phone would ring or my mother, suddenly needing her for something, would call out for her. It then fell to me to run straight to my mother to tell her our maid was praying. Sometimes I did this out of the goodness of my heart, and sometimes I was driven more by that strange disquiet, that envy, and a desire to make trouble just to see what would happen. There was a certain desire to know which was stronger, this maid's loyalty to us or her loyalty to God; part of me was keen to wage war with this other world into which she escaped, sometimes returning with angry threats.

"If you tug at my scarf when I'm praying, your hands will turn to stone!" I still kept tugging her scarf, and nothing happened. But like my elders, who, while claiming not to believe in any of this nonsense, still watched their step—just in case time proved them wrong—I knew there was a point beyond which I dared not tease her. While I hadn't turned to stone this time, like everyone else in my prudent family I learned that it was always wise, if you'd just derided religion or expressed your lack of interest in it, to change the subject right away; we equated piety with poverty but never in too loud a voice.

To me, it seemed as if it was *because* they were poor that God's name was always on their lips. It's entirely possible that I reached this false conclusion by watching the disbelief and mockery with which my family viewed anyone religious enough to pray five times a day.

If God gradually ceased to manifest Herself as a white-scarved worthy, if my bond with Her was a subject that aroused a fleeting fear and caution, it was partly because no one in my family saw fit to give me any religious instruction. Perhaps they had nothing to teach me: I never saw anyone in my family bowing down on prayer rugs or fasting or whispering prayers. In this sense, you could say that families like mine were like those godless bourgeois families of Europe who lack the courage to make the final break.

This might seem unprincipled cynicism, but in the secular fury of Atatürk's new Republic, to move away from religion was to be modern and western; it was a smugness in which there flickered from time to time the flame of idealism. But that was in public. In private life, nothing came to fill the spiritual void. Cleansed of religion, home became as empty as the city's ruined *yalıs* and as gloomy as the fern-darkened gardens surrounding them.

So in our house, it was left to the maids to fill in the void (and satisfy my curiosity—if God didn't matter, why did they build so many mosques?). It wasn't difficult to see the foolishness of superstition. ("Touch this and you'll turn to stone," our maid would say. "His tongue's been tied." "An angel came and took him up to heaven." "Never put your left foot first.") All those pieces of cloth people tied to the sheikhs' *türbes*—tombs—the candles they lit for Sofu Baba in Cihangir, the old wives' remedies the maids concocted because no one would send them to the doctor, and the legacy of centuries of dervish orders that found its way into our republican, European household in the form of proverbs, sayings, threats, and suggestions: They might all be nonsense, but they had left their imprint on everyday life all the same. Even now, when in a large square or walking down a corridor or pavement, I'll suddenly remember not to step on the cracks between the paving stones or on the black squares, and find myself hopping rather than walking.

Many of these religious injunctions became confused in my mind with my mother's rules (like "Don't point"). Or, when she told me not to open a window or the door because it would cause a draft, I imagined that a draft was a saint like Sofu Baba, whose soul was not to be disturbed.

So rather than see it as a system by which God spoke to us through prophets, books, and laws, we reduced religion to a strange and sometimes amusing set of rules on which the lower classes depended; having stripped religion of its power, we were able to accept it into our home as a strange sort of background music to accompany our oscillations between East and West. My grandmother, my mother, my father, my aunts and uncles—none of them ever fasted for a single day, but at Ramadan they awaited sunset with as much hunger as those keeping the fast. On winter days, when night fell early and my grandmother was playing bezique or poker with her friends, the breaking of the fast would be an excuse for a feast, which meant more treats from the oven. Still, there were concessions. On any other month of the year, these gregarious old women would nibble continuously as they played, but during Ramadan, as sunset approached, they'd stop gorging themselves and stare longingly at a nearby table laden with all sorts of jams, cheeses, olives, flaky *böreks,* and garlic sausages; when the flute music on the radio indicated that the time for breaking the fast was near, they would eye the table as hungrily as if they, like the ordinary Muslims who made up 95 percent of the country, had gone without food since dawn. They'd ask one another, "How much more is there?" When they heard the cannon fire, they waited for Bekir the cook to eat something in the kitchen, before they too set upon the food. Even today, whenever I hear a flute, my mouth waters.

My first trip to a mosque helped confirm my prejudices about religion in general and Islam in particular. It was almost by chance: One afternoon when there was no one home, Esma Hanım took me off to the mosque without asking anyone's permission; she was not so much burning with a need to worship as tired of being inside. At Teşvikiye Mosque we found a crowd of twenty or thirty people— mostly owners of the small shops in the back streets or maids,

cooks, and janitors who worked for the rich families of Nişantaşı; as they gathered on the carpets, they looked less like a congregation of worshipers than a group of friends who had gathered to exchange notes. As they waited for the prayer time, they gossiped with one another in whispers. As I wandered among them during prayers, running off to the far corners of the mosque to play my games, none of them stopped to scold; instead, they smiled at me in the same sweet way most adults smiled at me when I was a young child. Religion may have been the province of the poor, but now I saw that—contrary to the caricatures in newspapers and my republican household—religious people were harmless.

Nevertheless, I was given to understand by the high-handed ridicule directed at them in the Pamuk Apartments that their good-hearted purity carried a price. It was making the dream of a modern, prosperous, westernized Turkey more difficult to achieve. As westernized, positivist property owners, we had the right to govern over these semiliterates, and we had an interest in preventing their getting too attached to their supersititions—not just because it suited us privately but because our country's future depended on it. If my grandmother discovered that an electrician had gone off to pray, even I could tell that her sharp comment had less to do with the small repair job he had left unfinished than with the "traditions and practices" that were impeding "our national progress."

The staunch disciples of Atatürk who dominated the press, their caricatures of black-scarved women and bearded reactionaries fingering prayer beads, the school ceremonies in honor of the Martyrs of the Republican Revolution—all reminded me that the nation-state belonged more to us than to the religious poor, whose devotion was dragging the rest of us down with them. But feeling at one with the mathematics and engineering fanatics in our own household, I would tell myself that our mastery did not depend on our wealth but on our modern western outlook. And so I looked down on families that were as rich as we were but not as western. Such distinctions became less tenable later on, when Turkey's democracy had matured somewhat and rich provincials began flocking to Istanbul to present themselves to "society"; by then my father's and my uncle's business failures had taken their toll, subjecting us to the indignity of being outclassed by people who had no taste for secularism and no understanding of western culture. If enlightenment entitled us to riches and privilege, how were we to explain these pious parvenus? (At the time I knew nothing about the refinements of Sufism or the Mevlana or the great Persian heritage.) For all I knew, the new class denounced as "rich peasants" by the political left held views no different from those of our chauffeurs and cooks. If Istanbul's westernized bourgeoisie gave support to the military interventions of the past forty years, never strenuously objecting to military interference in politics, it was not because it feared a leftist uprising (the Turkish left in this country has never been strong enough to achieve such a feat); rather, the elite's tolerance of the military was rooted in the fear that one day the lower classes would combine forces with the new rich pouring in from the provinces to abolish the westernized bourgeois way of life under the banner of religion. But if I dwell any longer on military coups and political Islam (which has much less to do with Islam than is commonly thought), I risk destroying the hidden symmetry of this book.

I find the essence of religion to be guilt. As a child I felt guilty—about not being fearful enough of the honorable white-scarved woman who entered my daydreams from time to time and about not believing in Her enough. There was also the guilt of keeping myself apart from those who did believe in Her. But just as I embraced the imaginary world into which I so often slipped, I welcomed that guilt with all my childish might, certain my disquiet would deepen my soul, sharpen my wits, and bring color to my life. As for the other, happier Orhan in that other house in Istanbul—in my daydreams, religion caused him no disquiet whatsoever. Whenever I grew tired of religious guilt, I'd want to seek out this Orhan, knowing he would not waste time on such thoughts and would sooner head for the movies.

Still, my childhood was not without capitulations to the dictates of religion. In the last year of primary school, there was a teacher I now remember as disagreeable and authoritarian, though at the time it made me happy just to see her; if she smiled at me I was ecstatic, and if she so much as raised an eyebrow I was crushed. When describing to us "the beauties of religion," this elderly white-haired sullen woman overlooked the vexing questions of faith, fear, and humility, choosing instead to see religion as rationalist utilitarianism. According to her, the Prophet Muhammad had thought fasting was important not just to strengthen one's will but also to improve one's health. Centuries later, western women inimical to the other beauties of religion nevertheless availed themselves of the healthy joys of fasting. Praying raised your pulse; like gymnastics, it kept you alert. In our own time, in countless Japanese offices and factories, the blow of a whistle signals the stop of work when everyone does five minutes of exercise, rather as Muslims take five-minute breaks for prayers.

My teacher's rationalist Islam confirmed the secret longing for faith and self-denial that the little positivist inside me was nurturing, so one day during Ramadan, I decided I would fast too. Although I was doing this under the teacher's influence, I didn't inform her. When I told my mother, I saw she was surprised but glad, as well as a little worried. She was the sort of person who believed in God "just in case"; even so, fasting was in her view something only backward people did. I did not raise the subject with my father or my brother. Even before I made my first fast, my hunger for belief had metamorphosed into a shame best kept secret. I was well acquainted with my family's touchy, suspicious, and mocking class attitudes, and I knew what they were likely to say. So I did my fast without anyone noticing or patting me on the back and saying, "Well done." Perhaps my mother should have told me that an eleven-year-old was under no obligation to fast at all. Instead, she had all my favorite things waiting for me—braided cakes and anchovy toasts—when my fast was over. Part of her was glad to see the fear of God in such a young boy, but I could see in her eyes that she already worried whether this was evidence of a self-destructive streak liable to condemn me to a life of spiritual suffering.

My family's ambivalence about religion was most evident at Kurban Bayram, the Feast of Sacrifice. Like all wealthy Muslim families, we'd buy a ram and keep it in the small garden behind the Pamuk

Apartments until the first day of the holiday, when the neighborhood butcher would come and slaughter it. In contrast to the
golden-hearted child heroes in my Turkish comics who longed for
the ram to be spared, I didn't much like sheep, so my heart didn't
bleed every time I saw the doomed ram frolicking in our yard. I
would even feel glad that we'd soon be disposing of this ugly, stupid,
foul-smelling animal; I do remember, however, having a troubled
conscience about the way we did it: After distributing the meat
among the poor, we ourselves would sit down to a great family feast
at which we drank the beer our religion forbade us and feasted on
meat from the butcher, because the fresh meat of our sacrifice had
too powerful an odor. The point of the ritual is to prove our bond
with the Almighty by sacrificing an animal *in the place of a child,*
thereby delivering us from guilt; and so it followed that people like
us, who ate nice meat from the butcher *in the place of the animal we had
sacrificed,* had cause to feel all the guiltier.

In our household, doubts more troubling than these were suffered in silence. The spiritual void I have seen in so many of Istanbul's rich, westernized, secularist families is evident in these silences.
Everyone talks openly about mathematics, success at school, soccer,
and having fun, but they grapple with the most basic questions of
existence—love, compassion, religion, the meaning of life, jealousy,
hatred—in trembling confusion and painful solitude. They light a
cigarette, give their attention to the music on the radio, and return
wordlessly to their inner worlds. The fast I undertook to express my
secret love of God was conducted in much the same spirit. As it was
winter and the sun set early, I don't think I suffered much hunger.
Even so, while eating the meal my mother had prepared for me (the
anchovies and mayonnaise and fish roe salads bore little resemblance to the traditional Ramadan feast) I felt happy and at peace.
But my joy had less to do with knowing I had honored God than the
simple satisfaction of having set myself a test and succeeded. After
I had eaten my fill, I went off to the Konak Cinema to see a Hollywood film and put the whole thing out of my mind. I never again
entertained the slightest desire to keep a fast.

Even if I didn't believe in God as much as I might have wished, part of me still hoped that if God was omniscient, as people said, She must be clever enough to understand why it was that I was incapable of faith—and so forgive me. So long as I did not broadcast my faithlessness or indulge in erudite attacks on faith, God would understand and ease the guilt and suffering of my disbelief, or at least not trouble Herself overmuch about a child like me.

What I feared most was not God but those who believed in Her to excess. The stupidity of the pious, whose judgment could never be compared with those of the God—God forbid—they adored with all their heart: This was the second thing that scared me. For years, I carried around the dread that one day I would be punished for not being "like them," and this dread had a far greater impact on me than any of the political theory I read during my leftist youth. What surprised me later on was finding out how few of my fellow secularist, half-believing, half-westernized *İstanbullus* shared my secret guilt. But it pleased me to imagine that—after a traffic accident, as they're lying in a hospital bed—people who have never performed their religious duties—who have always looked on the pious with contempt—will enter into a secret understanding with God.

At middle school I had a classmate courageous enough to shun this sort of secret understanding. He was a devilish boy from an ultra-rich family that had made its fortune in real estate; he rode horses in the gigantic gardens of their gorgeous houses in the hills above the Bosphorus and even represented Turkey in international equestrian events. One time we were talking metaphysics at recess, in the way children sometimes do, when he saw I was quivering with fear. He looked up at the sky and cried, "If God exists, let Him strike me dead!" and then, with a confidence that shocked me, he added, "But as you see, I'm still breathing." I felt guilty about lacking such courage and guilty, too, for secretly suspecting he was right, though even in my confusion, I felt glad without quite understanding why.

After I turned twelve, and my interests—and guilt—came to revolve more around sex than religion, I was less concerned about the imponderable tensions between the desire to believe and the desire to belong. The pain, it seemed from then on, was not in being far from God but from everyone around me, from the collective spirit of the city. Even so, whenever I am in a crowd, on a ship, or on a bridge and come face-to-face with an old woman in a white scarf, a shiver still passes through me.

CHAPTER TWENTY-ONE

The Rich

During the mid-sixties, my mother would go to the news-agent every Sunday morning to buy a copy of *Evening*. Unlike our daily newspapers, it wasn't delivered to our house, and—knowing that my mother went to the trouble of getting it for the sake of the society gossip column entitled "Have You Heard?" written anonymously under the pen name Gül-Peri (Rose Nymph)—my father never passed up an opportunity to tease her about it. His mockery gave me to understand that an interest in society gossip was a sign of personal weakness. It was to ignore that the journalists hid behind pen names to vent their resentment of the "rich" (including those with whom we socialized or wished to be classified) by making up lies about them. And even if they weren't lies, rich people inept enough to draw the attention of a society columnist were not leading exemplary lives. These insights, however, did not stop my father from reading these columns and believing them:

- Poor Feyziye Madenci! Her Bebek house has been robbed, but no one seems to know what's missing. Let's see if the police manage to solve this riddle.
- Aysel Madra didn't get to go swimming in the sea once last summer—and all because she had her tonsils taken out. This summer she's enjoying herself on Kuruçeşme Island— although we hear she's still a bit irritable. Let's not ask why.
- Muazzez İpar is off to Rome! We've never seen this Istanbul

socialite looking quite this happy. What's cheered her up? we wonder. Could it be the dashing man at her side?

• Semiramis Sarıay used to spend her summers on Büyükada, but now she's turned her back on us and returned to her villa in Capri. It's soooo much closer to Paris, after all. We hear she's going to do a few exhibitions of her art. So when's she going to show us her statues?

• Istanbul society has been undone by the evil eye! Many illustrious personages who have made frequent appearances in this column have been falling ill and rushing into hospital for operations. The latest bad news comes to us from the Çamlıca home of the much lamented Ruşen Eşref, where Harika Gürsoy was having *such* a good time at a moonlit party. . . .

"So Harika Gürsoy's had her tonsils out now too, eh?" my mother would say.

"She'd have been better off getting those nobs taken off her face first," my father would say, with idle malice.

Some of these socialites were named and others weren't, but from the back-and-forth I deduced they were people my parents knew and were interesting to my mother because they were richer than we were. My mother envied them—while also disapproving of their wealth, a rebuke clear from the way she sometimes talked about their "falling into the papers." It was not my mother's unique view. That the rich should not flaunt themselves in public was a belief then held just as strongly by most *İstanbullus*.

From time to time they even said it out loud; it was not, however, a cry for humility or an attempt to avoid the pitfalls of pride; neither did it suggest, as it were, a Protestant work ethic. It simply sprang from a fear of the state. For centuries, ruling Ottoman pashas had eyed all other rich persons—most of whom were themselves powerful pashas—as threats and would seize any excuse to kill them and confiscate their property. As for the Jews, those who were in a position to loan money to the state during the last centuries of the empire—they shared with the Greeks and Armenians who gained prominence as businessmen and artisans the bitter memory of the punitive Wealth Tax imposed on them during the Second World War, paving the way for the seizure of their land and factories, and of the riots of September 5 and 6, 1955, during which so many of their shops were pillaged and burned.

So the big Anatolian landowners and the second-generation industrialists now pouring into Istanbul were quite daring to flaunt their riches. Naturally, those still fearful of the state, or people like us who had failed through our own ineptitude to preserve our wealth for more than a generation, found such daring not just foolish but vulgar. One such second-generation industrialist, Sakıp Sabancı, now the head of Turkey's second richest family, was derided for his nouveau-riche ostentation, his odd opinions, and his unconventional behavior (though none of the papers wrote about it, for fear of losing advertising revenue), but it was his provincial courage in the 1990s that allowed him to follow Henry Clay Frick's example and turn his home into Istanbul's finest private museum.

Nevertheless, the anxieties that gripped the Istanbul rich of my childhood were not unfounded, their discretion not unwise. The state bureaucracy maintained a greedy interest in all aspects of production, and because it was impossible to become seriously wealthy without entering into deals with politicians, everyone assumed that even the "well-meaning" rich had tainted pasts. After my grandfather's money ran out and my father was forced to work for many years for Vehbi Koç, the head of Turkey's other leading industrialist family, he did not content himself with making fun of his boss's provincial accent or the intellectual shortcomings of his less-than-brilliant son. In his moments of anger, my father would say that the family had made its fortune during the Second World War and had not a little to do with the famines and food lines that the country had had to endure during that period.

Through my childhood and youth, I never saw the rich of Istanbul as beneficiaries of their own ingenuity but as people who long ago had seized some opportunity to bribe someone in the state bureaucracy and then struck it rich. Until the 1990s, when the fear of the state abated, I assumed that most of them had made quick fortunes and devoted the rest of their lives to keeping their money well hidden, while at the same time seeking to legitimize their social standing. Since no intellectual application was required to get rich, these people had no interest in books or reading or even chess. This was a far cry from the meritocratic Ottoman period, when only by dint of an education could a man of humble background hope to rise through the ranks, get rich, and become a pasha. With the closing of the Sufi *tekkes* in the early years of the Republic, the repudiation of religious literature, the alphabet revolution, and the voluntary shift to European culture, all mobility through acculturation ended.

As the new rich came (with good reason) to fear the state, these timid families had only one way to advance themselves, and that was to show themselves to be more European than they really were. So they amused themselves by going to Europe and buying clothes, luggage, and the latest appliances (everything from juicers to electric shavers), taking great pride in these trappings. Sometimes an older Istanbul family would set up a business and strike it rich again (as happened to a famous columnist and newspaper owner who was a close friend of my paternal aunt). But they had already learned their lesson; even if they had broken no laws and offended no official and had no reason to fear the state, it was not uncommon for such people to sell everything and move to a nondescript London flat, from which they'd stare either at the neighbors' walls across the way or their inscrutable English television, which they never quite understood, but somehow this was still an improvement over the uncertain comforts of an apartment in Istanbul with a Bosphorus view. Often, too, the western longing produced tales with echoes of *Anna Karenina*: a rich family would hire a foreign nanny to teach the children her language, only for the man of the house to run off with her.

The Ottoman state had no hereditary aristocracy, but with the coming of the Republic, the rich worked hard to be seen as its rightful heirs. So in the 1980s, when they suddenly became interested in the last remnants of Ottoman culture, they struggled to collect the few "antiques" that had survived the burning of the wooden *yalıs*. Since we had once been rich and were still seen to be, we loved to gossip about how the rich had made their fortunes (my favorite story was the one about the man who had brought in a boat full of sugar in the middle of the First World War, becoming rich overnight and enjoying the proceeds until the day he died). Perhaps it was the glamour of such stories, or perhaps it was the startled tragic air or the desperate uncertainty as to what to do with their sudden wealth and how to keep it from vanishing as mysteriously as it had come; whatever the reason, whenever I met someone rich—a distant relation, a family friend, a childhood friend of one of my parents, a Nişantaşı neighbor, or one of those soulless and uncultured rich people who ended up in "Have You Heard?"—I had the insatiable urge to probe their empty lives.

There was a childhood friend of my father's, a chic avuncular man who had inherited a great deal of property from his father (a vizier in the last years of the Ottoman Empire); the income he derived from his inheritance was so large that—and I could never tell if people were praising or damning him when they said it—"he never had to work for a day in his life." This man did little but read the paper and watch the streets from his Nişantaşı apartment. In the afternoon he would take a very long time shaving and combing his mustache; then, donning an elegant outfit made in Paris or Milan, he would set out on his one mission of the day, which was to sip tea for two hours in the lobby or the pastry shop of the Hilton Hotel. As he once explained to my father with raised eyebrows, as if he were sharing a great secret, and wearing a mournful face to suggest deep spiritual pain, "Because it's the only place in the city that feels like Europe." From the same generation there was a friend of my mother's, a very rich and very fat woman who, in spite of (or perhaps because of) looking an awful lot like a monkey herself, would greet everyone with the words, "How are you, monkey?"—an affectation my brother and I loved to imitate. She spent most of her life rejecting suitors, complaining they weren't refined or European enough; when she was approaching fifty, she gave up on men who were too rich or too elegant to want a woman as plain as she and married a "very distinguished, very refined" thirty-year-old policeman. After a short spell, this marriage failed, and she spent the rest of her life advising girls of her class to marry only rich men who were their social equals.

The westernized rich of the last Ottoman generation by and large failed to capitalize on their inherited wealth and share in the great commercial and industrial boom that Istanbul was entering. All too often, scions of these old families not only refused to sit down at a table to do business with the "vulgar businessmen" who tempered their swindling and deception with a capacity for "true and sincere" friendship and community spirit, they refused even to drink tea with them. These old Ottoman families were also (without knowing it) being swindled by the lawyers they hired to protect their interests and collect their rents. Whenever we went to visit members of this dying breed in their mansions or their Bosphorus *yalıs*, it was clear to me that most of them usually preferred their cats and dogs to people, so I always particularly valued the special affection they showed me. When, five or ten years later, the dealer Rafi Portakal would display in his antiques shop the same furniture that had surrounded these people—lecterns, divans, tables inlaid with mother-of-pearl, oil paintings, framed calligraphy, old rifles, historic swords passed down from their grandfathers, tablets, and huge clocks—I remembered fondly the diminished lives they had led. They all had hobbies and eccentricities that distracted them from their troubled relations with the outside world. I remember one frail man who showed my father his collection of clocks and his collection of weapons as surreptitiously as one might reveal a cache of erotic drawings. When one aged aunt warned us to make a detour around a small but dangerous collapsed wall on our way down to the boat-house, we were amused to remember she'd used the same words when we visited her five years earlier; another would always whisper, to keep the servants from hearing her precious secrets; a third would annoy my mother by rudely asking where my paternal grandmother was from. One of my fat maternal uncles got into the habit of taking guests around his house as if it were a museum; he would then discuss seven-year-old corruption scandals and disasters as if they'd been reported only that morning in *Hürriyet* and had left the

entire city agog. As we negotiated these strange rituals, as I tried to
catch my mother's eye to make sure we weren't misstepping, it
would slowly dawn on me that we were not important people in the
eyes of these rich relatives of ours who were working so hard to
impress us, and then I'd suddenly want to leave their *yalı* and go
home. It was when someone got my father's name wrong or mis-
took my grandfather for a provincial farmer or—as I often saw
among the reclusive rich—exaggerated some small inconsequential
annoyance—the maid who brought sugar cubes instead of loose
sugar as requested; the servant girl wearing socks of a disagreeable
color; the speedboat that came too close to the house—that I
sensed the difference in our social standing. But for all their snob-
beries, the sons and grandsons—boys my age with whom I had to
be friendly—were uniformly considered "difficult"; many would
end up arguing with the fishermen in the coffeehouse, beating up
priests in the French school downtown, or (if they weren't locked
up in a Swiss asylum) committing suicide.

These families were locked into petty but intractable disputes
that often landed them in court, and in this, I felt, they bore some
resemblance to my own family. Some managed to live together in
their great mansions for years and years and—even as they were
bringing legal action against one another—still gathering together
for family meals (as my father, aunts, and uncles did). Those who
took their grievances too seriously and matched emotion with deed
would suffer more, refusing to speak to one another for years on
end, even though they continued to live in the same *yalı;* some, who
could not bear the sight of their loathsome relations, would partition
their *yalı*'s most beautiful room, disrupting the flow of its high ceilings and its sweeping view of the Bosphorus with ugly makeshift
plaster walls so thin they were still forced to listen to their hated relatives' coughs and footsteps all day long; if they divided up the rest of
the *yalı* ("you take the harem; I'll keep the annex") it was less for their
own comfort than for the pleasure of knowing that they were causing discomfort to their unloved ones. I've even heard of some who
used legal maneuvers to block their relatives' access to the garden.

As I watch a new wave of similar disputes raging in the same families a generation later, I've begun to wonder whether the rich of Istanbul have some special genius for blood feuds. In the early days of the Republic, when my grandfather was amassing his fortune, a wealthy family moved to Nişantaşı not far from where we lived on Teşvikiye Avenue; the children took a lot their father had bought from one of Abdülhamit's pashas and divided it into two. The first brother built an apartment that was set back from the pavement in accordance with city regulations. A few years later, the other built an apartment on his half of the lot; and while still acting within city regulations, he deliberately set it ten feet closer to the pavement, just to block his brother's view. Whereupon the first brother erected a wall five stories high, which—as everyone in Nişantaşı knew— served no purpose other than to obstruct the view from the side windows of his brother's house.

You rarely hear of such disputes in families that moved to Istanbul from the provinces: Their norm is mutual support, especially if they are not very rich. After the 1960s, when the city's population was skyrocketing and, with it, the price of land, anyone whose family had been living in Istanbul for several generations and who had managed to acquire an amount of property enjoyed large windfalls. To prove that they belonged to "old Istanbul money," the first thing they did, of course, was to enter into disputes over dividing the property. There were two brothers whose land in the barren hills behind Bakırköy made them a colossal fortune when the city expanded in that direction; this may explain why the younger brother picked up a gun in the early 1960s and shot the older brother dead. The newspapers, I recall, insinuated that the older brother was in love with the younger brother's wife. As it happened, the murderer's green-eyed son was a classmate of mine at Şişli Terakki, so I followed this scandal with great interest. For days, it was front-page news, and as the city immersed itself in the minutiae of this tale of greed and passion, the murderer's fair-skinned redheaded son would arrive in class in his customary lederhosen, clutching a handkerchief, to spend the day in sobbing silence. In the forty years since, whenever I pass the part of the city—now home to 250,000—that bears my lederhosen-wearing classmate's last name, or I hear the family mentioned (for in the end, Istanbul is one big village), I remember how red my red-haired friend's eyes would become and how quiet his tears.

The great shipbuilding families (all from the Black Sea coast) were disinclined to take their disputes to court, preferring the naked passion that only weapons can satisfy. They'd begun with fleets of small wooden boats, competing for government contracts, but this did not lead to free competition in the western sense; instead, each sent out bands of brigands to intimidate the others; from time to time, when they tired of killing one another, they would do as the princes of the Middle Ages had done and exchange their daughters in marriage, but the ensuing periods of peace would never last long, and soon they'd be shooting at one another again, much to the distress of the girls, who now belonged to both families. After they began to buy up barges and build fleets of small cargo ships, and one of their daughters had married the president's son, they became regulars in "Have You Heard?"—whereupon my mother would carefully follow Rose Nymph's descriptions of their "splendiferous caviar and champagne-drenched" parties.

At parties, weddings, and balls of this sort—which my parents often attended, as well as my uncles and my grandmother—there were always plenty of photographers; my relatives would bring home any photographs in which they had appeared and display them for a few days on a buffet table. In them I recognized a few people who visited our house, plus a few celebrities I'd seen in the paper, along with a few of the politicians who had helped them on their way. When my mother compared notes on the phone with her sister, who attended such events more often, I would try to imagine what it had been like. Since the 1990s, society weddings have become grand affairs, attended by the press, television crews, and the country's most famous models; they are advertised with sky-rockets that can be seen throughout the city. But a generation ago, things were very different. The point was not ostentation but to allow the rich to gather together and forget, if only for an evening, their fears and worries about the meddlesome and rapacious state. When I attended such weddings and parties as a boy, I would,

despite my confusion, feel pleasure at finding myself in such august company. I'd read this same pleasure in my mother's eyes as she stepped out of the house to go to the party, having spent the whole day getting dressed. It was not so much the happy prospect of a fun night out; rather, it was the satisfaction of spending the evening with the rich—knowing that, for whatever reason, you belonged to their set.

Upon entering the great, brilliantly lit reception hall, or (in summer) the sumptuous garden, while walking among the beautifully arranged tables, tents, flower beds, waiters, and manservants, I would notice that the rich, too, enjoyed one another's company, even more so when celebrities were on hand as well. Surveying the crowd, as my mother did, to see "who else" was there, they were cheered to see "the right sort of people." Most had not made their money by dint of hard work or ingenuity but through a stroke of luck or a swindle they now wished to forget, and their confidence rested in the knowledge that they had more money than they could ever hope to spend. They were, in other words, the sort of people who could only relax, only feel good about themselves, if they were in the same place with others like them.

Once I'd taken my first stroll through the crowd, a strange wind would blow in out of nowhere and I'd begin to feel out of place. Either I'd see some extravagant piece of furniture or a luxury appliance (say, an electric carving knife) that we couldn't afford, and my spirits would drop; seeing my parents on intimate terms with people who by their own smug account owed their fortunes to some disgrace, disaster, or swindle only added to my unease. Later I would discover that my mother, who was genuinely pleased to be in their company, and my father, who was probably flirting with one of his mistresses, had not exactly forgotten the sordid gossip they talked about at home but had put it aside, if only for the night. After all, didn't all the rich do likewise? Perhaps, I thought, this was part of being rich: always acting "as if." The rich spent these parties complaining at length about the food they'd been served on their last plane flight—as if this were a matter of great concern and grave importance and as if most of the food they ate were not of the same low quality. And then there was the way their money was deposited in (or, to use my parents' word, siphoned into) accounts in Swiss banks. The knowledge that their money was in a faraway and hard-to-reach place endowed them with a lovely confidence that I envied.

That the distance between us was not quite as great as I had thought was made clear to me once by an insinuation of my father's. I was twenty years old and had just launched into a long diatribe against the stupidities of the soulless, brainless rich, who went to such pretentious lengths to show how "western" they were, who— instead of sharing their art collections with the public, endowing a museum, or following their passions—lived timid, mediocre lives; I singled out a number of family acquaintances, several of my parents' childhood friends, and the parents of some of my own friends. My father interrupted me mid-rant and—perhaps because he feared I might be heading for a life of unhappiness or perhaps simply to warn me—he said that "actually" the lady I'd just mentioned (a very beautiful woman) was a good-hearted, well-meaning "girl," and if I ever had a chance to know her intimately I'd have no trouble understanding why.

CHAPTER TWENTY-TWO

On the Ships That Passed Through the Bosphorus, Famous Fires, Moving House, and Other Disasters

My father and my uncle's string of business failures, my parents' arguments, the smoldering disputes between the various branches of the extended family over which my grandmother presided—these were some of the things that had prepared me for the knowledge that, despite everything the world had to offer (painting, sex, friendship, sleep, love, food, playing games, watching things), and although the opportunities for happiness were limitless and hardly a day passed without my discovering a new pleasure, life was also full of sudden, unexpected, fast-flaming disasters of every size and shade of importance. The randomness of these disasters reminded me of the radio maritime announcements, warning all shipping (and the rest of us too) about "free-floating mines" at the mouth of the Bosphorus and giving their precise location.

At any moment, my parents could begin to argue about something utterly predictable, or else a property dispute could flare up with the relatives upstairs, or my brother would lose his temper and decide to teach me a lesson I'd never forget. Then again, my father might come home and mention in passing that he'd sold our house, or they'd slapped a restraining order on him, or we had to move, or he was going off on a trip.

We moved a great deal in those days. Each time, the tension at home grew, but because my mother had to give so much attention to the wrapping of each pot and pan with old newspapers, as was then the custom, she had less time to keep watch over us, and this meant my brother and I could have the run of the house. As we watched the movers pick up the cabinets, cupboards, tables that we'd begun to see as the only constants in our lives and prepared to leave the apartment that had been our home, I'd begin to feel melancholy, the only consolation being that I might find a long-lost pencil, a marble, or a dear toy of great sentimental value that had gone missing under a piece of furniture. Our new homes may not have been as warm or as comfortable as the Pamuk Apartments in Nişantaşı, but the ones in Cihangir and Beşiktaş had beautiful views of the Bosphorus, so I never felt unhappy to be there, and as time passed I was less and less concerned about the decline in our fortunes.

I had a number of strategies to keep these small disasters from unsettling me. I'd established strict regimes of superstition for myself (like not stepping on sidewalk cracks and never closing certain doors all the way); or I'd have myself a quick adventure (meet up with the other Orhan, escape to my second world, paint, fall into a disaster of my own by picking a fight with my brother); or I'd count the ships passing through the Bosphorus.

In fact I'd been counting the ships going up and down the Bosphorus for some time. I'd been counting the Romanian tankers, the Soviet warships, the fishing boats coming in from Trabzon, the Bulgarian passenger ships, the Turkish Maritime passenger liners heading into the Black Sea, the Soviet meteorological vessels, the elegant Italian ocean liners, the coal boats, the frigates, the rusting neglected Varna-registered cargo ships, and the decaying vessels that kept their flags and countries of origin under cover of darkness. This is not to say I counted everything; like my father, I didn't bother with the motor launches that crisscrossed the Bosphorus, taking businessmen to work and transporting women with fifty bags of shopping, nor did I count the city ferries that darted shore to shore from one end of Istanbul to the other, carrying gloomy passengers who spent the journey lost in thought, smoking and drinking tea; like the household furniture, these were already fixtures in my everyday life.

As a child I counted these ships heedless of the disquiet, agitation, and mounting panic they induced in me. By counting I felt as if I was giving order to my life; at times of extreme rage or sadness, when I fled myself, my school, and my life to wander in the city streets, I stopped counting altogether. It was then I longed most keenly for disasters, fires, the other life, the other Orhan.

Perhaps if I explain how I got into the habit of ship-counting, it might make more sense. At the time—we are talking about the early sixties—my mother, father, brother, and I were living in a small Bosphorus-facing apartment in my grandfather's building in Cihangir. I was in the last year of primary school, so I was eleven years old. About once a month, I would set my alarm clock (with the image of a bell on it) for a few hours before dawn, waking up in the last hours of the night. The stove would have been put out before bedtime and I couldn't light it on my own, so to keep myself warm on a winter's night, I would go into the empty bed in the rarely used maid's room, take out my Turkish textbooks, and begin to recite the poem I had to have memorized by the time I got to school.

> "O flag, O glorious flag,
> Waving in the sky!"

As anyone who has had to memorize a prayer or a poem will know, if you're trying to engrave words into your memory, it's better not to pay much attention to what you see before your eyes. Once the words imprint themselves, your mind is free to go in search of images that can serve as aide-mémoires. Your eyes can be entirely disengaged from your thoughts and watch the world for their own amusement. On cold winter mornings, while I shivered under the covers and memorized my poem, I'd gaze through the window at the Bosphorus, shimmering in the darkness like a dream.

I could see the Bosphorus through the gaps between the four- and five-story apartment buildings below us, above the roofs and chimneys of the rickety wooden houses that would burn down over the next ten years, and between the minarets of Cihangir Mosque; no ferries ran at this hour, and the sea was so dark that no searchlight or lamp could pierce it. Over on the Asian side, I could see the old cranes of Haydarpaşa and the lights of a silently passing cargo

ship; with the help of faint moonlight or the lamp of a lonely motorboat, I could sometimes see huge, rusty, mussel-encrusted barges, a solitary fisherman in a rowboat, the ghostly white contours of Kızkulesi. But mostly the sea would be engulfed in darkness.

Even when—long before sunrise—the apartment buildings and cypress-filled cemeteries on the Asian side began to grow light, the Bosphorus would remain pitch-black—it looked to me as if it would stay that way forever.

As I continued memorizing my poem in the dark, as my mind occupied itself with recitation and strange memory games, my eyes would fix on something moving very slowly through the currents of the Bosphorus—a strange-looking ship, a fishing boat setting out early. Although I paid this object no mind, my eyes did not refrain from their usual habits; they'd spend a moment studying this thing passing before them and only when they'd established what it was would they acknowledge it. Yes, that's a cargo ship, I'd say to myself; yes, this is a fishing boat that has not lit its only light; yes, this is a motor launch taking the day's first passengers from Asia to Europe; yes, that is an old frigate from a remote Soviet port. . . .

On one such morning, when I was shivering and memorizing poetry under the blanket as usual, my eyes lit on an amazing sight, the likes of which I'd never seen. I remember well how I just sat there, frozen, my forgotten book in hand. A great hulk, growing larger and larger as it rose from the pitch-dark sea and approached the closest hill—the hill from which I was watching—this was a colossus, a leviathan, in shape and size a specter from my worst nightmares, a Soviet warship!—rising out of the night and the mist as if in a fairy tale, a vast floating fortress. Its engine was running low, the warship passing silently, sluggishly, but so powerfully that it shook the windowpanes, the woodwork, and our furniture; the tongs that someone had hung wrongly next to the stove, the pots and saucepans lined up in the dark kitchen, the windows in the bedrooms where my mother, my father, and my brother were sleeping were all trembling too, and so was the cobblestoned alley that went down to the sea; even the garbage cans in front of the houses were making such a clatter you might have thought this peaceful neighborhood was suffering a minor earthquake. It meant that what *İstanbullus* had been discussing in whispers since the Cold War began was actually true: The biggest Russian warships passed through the Bosphorus after midnight, under cover of darkness.

For a moment I panicked, thinking I should do something. The rest of the city was asleep and I was the only one to have seen this Soviet vessel heading who knew where to commit who knew what terrible act. I had to spring into action, to warn Istanbul, to warn the whole world. This was the sort of thing I'd seen so many brave child heroes do in magazines—stir cities from their sleep to save them from floods, fires, and invading armies. But I could not find the will to leave my warm bed.

As anxiety overtook me, I hit on a frantic stopgap measure that would become a habit: I applied my full mind, sharpened as it was by memorization, to the Sovet ship, committed it to memory, and counted it. What do I mean to say? I did the same as those legendary American spies rumored to live on hilltops overlooking the Bosphorus, who photographed every passing Communist ship (and this is probably another Istanbul myth that had some basis in reality, at least during the Cold War): I mentally cataloged all the salient features of the vessel in question. In my imagination, I collated my new data with existing data about other ships, the Bosphorus currents, and perhaps even the rate at which the world was turning; I counted it and in so doing turned the giant hulk into something ordinary. And not just the Soviet ship: By counting all ships "of note" I could reassert my picture of the world and my own place within it. So it was true, what they taught us in school: The Bosphorus was the key, the heart of the geopolitical world, and this was why all the nations of the world and all their armies and most especially the Russians wanted to take possession of our beautiful Bosphorus.

All my life, starting in childhood, I've always lived on hills overlooking the Bosphorus—if only from a distance and between apartments, the domes of mosques, and hills. To be able to see the Bosphorus, even from afar—for *İstanbullus* this is a matter of spiritual import that may explain why windows looking out onto the sea are like the mihrabs in mosques, the altars in Christian churches, and the *tevans* in synagogues, and why all the chairs, sofas, and dining tables in our Bosphorus-facing sitting rooms are arranged to face the view. Another result of our passion for Bosphorus views: If you are on a ship sailing in from the Marmara, you are met with Istanbul's millions of greedy windows mercilessly crowding one another out to get a better look at your ship and the waters through which it is moving.

Counting ships passing through the Bosphorus might be a strange habit, but once I began discussing it with others, I discovered that it's common among *İstanbullus* of all ages. In the course of a normal day, a large number of us make regular trips to our windows and balconies to take account, and we do so to get some sense

of the disasters, deaths, and catastrophes that might or might not be heading down the strait to turn our lives upside down. In Beşiktaş, where we would move when I was an adolescent, there lived, in a house in Serencebey on a hill overlooking the Bosphorus, a distant relation who took notes about every passing ship so diligently you might have thought it was his job. And there was a lycée classmate of mine who was sure that every suspicious-looking ship—anything that was old, rusty, in poor repair, or of unknown origin—was either smuggling Soviet arms to insurgents in such-and-such a country or carrying oil to some other country to wreak havoc on the world markets.

In the days before television, this was a pleasant way to pass the time. But my ship-counting habit, this habit I share with so many others, is essentially fed by fear, one that eats away at many others in the city too. After seeing all the wealth of the Middle East seep out of their city, after witnessing the slow decline that began with the

Ottoman defeats at the hands of Russia and the West and ended with their city falling into poverty, melancholy, and ruin, *İstanbullus* became an inward-looking nationalist people; we are therefore suspicious of anything new and most especially of anything that smacks of foreignness (even if we also covet it). For the past 150 years, we have lived in timorous anticipation of catastrophes that will bring us fresh defeats and new ruins. It's still important to do something to fight off the dread and the melancholy, and that is why the idle contemplation of the Bosphorus can seem like a duty.

The types of disasters that the city remembers best and awaits with greatest trepidation are, of course, the accidents involving ships in the Bosphorus. These bring the city together and make it feel like a large village. Because these disasters suspend the rules of everyday life and because, in the end, they spare "people like us," I secretly (if also guiltily) enjoy them.

I was only eight on the night I deduced—from the noise and the fires piercing the starry night—that two tankers laden with petroleum had collided in the middle of the Bosphorus and had, after a huge explosion, burst into flames; but I was more thrilled than terrified. It was only much later that we found out by phone that the burning ships had set off explosions in neighboring petroleum depots, and there was a danger that the fire might spread and consume the entire city. As with all spectacular fires of that era, there was a preordained order: First we saw a few flames and a bit of smoke, then rumors circulated, most of them false, and then, in spite of the pleas of mothers and aunts, we were gripped by an undeniable desire to see the fire for ourselves.

That night it was my uncle who awakened us, piled us into the car, and took us to Tarabya via the hills behind the Bosphorus. Just in front of the big hotel (still under construction), the road had been blocked off; that saddened and elated me as much as the fire itself. Later, I was very jealous to hear a swaggering school friend of mine claim that he had been able to pass through the cordon after his father had flashed a card and cried "Press!" And so it was that in the year 1960, just before dawn on an autumn night, I ended up watching the Bosphorus burn with a curious, even joyous, crowd of people in pajamas, hastily fastened trousers, and slippers, holding babies on their laps and bags in their hands. As I would see so often during the magnificent fires that ravaged *yalis* and ships and sometimes the very surface of the sea in the years that followed, there appeared out of nowhere street sellers wandering among the crowds, selling paper helva, *simits,* bottled water, seeds, meatballs, and sherbets.

According to newspaper reports, the *Peter Zoranich,* a tanker carrying more than ten tons of heating oil from the Soviet port of Tvapse to Yugoslavia, was traveling down the wrong lane when it collided with *World Harmony,* a Greek tanker in the proper lane and bound for the Soviet Union to load up on fuel; a minute or two after the collision, the fuel that had leaked from the Yugoslavian tanker exploded with such violence it could be heard all over Istanbul. Either because the captains and their crews had immediately abandoned ship or died in the explosion, neither ship was manned, so both went out of control and began spinning in the fierce, mysterious currents and whirlpools; swaying left and right, they turned into fireballs threatening Kanlıca, the *yalis* of Emirgân and Yeniköy, the Çubuklu petroleum and gas depots, and the wooden houses lining the Beykoz shore. The shores Melling had once depicted as heaven on earth and A. Ş. Hisar had called the Bosphorus Civilization were aflame and choked with black smoke.

Wherever the ships came too close to the shore, people fled their *yalis* and wooden houses, quilts under one arm, children under the other, racing away from the water as fast as their legs could take them. When the Yugoslavian tanker drifted from the Asian to the European side, it collided with the *Tarsus,* a Turkish passenger ship that was anchored at Istinye, and before long this ship too was in flames. As the burning ships drifted past Beykoz, crowds of people carrying quilts and wearing raincoats thrown hastily over nightclothes were rushing up into the hills. The sea was alight with brilliant yellow flames. The ships were great red heaps of molten iron, their masts, smokestacks, and bridges lurching as they melted. The

sky glowed with a reddish light that seemed to radiate from within. From time to time there was an explosion and great sheets of burning iron would float into the sea; from the shore and the hills came shouts, screams, and the sound of children crying.

How heartbreaking and yet enlightening to contemplate this paradise of cypress and pine groves, of gardens shaded by mulberry trees and thick with the perfume of honeysuckle and judas blossoms, this moonlit world where on summer evenings the sea had shimmered like silk, the air had echoed with music, where a young man rowing slowly through a maze of boats might see silver droplets at the ends of his oars—to see all of it vanish into smoke as people in their nightclothes, weeping and clutching one another, rushed from the last of the great wooden *yalıs* set against the reddened sky.

This disaster could have been prevented, I would later think, if only I'd been counting ships. Feeling personally responsible for disasters, I had no wish to run away from them and, indeed, felt compelled to get as close as I could, to see them with my own eyes.

Later, like so many other *İstanbullus,* I came almost to wish for disasters, and that wish made me feel even guiltier when the next disaster occurred.

Even Tanpınar—whose books offer the deepest understanding of what it means to live in a rapidly westernizing country among the ruins of Ottoman culture, and who shows how it is, in the end, the people themselves who, through ignorance and despair, end up severing their every link with the past—admits to taking pleasure from the sight of an old wooden mansion burning itself into the ground, and in the Istanbul section of *Five Cities* he compares himself, as Gautier does, with Nero. Even stranger, a few pages earlier, Tanpınar mournfully writes: "One after the other, the masterpieces I see before my eyes melt as fast as watered rock salt until all that's left are piles of ash and earth."

Tanpınar wrote those lines in the 1950s, when he was living in Chickens Can't Fly Alley—the street where we would be living when I counted that Soviet warship. It was from here he watched the fire that destroyed the waterfront palace of Princess Sabiha and the wooden building that had once housed the Ottoman Assembly and later became the Fine Arts Academy, where he was an instructor. The fire had raged for an hour, casting a fine shower of sparks

with each new explosion, and with "the leaping flames and columns of smoke, there was something in the air that suggested the Day of Judgment had arrived." Perhaps he felt a need to reconcile his pleasure at the spectacle with his despair at seeing one of the most beautiful buildings from the reign of Mahmud II destroyed, taking its priceless collections with it (including that of the architect Sedad Hakkı, whose archives and detailed plans of Ottoman monuments were said to be the best of his age), for he went on to tell how Ottoman pashas took a similar pleasure in watching the great fires of their time. Hearing someone cry "Fire!" they would jump into their horse-drawn carriages and rush to the scene, a strangely guilty Tanpınar tells us, and he goes on to itemize the things they took with them to fend off the cold: blankets, fur rugs, and—if they expected the spectacle to go on for some time—stoves and pots for making coffee and heating up food.

It wasn't just pashas, looters, thieves, and children who ran to watch the old Istanbul fires; western travel writers felt compelled to observe and describe them too. One such writer is Théophile Gautier, who witnessed five fires during his two-month stay in 1852 and described them all in ecstatic detail. (He was sitting in Beyoğlu Cemetery writing a poem when news of the first fire reached him.) If he preferred fires that started at night, it was because they made for better viewing. He describes the "wondrous sight" of the multicolored flames bursting from a paint factory on the Golden Horn, and his painterly eye remains attentive to the details: the shadows playing on the ships in the water, the cracking beams, the undulating crowds of onlookers, the wooden houses bursting into flame. Later, he would visit the smoldering scene to find hundreds of families struggling to survive in shelters they had built in the space of two days with whatever carpets, mattresses, pillows, and pots and pans they had managed to salvage; upon learning that they accepted their misfortunes as fate, he felt he had stumbled on yet another strange Turkish-Muslim custom.

Although fires were many and frequent through the five hundred years of Ottoman rule, it was during the nineteenth century particularly that people began to prepare for them. The residents of wooden houses in Istanbul's narrow streets did not think of fires as avoidable disasters so much as grim certainties they had no choice but to face. Even if the Ottoman Empire had not fallen, the fires that ripped through the city during the early years of the twentieth century—destroying thousands of houses, entire neighborhoods, vast stretches of the city, leaving tens of thousands of people homeless, helpless, and penniless—would have sapped its strength and left little to remind us of past glories.

But for those of us who watched the city's last *yalıs,* mansions, and ramshackle wooden houses burn during the 1950s and 1960s, the pleasure we derived had its roots in a spiritual ache different

from that of the Ottoman pashas, who thrilled to them as spectacles; ours was the guilt, loss, and jealousy felt at the sudden destruction of the last traces of a great culture and a great civilization that we were unfit or unprepared to inherit, in our frenzy to turn Istanbul into a pale, poor, second-class imitation of a western city.

During my childhood and youth, whenever one of the Bosphorus *yalıs* caught fire, crowds would immediately form around it and those hoping for a closer look would take to rowboats and motorboats to watch from the sea. My friends and I would immediately phone one another, hop into cars, and go out to Emirgân, say, and park our cars on the pavement, turn on our tape decks (the latest consumer rage), and listen to Creedence Clearwater Revival, ordering tea, beer, and cheese toasts from the teahouse next door as we watched the mysterious flames rising from the Asian shore.

We'd tell stories about how, in the old days, the nails in the beams of the old wooden houses had burst incandescent into the Asian sky and flown across the Bosphorus to ignite other wooden houses on the European shore. But we'd also talk about our latest infatuations, exchange political gossip and soccer news, and complain about all the stupid things our parents had been up to. Most important, even if a dark tanker passed before the burning house, no one would pay it the slightest attention, let alone count it: There was no need; the disaster had already happened. When the fire was at its apex and the extent of the damage was clear, we'd all fall silent, and I would imagine each of us thinking of a special private disaster lurking just ahead.

The dread of a new disaster, a disaster that everyone who lives in Istanbul knows will come from the Bosphorus: I think about it most while in bed. In the early hours of the morning, a ship's horn will interrupt my sleep. If I hear a second blast—long and deep, and so powerful that it echoes in the surrounding hills—I know there's fog on the straits. At regular intervals on foggy nights, I'll hear the gloomy horn from the Ahırkapı lighthouse, where the Bosphorus opens out into the Sea of Marmara. And as I swim in and out of sleep, an image will form in my mind of a huge ship struggling to find its way through the treacherous currents.

In what country is this ship registered, how big is it, and what is its cargo? How many people are there on the bridge with the pilot, and why are they so concerned? Are they caught in a current, or have they spotted a dark silhouette coming at them out of the fog? Have they strayed from the shipping lane and, if so, are they sounding the horn to warn any ships that might be near? When *İstanbullus* hear ship horns as they're tossing and turning in their sleep, the pity they feel for the men on the ship merges with their dread of disaster to create a fearsome dream about everything that could ever go wrong on the Bosphorus. On stormy days, my mother used to say, "God help anyone setting out to sea in this weather!" On the other hand, the best medicine for those who wake up in the night is a disaster too distant to touch their own lives. For those who wake up in the night in Istanbul, most get back to sleep by counting the horn blasts. And perhaps in their dreams, they imagine themselves on a ship moving through the fog to the brink of disaster.

Whatever their dreams may be, most awake the next morning with no memory of the ships they heard in the night; these will have gone the way of all nightmares. Only children and childish adults remember such things. Then, in the middle of an ordinary day, while you're waiting in the queue at the pastry shop or eating lunch, such a person will turn around and say, "Last night a foghorn woke me from a dream."

That's when I know that there are millions of people living on the hills of the Bosphorus haunted by the same dream on foggy nights.

There is something else that haunts those of us living on the shores, and it is bound up with another accident as indelible as the great tanker fire. One night when the fog was so thick you couldn't see more than ten yards ahead—at four a.m. on September 4, 1963, to be exact—a 5,500-ton Soviet freighter carrying military supplies to Cuba went thirty feet into the darkness of Baltıliman and crushed two wooden *yalıs,* killing three people.

"We were awoken by a terrifying noise. We thought the *yalı* had been struck by lightning; the building had split in two. It was only luck that saved us. When we pulled ourselves together, we went into

our third-floor sitting room and found ourselves nose to nose with
a huge tanker."

The papers supplemented the survivors' accounts with photographs of the tanker in their sitting room: Hanging on the wall was
a photograph of their pasha grandfather; sitting on the sideboard
was a bowl of grapes. Because half the room was gone, the carpet
spilled down like a curtain and flapped in the wind, and there,
among the sideboards, the tables, the framed calligraphy, and the
overturned divan was the prow of the deadly tanker. What made
these photographs intriguing and horrifying was that the furnishings of room into which the tanker had brought death and destruction—chairs, sideboards, tables, screens, tables, and sofas—were
identical to the ones in our own sitting room. As I read the forty-
year-old news accounts of the beautiful, newly engaged lycée student who died in the accident—what she talked about the night
before the accident with the people who survived it, the sorrow of
the neighborhood youth who found her body in the rubble—I
remember how no one in Istanbul spoke of anything else for days.

At that time the population of the city was only a million, and
the stories we told grew to epic proportions as rumors spread.
When I told people I was writing about Istanbul, I was surprised at
the longing in their voices when the conversation turned to those
old Bosphorus disasters. Even as tears formed in their eyes, it was as
if they were recounting their happiest memories, and there were
even some who insisted that I include *their* favorites.

It is to satisfy one such request that I am obliged to report that in
July 1966, a motor launch carrying members of the Turkish-
German Friendship Society collided with another vessel carrying
lumber between Yeniköy and Beykoz, and three people fell into the
dark waters of the Bosphorus and died.

I have also been asked to mention that an acquaintance of mine
happened to be on the balcony of his *yalı* one night, counting ships
with his usual resignation, when right before his eyes a fishing boat
bumped into the *Ploiesti,* a Romanian tanker, and split in two.

As for more recent disasters, there was that Romanian tanker
(the *Indepente*) that collided with another ship (a Greek freighter

called *Euryali*) in front of Haydarpaşa (the Asian city's main train station), and when the leaking fuel caught fire, the tanker, which was carrying a full load, exploded loud enough to wake us all—I promised not to omit that one. I haven't, and with good reason: Although we were living many miles from the scene of the accident, half the windows in our neighborhood were shattered by that explosion, and the street was knee-deep in jagged glass.

Then there was the shipload of sheep. On November 15, 1991, a Lebanese animal transporter called the *Rabunion,* carrying more than twenty thousand sheep it had picked up in Romania, collided with the *Madonna Lili,* a Philippines-registered cargo ship ferrying wheat from New Orleans to Russia; it sank, taking most of its sheep with it. It was reported that a few managed to jump off the boat and swim to shore, where they were rescued by a number of men who happened to be in a nearby teahouse, reading newspapers and drinking coffee, but the rest of the luckless twenty thousand are still waiting for someone to pull them out of the depths.

This collision occurred just below Fatih Bridge, the second Bosphorus bridge; it's the first bridge that *İstanbullus* prefer when committing suicide.

While writing this book I spent quite a bit of time in archives reading the very newspapers I'd read as a child, and in a paper that came out around the time I was born, I found many articles about another form of suicide that was even more popular than jumping off a Bosphorus bridge. For example:

A car driving through Rumelihisarı has flown into the sea. Yesterday's [May 24, 1952] lengthy searches failed to recover either the car or its passengers. As the car was flying into the sea, the driver was reported to have opened the door and cried "Help!" but then, for reasons unknown, he closed the door again and plunged into the sea with his car. It is thought that the currents may have pushed the car away from shore and into the watery depths.

Here is another article from forty-five years later, November 3, 1997:

Having stopped on his way home from a wedding to make an offering to Tellibaba, the drunk driver of a car carrying nine people lost control of the steering while driving into Tarabya and flew into the sea. The accident claimed the life of the mother of two children.

However many cars that have flown into the Bosphorus over the years, the story is always the same: Its passengers are dispatched to the watery depths, from which there is no return. Not only have I heard and read this, I've seen a few go down with my own eyes! No matter who the passengers are—screaming children; a pair of quarreling lovers; a gang of obnoxious drunks; a husband speeding home; an old man who can't see in the dark; a sleepy driver who stopped on the quay for tea with his friends and then went into first gear instead of reverse; Şefik, the old treasurer, with his beautiful secretary; policemen counting the ships passing through the Bosphorus; a novice chauffeur who's taken his family out in the factory car without permission; a nylon stocking manufacturer who happens to be an acquaintance of a distant relation; a father and son wearing identical raincoats; a famous Beyoğlu gangster and his lover; a Konya family seeing the Bosphorus bridges for the first time—when the cars fly into the water, they never sink like stones. For a moment they waver, almost as if sitting on the surface. It might be daylight, or the only light might be coming from a nearby *meyhane,* but when people on the living side of the Bosphorus look into the faces of those about to be engulfed, they see a knowing terror. A moment later the car sinks slowly into the deep, dark, fast-flowing sea.

I should remind readers that, once the cars start sinking, it's impossible to open their doors because the pressure of the water against them is too great. At a time when an unusual number of cars were flying into the Bosphorus, one refined and thoughtful journalist, wishing to remind his readers of this fact, did something rather clever: He published a survival guide, complete with beautifully drawn illustrations:

HOW TO ESCAPE FROM A CAR THAT'S FALLEN INTO THE BOSPHORUS

1. Don't panic. Close your window and wait for your car to fill with water. Make sure the doors are unlocked. Also ensure that all passengers stay very still.

2. If the car continues to sink into the depths of the Bosphorus, pull up your hand brake.

3. Just as your car has almost filled with water, take one final breath of the last layer of air between the water and the car roof, slowly open the doors, and, without panicking, get out of the car.

I'm tempted to add a fourth pointer: With God's help, your raincoat won't get caught on the hand brake.

If you know how to swim and manage to find your way up to the surface, you'll notice that, for all its melancholy, the Bosphorus is very beautiful, no less than life.

CHAPTER TWENTY-THREE

Nerval in Istanbul: Beyoğlu Walks

Melling's paintings depict the hills where I've lived all my life, but as they were before a single building stood on them. In Yıldız, Maçka, or Teşvikiye, gazing at the edges of Melling's landscapes, at those empty hills with their poplars, plane trees, and kitchen gardens, I'd imagine what the *İstanbullus* of his day would think if they could see what had become of their paradise, and I would feel the same pain as I did at the sight of gardens, crumbling walls, arches, and charred remains of burned-down mansions. To discover that the place in which we have grown up—the center of our lives, the starting point for everything we have ever done—did not in fact exist a hundred years before our birth is to feel like a ghost looking back on his life, to shudder in the face of time.

I had a similar sensation at a certain point in the Istanbul section of Gérard de Nerval's *Voyage en Orient*. The French poet came to Istanbul in 1843, a half century after Melling did his paintings, and in his book he recalls walking from the Mevlevi Dervish Lodge in Galata (which would be renamed Tünel in fifty years' time) to the area we today call Taksim—the same walk I would make over a hundred years later, holding my mother's hand. We now know this area as Beyoğlu; in 1843, its main thoroughfare (renamed İstiklâl after the founding of the Republic) was known as the Grand Rue de Pera, and it looked then almost as it does today. Nerval describes the

avenue leading away from the lodge as resembling Paris: fashionable clothes, laundries, jewelers, sparkling display windows, candy shops, English and French hotels, cafés, embassies. But beyond the place the poet identifies as the French Hospital (today's French Cultural Center) the city came to a shocking, confusing, and to me terrifying, end. Because in Nerval, today's Taksim Square, the center of my life and the biggest square in this part of the city, around which I have lived all my life, is described as a vast plain where horse-drawn carriages mingled with vendors selling meatballs, watermelon, and fish. He speaks of the cemeteries lying here and there in the fields beyond; a hundred years later, these would be gone. But there is one phrase of Nerval's that never leaves my mind, when he describes this "plain" where for my whole life I've only known an expanse of old apartment buildings as "a vast, infinite pasture shaded by pine and nut trees."

Nerval was thirty-five years old when he came to Istanbul. Two years earlier, he had suffered the first of the depressions that would ultimately lead to him hang himself in twelve years, after stays in several insane asylums. Six months earlier, before his arrival, the actress Jenny Colon, the great but never requited love of his life, had died. *Voyage en Orient,* which takes him from Alexandria and Cairo to Cyprus, Rhodes, Izmir, and Istanbul, bears the marks of these sorrows as well as of the exotic oriental dreams that Châteaubriand, Lamartine, and Hugo were fast turning into a great French tradition. Like the writers before him, he wished to describe the East, and since Nerval is identified with melancholy in French literary culture, one might assume he'd found melancholy in Istanbul.

But when Nerval came to Istanbul in 1843, he paid attention not to his own melancholy but to the things that helped him forget it. In a letter to his father, he vowed that his spell of madness two years earlier was never going to recur and this would "help me to prove to people that I was only the victim of an isolated accident"; he added hopefully that his health was excellent. We can assume that Istanbul, as yet not eaten away by defeat, poverty, and the shame of being thought weak by the West, had not shown the poet its melancholic aspect. Let us not forget that gloom did not descend on the city until after its great defeats. Here and there in his travel book, Nerval does report seeing in the East what he would call in his most famous poem "the Black Sun of Melancholy"—for example, on the shores of the Nile. But in the rich exotic Istanbul of 1843, he is a hurried journalist in search of good material.

He'd come to the city during the month of Ramadan. In his eyes, this was like going to Venice for *carnevale.* (Indeed, he describes Ramadan as a fast *and* a carnival.) Nerval spent his Ramadan evenings watching Karagöz shadow theater, taking in the lamplit city views, and going to cafés to listen to storytellers. The spectacle he describes was to inspire many other western travelers to follow in his footsteps; while it is no longer to be seen in poor, westernized, technically minded modern Istanbul, it left a deep impression on many Istanbul writers, who have written a great deal on "Old Ramazan Nights." Underlying this literature, which I read with such nostalgia around the time of my own childhood fast, is an image of Istanbul that owes much to the exoticism first contrived by Nerval and continued by the the travel writers he influenced. Although he mocks the English writers who come to Istanbul for three days, visit all the "tourist sights," and then immediately set to work on a book, Nerval does not neglect to see the whirling dervishes, take in a distant view of the sultan leaving the palace (Nerval claims touchingly that when they came face-to-face, Abdülmecit noticed him), and take long walks in cemeteries, reflecting all the while on Turkish clothes, customs, and rituals.

In his spine-tingling *Aurelia, or Life and Dreams,* which he likened to Dante's *New Life* and which was greatly admired by the surrealists André Breton, Paul Éluard, and Antonin Artaud, Nerval confesses outright that after his rejection by the woman he loved, he'd decided there was nothing to live for but "vulgar distractions" and that he had sought the inane distraction of wandering all over the world gazing at the clothes and strange customs of distant countries. Nerval knew his accounts of customs, views, and eastern women, like his reports of Ramadan evenings, were cheap and coarse, and in *Voyage en Orient*—like so many writers do when they feel the power of the story waning—he added long stories of his own invention to step up the pace. (In a long piece on the city's seasons for *Istanbul,* a book he wrote with his fellow melancholics, Yahya Kemal and A. Ş. Hisar, Tanpınar reports having done a great deal of research to find out which of these stories were inventions and which were genuinely Ottoman.) The inventions, which reveal much about Nerval's deep powers of imagery but little of Istanbul, provide a frame in the manner of Sheherazade. Indeed, whenever he felt a tableau lacked verve, Nerval would remind readers that the city was "just like *One Thousand and One Nights*"; it was just after explaining why he "had felt no need to discuss the palace, mosques, and hamams already described by so many others" that he made the remark that writers like Yahya Kemal and Tanpınar would echo almost a century later and that western travelers would then turn into a cliché: "Istanbul, which has some of the most beautiful scenery in the world, is like a theater and best seen from the hall, avoiding the poverty-stricken and sometimes filthy neighborhoods in the wings."

Eighty years later, when Yahya Kemal and Tanpınar created an image of the city that resonated for *İstanbullus*—something they could do only by merging those beautiful views with the poverty "in the wings"—they must have had Nerval in mind. But to understand what these two great writers (both of whom greatly admired Nerval) discovered, what they discussed, and what they went on to invent—to see how the generation of Istanbul writers that followed simplified and popularized this invention and to understand how their concept conveyed not so much the city's beauty as their melancholy about the city's decline—we must look at the work of another writer who came to Istanbul after Nerval.

CHAPTER TWENTY-FOUR

Gautier's Melancholic Strolls Through the City

Writer, journalist, poet, translator, and novelist, Théophile Gautier was a lycée friend of Nerval's. They spent their youths together, they both admired the romanticism of Victor Hugo, and for a time they lived very close to each other in Paris, never to fall out. A few days before his suicide, Nerval paid Gautier a visit, and after Nerval had hanged himself from a streetlamp, Gautier wrote a soul-searching memorial about his lost friend.

Two years before this, in 1852 (nine years after Nerval's trip and exactly a hundred years before my birth), events that would later set Russia against England, bring France closer to the Ottoman Empire, and pave the way for the Crimean War once again made voyages to the East interesting to French readers. While Nerval dreamed of a second eastern voyage, it was Gautier who arrived in Istanbul. (Thanks to the swift steamboats plying the Mediterranean by then, he made the trip from Paris in eleven days.)

Gautier stayed seventy days. He published his accounts of the visit first in the newspaper, for he was the chief *feuilletoniste,* and later in a book entitled *Constantinople.* This very popular tome was translated into many languages and set the standard for books written about Istanbul in the nineteenth century (along with Edmondo de Amici's *Constantinopoli,* published in Milan thirty years later).

Compared to Nerval, Gautier is the more skillful, organized, and fluent. Not surprisingly: Being a *feuilletoniste,* a critic and arts journalist who also wrote serialized fiction, Gautier had the acquired speed and liveliness born of having to write every day for a newspaper. (Flaubert criticized him for this.) But if we overlook the usual stereotypes and clichés about sultans, harems, and cemeteries, his book is a fine piece of reportage. If it resonated for Yahya Kemal and Tanpınar, helping them create an image of the city, it is because Gautier, seasoned journalist that he was, took an interest in what his

friend had called the city's "wings," venturing into its poorer quarters to explore their ruins and their dark filthy streets, to show western readers that poor neighborhoods were just as important as scenic views.

While passing through the island of Cythera, Gautier remembers Nerval telling him of a dead body he saw wrapped in oily clothes and hanging from a gallows. (This image, much loved by the two friends, perhaps rather too suggestive to one, would later be appropriated by Baudelaire in his poem "Journey to Cythera.") When he arrived in Istanbul, Gautier, like Nerval, donned "Muslim dress" to stroll about the city with greater ease. Like Nerval, he arrived during Ramadan, and he follows his example, too, in exaggerating the amusements of Ramadan nights. Likewise, he goes to Üsküdar to see the mystic ceremonies of the Rufai dervishes, wanders the cemeteries (where he sees children playing among the gravestones), goes to watch the Karagöz shadow theater, visits shops, and meanders through the city's busy markets, paying close and enthusiastic attention to passersby. Again aping Nerval, he makes a great effort to catch sight of Sultan Abdülmecit on his way to Friday prayers. Like most western travelers, he wheels out his theories about Muslim women—their closed-in lives, their inaccessability, their mystery (he advises his reader never, ever, to ask after the health of anyone's wife!). But he tells us all the same that the city's streets are full of women, some of them even alone. He discusses at length Topkapı Palace, the mosques, the Hippodrome, and all the other places Nerval eschewed as tourist traps. (Since these sights and subjects were de rigueur for western travelers, one perhaps ought not to exaggerate Nerval's influence in this respect.)

Despite his occasional arrogance, his fondness for sweeping gener-
alizations, and his interest in the bizarre, Gautier can be enjoyed for
his fine irony and, of course, his painterly eye.

Until he read the poems in Hugo's *Orientales* at the age of nineteen, Théophile Gautier had dreamed of becoming a painter. As an
art critic, he was highly regarded in his time. To describe Istanbul's
views and landscapes, he drew from a critical vocabulary never
before applied to Istanbul. Writing of Istanbul's silhouette and the
Golden Horn as seen from the Galata Mevlevi Lodge hilltop (the
same place Nerval had described nine years earlier: the end point of
shopping trips with my mother to Beyoğlu, the Maçka-Tünel
tramway, and today's Tünel Square), he observes, "The view is so
strangely beautiful that it seems unreal," but then he goes on to
describe the minarets and domes of Hagia Sophia, Beyazıt, Süleymaniye, Sultanahmet, the clouds, the waters of the Golden Horn,
the cypress-filled gardens of Sarayburnu, and, behind them, the
"inconceivably delicate bluish tints" of the sky and the plays of light
between them—all with the pleasure of an artist admiring the
refinements of his own painting and the confidence of an experi-
enced writer. Even the reader who has never seen this view can take
pleasure in it. Tanpınar, the Istanbul writer most alert to the changes
wrought by the "vast light show" that is the Istanbul landscape,
acquired his vocabulary and his eye for detail from Gautier. In an
article he wrote during the Second World War, Tanpınar criticized
other novelists in his circle for their unwillingness to see or describe
the things around them, and while extolling the painterly style of
writers like Stendhal, Balzac, and Zola, he added that Gautier was
himself a painter.

Gautier knew how to put views into words, how to convey the
feelings evoked by the contours, the arresting detail, the playing
lights; he is at the height of his powers when recounting his walks
through the "wings." Before setting out to follow the city walls to
their outer limits, Gautier, drawing on the observations of friends
who preceded him, writes that the city's magnificent views need
light and a clear point of view, for like stage sets they lose their
attraction when seen at close range: Distance endows the scenery

with magnificence and allows its dull, narrow, steep, filthy streets and its disordered heaps of houses and trees to be "colored by the palette of the sun."

But Gautier also had the sort of eye that could find melancholic beauty amid dirt and disorder. He shared the excitement of romantic literature for Greek and Roman ruins and the remains of vanished civilizations, even as he mocked the awe. During his youth, while still dreaming of becoming a painter, Gautier found the

empty houses of the Doyenne cul-de-sac and the Saint-Thomas-du-Louvre Church (near the Louvre, next to which Nerval lived) very seductive on moonlit nights.

Leaving his hotel (in today's Beyoğlu) and walking down through Galata to the shores of the Golden Horn, then crossing Galata Bridge (newly erected in 1853, it was, he said, a "bridge of boats"),

Gautier and his French guide proceeded to Unkapanı and north-
west; soon they "plunged into a labyrinth of Turkish lanes." The
farther they went, the more isolated they felt and the larger the pack
of snarling dogs that followed them. Every time I read about the
unpainted, darkened, dilapidated wooden houses, the broken-down
fountains, the neglected tombs with their fallen-in roofs, and all the
other things they observed during their walks, I am amazed that
these places I saw while riding around in my father's car a hundred

years later were unchanged except for the cobblestones. It was because he, like me, thought they were beautiful that Gautier noticed the blackened, ruined wooden houses, the stone walls, the empty streets, and the cypresses without which no cemetery was complete. When I began my own wanderings around the same destitute and not yet westernized quarters (which, sadly, fire and concrete would soon obliterate), I found the view exhausting as he did, while still feeling urged on "from lane to lane, from square to square." The call to prayer seemed to him, as it would later to me, addressed to the "mute, blind, and deaf houses falling here in silence and solitude." He would think about the passage of time as he watched the people and creatures straggling past: an old woman, a lizard disappearing among the weeds, and two or three boys throwing stones into the basin of a broken-down fountain (this reminded him of a watercolor by Maxime du Camp, who'd visited the city two years earlier with Flaubert). When he grew hungry, he noticed how little the shops and restaurants in this part of the city had to offer, and he gobbled mulberries from the trees that brought color to the side streets and that, despite all the concrete, still do. He was attuned to the village atmosphere of the Greek neighborhoods of Samatya and Balat, the so-called Ghetto of Istanbul. The fronts of the houses in Balat were full of cracks, and the streets were dirty and muddy, but the Greek district of Fener was better cared for; whenever he saw the remains of a Byzantine wall or part of a great aqueduct, what he felt more than the durability of stone and brick was the impermanence of wood.

The most moving moments in these tiring, confusing walks come when Gautier catches sight of the Byzantine ruins running through these remote and destitute streets. Gautier conveys very powerfully the thickness and durability of walls: their upheaval, the

fissures and ravages of time; the cracks that run the whole length of a tower (as a child, that scared me too); the fallen fragments scattered at its base (between Gautier's time and ours, the great earthquake of 1894 caused considerable damage to the city walls). He describes the grass in the cracks and the fig trees, whose large green leaves soften the tops of the towers, the dullness of the abutting districts, the silence of these neighborhoods and their ramshackle houses. "It is difficult to believe there is a living city behind these dead ramparts!" wrote Gautier. "I do not believe there exists any-

where on earth [a thing] more austere and melancholy than this road, which runs for more than three miles between ruins on the one hand and a cemetery on the other."

What happiness do I derive from such confirmations of Istanbul's *hüzün*? Why have I devoted so much energy to convey to the reader the melancholy I feel in this city where I've spent my entire life?

In the last 150 years (1850–2000), I have no doubt that not only has *hüzün* ruled over Istanbul but that it has spread to the surrounding areas. What I have been trying to explain is that the roots of our *hüzün* are European: The concept was first explored, expressed, and poeticized in French (by Gautier, under the influence of his friend Nerval). So why is it that I care so much—why did my four melancholic writers care so much—about what Gautier and other Westerners have to say about Istanbul?

CHAPTER TWENTY-FIVE

Under Western Eyes

To some degree, we all worry about what foreigners and strangers think of us. But if anxiety brings us pain or clouds our relationship with reality, becoming more important than reality itself, this is a problem. My interest in how my city looks to western eyes is—as for most *İstanbullus*— very troubled; like all other Istanbul writers with one eye always on the West, I sometimes suffer in confusion.

When Ahmet Hamdi Tanpınar and Yahya Kemal were looking for an image of the city and a literature in which *İstanbullus* could see themselves, they studied Nerval's and Gautier's travel notes with great care. The Istanbul section of Tanpınar's *Five Cities* is the most important text by a native writer about the twentieth-century city, and it might be described as a conversation with Nerval and Gautier that sometimes degenerates into a quarrel. At one point, Tanpınar talks of Lamartine, the French writer and politician who also visited Istanbul; after noting his "painstaking portrait" of Abdülmecit and insinuating that Lamartine's *History of Turkey* (there was a fine eight-volume edition in my grandfather's library) may have been paid for by Abdülmecit himself, he went on to warn that Nerval and Gautier's assessments of Abdülmecit were less than penetrating because they were journalists whose readers "had made up their minds"; this gave the travelers no choice but to tell them what they wanted to hear. As for Gautier's boasts of the sultan's interest in the Italian lady accompanying the traveler and his fantasies of the sultan's harem—Tanpınar found these (like the accounts of so many subsequent western travelers) to be of "dubious morality," although he does allow that Gautier could not be blamed insofar as the harem "did indeed exist."

This uneasy aside conveys the ambivalence that besets literary *İstanbullus* on reading western observations. Because the country is trying to westernize, what western writers say is desperately important, but whenever a western observer goes too far, the Istanbul reader, having gone to great lengths to acquaint himself with that writer and the culture he represents, cannot help but feel heartbroken. Above all, no one can really say what counts as "going too far." A city, it may be said, owes its very character to the ways in which it "goes too far," and while an outside observer can take things out of proportion by paying excessive attention to certain details, these are often the same details that come to define that city's nature. (For example, when western travelers see cemeteries as part of the city's everyday life, they are going too far. But as Flaubert noted, they would disappear as the city tried to become more western; today it is only by reading western travelers' descriptions of cemeteries that we can understand how the city looked in their day.)

With the drive to westernize and the concurrent rise of Turkish nationalism, the love-hate relationship with the western gaze became all the more convoluted. The subjects that most obsessed western observers who set foot in Istanbul from the middle of the eighteenth century and throughout the nineteenth were the harem; the slave market (in *Innocents Abroad*, Mark Twain fantasized that the financial pages of big American papers might report the price and vital statistics of the latest crop of Circassian and Georgian girls); the beggars in the streets; the unimaginably huge burdens carried by hamals (during my childhood we were all uneasy when European tourists photographed the fearsome hamals I'd see crossing the Galata Bridge with tin piled high on their backs, but when an Istanbul photographer like Hilmi Şahenk chose the same subject, no one minded in the least); dervish lodges (one pasha told his friend and guest Nerval that the Rufai dervishes who ran around piercing themselves with skewers were "crazy" and advised him it was a waste of time to visit their lodges); and the seclusion of women.

Istanbul's westernized residents were all critical of these same things. But a western writer voicing even a mild objection would break their hearts and wound their nationalist pride.

The vicious circle is fed by westernizing intellectuals who long to hear the prominent writers and publishers of the West praise them for being like Westerners. Writers like Pierre Loti, by contrast, make no secret of loving Istanbul and the Turkish people for the opposite reason: for the preservation of their eastern particularity and their resistance to becoming western. In the days when Pierre Loti was criticizing *İstanbullus* for losing touch with their traditions, he had only a small following in Turkey, most of it, ironically, among the westernizing minority. But whenever the nation is embroiled in an international dispute, the westernized literary elite makes an indignant peace with Pierre Loti's highly sentimental and exotic "Turko-phile" writings.

André Gide's account of his travels through Turkey in 1914 offers nothing of this "Turk-loving" panacea. Quite the contrary: When he says he detests the Turks, he does not use the term in the proud nationalist way that is slowly coming into fashion but as a racial slur—the clothes the Turks wear are ugly, but the race deserves no better. He boasts that his travels have taught him that western civilization, particularly French civilization, is superior to all others. When *Marche Turque* was first published, Yahya Kemal, then the foremost Turkish poet, was deeply offended, but instead of publishing a response in the popular press as a writer might do today, he and other Turkish intellectuals hid their injury like a guilty secret and grieved in private. This can only mean that in their heart of hearts they feared Gide's insults might be well-founded. A year after Gide's book came out, Atatürk, the greatest westernizer of them all, instituted a revolution in dress, banning all clothing that wasn't western.

When western observers speak ill of the city, I often find myself in agreement, taking more pleasure in their cold-blooded candor than in the condescending admiration of Pierre Loti, forever going on about Istanbul's beauty, strangeness, and wondrous uniqueness. Most western travelers praise the city for its beauty and its people for their charms, but this is neither here nor there: What concerns us is what they read into what they see. In the mid-nineteenth century, French and English literature produced an ever richer image of Istanbul. Dervish lodges, fires, the beauty of cemeteries, the palace and its harem, the beggars, the packs of roaming dogs, the prohibition against drinking, the seclusion of women, the city's air of mystery, the Bosphorus tour, and the beauty of the skyline—these things gave the city its exotic allure, and because the writers who came often stayed in the same places and used the same guides, they rarely saw anything to destoy their illusions. A new generation of travelers did slowly become aware that the Ottoman Empire was crumbling, and so had little cause to wonder about the secret of the Ottoman army's success or the hidden workings of its government; instead of seeing the city as frightening and impenetrable, they came to see it as strange but amusing, a tourist attraction. For them, it was enough to have arrived; since they wrote mostly about the same things as their predecessors and saw travel as an end in itself, they were disinclined to dig deeper.

As trains and steamships brought Istanbul closer to the West, there were suddenly more western travelers wandering the streets, and this led many to speculate indulgently about what had brought them to this terrible place. Ignorance embroidered their pretensions and creative presumption prompted them to say exactly what they thought; even "cultivated" writers like André Gide saw no need to bother with cultural differences, the meaning of local rituals and traditions, or the social structures that underpinned them: A traveler, in his view, had the right to demand that Istanbul be amusing, distracting, upbeat. Having nothing of interest to say about the city, he and his ilk were confident enough to blame their boring, featureless subject, and they made notably little effort to hide their military and economic chauvinism from more "critical" western intellectuals. For them, the West set the standard for all humankind.

These writers came to Istanbul at a time when it had ceased to be exotic, due to westernization and the prohibitions of the Atatürk era—the banishing of the sultan, the closing of the harem and the dervish lodges, the tearing down of the wooden houses and other tourist attractions, and the replacement of the Ottoman Empire with the little imitative Republic of Turkey. After a long period when no one of consequence came to Istanbul, and local journalists interviewed all foreigners who turned up at the Hilton Hotel, the Russian-American poet Joseph Brodsky published a long piece entitled "Flight from Byzantium" in *The New Yorker*.

Perhaps because he was still smarting from W. H. Auden's brutal review of the book recounting his journey to Iceland, Brodsky began with a long list of reasons he'd come to Istanbul (by plane). At the time I was living far from the city and wanted to read only good things about it, so his mockery was crushing, yet I was glad when Brodsky wrote, "How dated everything is here! Not old, ancient, antique, or even old-fashioned, but dated!" He was right. When the empire fell, the new Republic, while certain of its purpose, was unsure of its identity; the only way forward, its founders thought, was to foster a new concept of Turkishness, and this meant a certain cordon sanitaire to shut it off from the rest of the world. It was the end of the grand polyglot multicultural Istanbul of the imperial age; the city stagnated, emptied itself out, and became a monotonous monolingual town in black and white.

The cosmopolitian Istanbul I knew as a child had disappeared by the time I reached adulthood. In 1852, Gautier, like many other travelers of the day, had remarked that in the streets of Istanbul you could hear Turkish, Greek, Armenian, Italian, French, and English (and, more than either of the last two languages, Ladino, the medieval Spanish of the Jews who'd come to Istanbul after the Inquisition). Noting that many people in this "tower of Babel" were fluent in several languages, Gautier seems, like so many of his compatriots, to be slightly ashamed to have no language other than his mother tongue.

After the founding of the Republic and the violent rise of Turkification, after the state imposed sanctions on minorities—measures that some might describe as the final stage of the city's "conquest" and others as ethnic cleansing—most of these languages disappeared. I witnessed this cultural cleansing as a child, for whenever anyone spoke Greek or Armenian too loudly in the street (you seldom heard Kurds advertising themselves in public during this period), someone would cry out, "Citizens, please speak Turkish!"—echoing what signs everywhere were saying.

My own troubled interest in even the most unreliable western travel writers does not issue from a simple love-hate relationship or blend of a confused anguish and a longing for approval. Leaving aside various official documents and the handful of city columnists who scolded *İstanbullus* for their poor comportment in the streets, *İstanbullus* themselves wrote very little about their city until the beginning of the twentieth century. The living, breathing city—its streets, its atmosphere, its smells, the rich variety of its everyday life—is something that only literature can convey, and for centuries the only literature our city inspired was penned by Westerners. We must look at Du Camp's photographs and the engravings of western artists to see how the streets of Istanbul looked in the 1850s and what sorts of clothes people wore; if I wish to know what was going on in the streets, avenues, and squares where I have spent my whole life, a hundred, two hundred, four hundred years before I was born; if I want to know which square was then just an empty field, and which of today's empty fields were once colonnaded squares; if I want to have some sense of how the people made their lives—unless I am prepared to spend years in the labyrinthine Ottoman archives, I can find my answers, however refracted, only in western accounts.

In "The Return of the Flaneur," Walter Benjamin begins his review of Franz Hessel's *Berlin Walks* by noting, "If we were to divide all the existing descriptions of cities into two groups according to the birthplace of the authors, we would certainly find that those written by natives of the cities concerned are greatly in the minority." According to Benjamin, the enthusiasm for seeing a city from the outside is the exotic or the picturesque. For natives of a city, the connection is always mediated by memories.

What I am describing may not, in the end, be special to Istanbul, and perhaps, with the westernization of the entire world, it is inevitable. Perhaps this is why I sometimes read Westerners' accounts not at arm's length, as someone else's exotic dreams, but drawn close by, as if they were my own memories. I enjoy coming across a detail that I have noticed but never remarked upon, perhaps because no one else I know has either. I love Knut Hamsun's description of the Galata Bridge I knew as a child—supported by barges and swaying under the weight of its traffic—just as I love Hans Christian Andersen's description of the "darkness" of the cypresses lining the cemeteries. To see Istanbul through the eyes of a foreigner always gives me pleasure, in no small part because the picture helps me fend off narrow nationalism and pressures to conform. Their occasionally accurate (and therefore somewhat embarrassing) descriptions of the harem, Ottoman dress, and Ottoman rituals are so distant from my own experience that even though I know they have some basis in fact, they seem to be describing someone else's city. Westernization has allowed me and millions of other *İstanbullus* the luxury of enjoying our own past as "exotic," of relishing the picturesque.

To see the city from many different points of view and thereby maintain the vitality of my connection to it, I sometimes fool myself. There are times—after I've gone for a long stretch without going outside or even bothering to look for that other Orhan waiting so patiently in that other house—when I worry that my attach-

ment to this place will ossify my brain, that isolation might kill the desire in my gaze. Then I take comfort in reminding myself that there is something foreign in my way of looking at the city, owing to all the time I've spent reading the accounts of western travelers. Sometimes, when I read about the things that never change—some of the main streets and side alleys, the wooden houses somehow still standing, the street vendors, the empty lots, and the *hüzün,* all that is as it was despite a tenfold increase in population—I will lull myself into believing that the accounts of western outsiders are my own memories.

If western travelers embroider Istanbul with illusions, fantasies about the East, there is in the end no harm done to Istanbul; we were never a western colony. So if Gautier mentions that the Turks don't cry when a disastrous fire strikes—that, unlike the French, who cry a great deal, they face adversity with dignity because they believe in fate—I might disagree entirely with what he says, but I still don't feel badly wronged. The disservice is done elsewhere: Any French reader who took Gautier at face value would be mystified as to why it is that *İstanbullus* have been unable to throw off their *hüzün.*

What grievance I feel when I read western travelers on Istanbul is above all that of hindsight: Many of the local features these observers, some of them brilliant writers, noted and exaggerated were to vanish from the city soon after having been remarked. It was a brutal symbiosis: Western observers love to identify the things that make Istanbul exotic, nonwestern, whereas the westernizers among us register all the same things as obstacles to be erased from the face of the city as fast as possible.

Here's a short list:

The Janissaries, those elite troops of great interest to western travelers until the nineteenth century, were the first to be dissolved. The slave market, another focus of western curiosity, vanished soon after they began writing about it. The Rufai dervishes with their waving skewers and the Mevlevi dervish lodges closed with the founding of the Republic. The Ottoman clothing that so many western artists painted was abolished soon after André Gide complained about it. The harem, another favorite, also gone. Seventy-five years after Flaubert told his beloved friend that he was going to the market to have his name written in calligraphy, all of Turkey moved from the Arabic to the Latin alphabet, and this exotic joy ended too. Of all these losses, I think the hardest for *İstanbullus* has been the removal of graves and cemeteries from the gardens and squares of our everyday lives to terrifying high-walled lots, bereft of cypress or view. The hamals and their burdens, noted by so many travelers of the republican period—like the old American cars that Brodsky noted—were no sooner described by foreigners than they vanished.

Only one of the city's idiosyncracies has refused to melt away under the western gaze: the packs of dogs that still roam the streets. After he abolished the Janissaries for not complying with western military discipline, Mahmut II turned his attention to the city's dogs. In this ambition, however, he failed. After the Constitutional Monarchy, there was another "reform" drive, this one aided by the Gypsies, but the dogs they removed one by one to Sivriada managed to find their way triumphantly back home. The French, who thought the dog packs exotic, found the cramming of all the dogs into Sivriada even more so; Sartre would joke about this years later in his novel *The Age of Reason*.

Les chiens des rues.
Le déjeuner.
Souvenir de

Éditeur Max Fruchtermann, Constantinople. 1078

Photogr. Abdullah.

Max Fruchtermann, the postcard artist, seems to have recognized the exoticism of the dogs' survival: In a series of Istanbul views he produced around the turn of the twentieth century, he was careful to include as many street dogs as he did dervishes, cemeteries, and mosques.

CHAPTER TWENTY-SIX

The Melancholy of the Ruins: Tanpınar and Yahya Kemal in the City's Poor Neighborhoods

Tanpınar and Yahya Kemal took long walks together through Istanbul's poorest sections. Revisiting them on his own during the Second World War, Tanpınar recalled how much he had learned strolling earlier through "those vast impoverished neighborhoods between Kocamustafapaşa and the city walls." These were the neighborhoods in which Gautier sensed the gloom that had fallen over the city by 1853; Tanpınar and Yahya Kemal began their excursions during the humiliating "armistice years."

When these two great Turkish writers set out on their first walk, seventy years had passed since the visits of Nerval and Gautier, the two French friends whose works they so admired; during that time the Ottoman Empire had slowly lost its territories in the Balkans and the Middle East, growing smaller and smaller until it finally disappeared; the sources of income that had nurtured Istanbul dried up; despite the steady steam of Muslim refugees fleeing from the ethnic cleansing in the new Balkan republics, the death toll of the First World War ran into the hundreds of thousands, so both the city's population and its wealth were much diminished. During the same period, Europe and the West were getting richer, thanks to huge technological advances. As Istanbul grew ever poorer, it lost its importance in the world and became a remote place burdened with high unemployment. As a child I had no sense of living in a great world capital but rather in a poor provincial city.

When Tanpınar wrote "A Stroll Through the City's Poor Neighborhoods," he was not just describing his own most recent visit and his earlier walks. His purpose was more than merely to reacquaint himself with the poorest and most remote areas of Istanbul; he was attempting to accustom himself to the fact of living in an impoverished country, in a city that no longer mattered in the eyes of the world. To explore the poor neighborhoods as a landscape, then, was to address the reality that Istanbul and Turkey were themselves poor neighborhoods.

Tanpınar writes at length about the burned-out streets, the ruins, and the crumbling walls familiar to me as a child. Later during his

stroll he hears women's voices (out of habit Tanpınar refers to this as the "chirping of the harem") coming from "a big wooden mansion from the Abdülhamit period that is only just managing to stay in one piece," but in keeping with the political-cultural program he has set himself, he is obliged to explain that these are not Ottoman sounds but rather those of poor women working in the city's new cottage industries—"a stocking factory or a textile weaving shop." On every page, Tanpınar repeats the phrase "as we've all known since childhood"; he describes a neighborhood Rasim once mentioned in a column as "a fountain shaded by a trellis of vines or grapes, clothes hanging in the sun to dry, cats with dogs, little

mosques and cemeteries." The melancholy Tanpınar first discovered in Nerval's and Gautier's arresting observations about the poor neighborhoods, the ruins, dingy residential districts, and city walls, he transforms into an indigenous *hüzün* through which to apprehend a local landscape and, most particularly, the everyday life of a modern working woman.

We cannot know if he was fully aware of doing this. But he was aware that the burned-out lots, workshops, depots, and ramshackle wooden mansions he found in the crumbling and forgotten empty streets of these "isolated" sections carried a special beauty and significance. Because in the same piece, Tanpınar writes:

> I see the adventures of these ruined neighborhoods as symbolic. Only time and the sharp shocks of history can give a neighborhood such a face. How many conquests, how many defeats, how many miseries did its people have to suffer to create the scene before us?

We can give an answer that is probably already nestling in the reader's mind: If people were preoccupied by the destruction of the Ottoman Empire and the decline of Istanbul in the eyes of Europe, on the one hand, and on the other by the melancholy-*hüzün* that all great losses awaken, why did they not transform their Nervalian suffering into the sort of "pure poetry" to which it was so well suited? In Nerval's *Aurelia,* when he loses his love and his melancholy darkens, we can understand his claim that there is nothing left to life but "vulgar distractions." Nerval came to Istanbul to leave his melancholy behind. (Without knowing it, Gautier allowed this melancholy to

seep into his own observations.) When Tanpınar, Turkey's greatest twentieth-century novelist, and Yahya Kemal, its greatest twentieth-century poet, strolled together through the city's poor neighborhoods, they did so to feel their losses and their melancholy all the more keenly. Why?

They had a political agenda. They were picking their way through the ruins looking for signs of a new Turkish state, a new Turkish nationalism: The Ottoman Empire might have fallen, but the Turkish people had made it great (like the state, the two were happy to forget the Greeks, the Armenians, the Jews, the Kurds, and many other minorities), and they wanted to show that though suf-

fused in melancholy they were still standing tall. Unlike the ideologues of the Turkish state who expressed their nationalism in unlovely and unadorned authoritarian rhetoric, *they* expressed their patriotism in a poetic language far removed from decrees and force. Yahya Kemal had spent ten years in Paris studying French poetry; "thinking like a Westerner," he longed for a western-style image that would make nationalism "look more beautiful."

When the Ottoman Empire emerged defeated from the First World War, the Allies occupied Istanbul, and French and English battleships were sitting on the Bosphorus in front of Dolmabahçe Palace, there were various political projects in play that did not put Turkish identity at the forefront. While the war was raging in Anatolia with the Greek army, Yahya Kemal, who was not very fond of war, politics, or armies, stayed away from Ankara. He chose to remain "offstage" in Istanbul, where he devoted himself to poetry about past Turkish victories and also to creating an image of "Turkish Istanbul." The literary aspect of his successful political program was to use traditional poetic forms and metrical rules (the *aruz*) in such a way as to evoke the manners and atmosphere of spoken Turkish, while also confirming the Turks to be a people who had seen great victories and produced great works. In presenting Istanbul as the people's greatest work of art, he had two aims. First, if, following the First World War, during the armistice years, Istanbul was to become a colony of the West, it was important to explain to the colonizers that this was not just a place to be remembered for Hagia Sophia and its churches; they had to be made aware of the city's "Turkish" identity. And second, after the War of Independence and the founding of the Republic, Yahya Kemal emphasized Istanbul's Turkishness to herald "the creation of a new nation." Both writers wrote long articles that overlooked Istanbul's multilingual, multireligious heritage to support this "Turkification."

Tanpınar recalls this in a piece he wrote many years later entitled "How We Embraced the Great Works of Our Past During the Painful Armistice Years!" In an essay entitled "On the City Walls of Istanbul," Yahya Kemal recounts how he and his students boarded

the tramway at Topkapı and walked "from the Marmara to the Golden Horn along the walls, whose towers and crenelations spread as far as the eye could see," and paused to rest on "great lumps of fallen wall." To prove that theirs was a Turkish city, these two writers knew it was not enough to describe the skyline so beloved of western tourists and writers, or the shadows cast by its mosques and churches. Dominated as it was by Hagia Sophia, the skyline noted by every western observer from Lamartine to Le Corbusier could not serve as a "national image" for Turkish Istanbul; this sort of beauty was too cosmopolitan. Nationalist *İstanbullus* like Yahya Kemal and Tanpınar preferred to look to the poor, defeated, and deprived Muslim population, to prove they had not lost one bit of their identity and to satisfy their craving for a mournful beauty expressing the feelings of loss and defeat. This is why they went out on walks to poor neighborhoods in search of beautiful sights that endowed the city's dwellers with the *hüzün* of the ruined past; they found it by following in the footsteps of Gautier. All his nationalist fervor notwithstanding, Tanpınar sometimes resorted to words like "picturesque" and "paysage"; to convey these neighborhoods as traditional, unspoiled, and untouched by the West, he wrote that "they were ruined, they were poor and wretched," but they had "retained their own style and their own way of life."

So this is how two friends living in Istanbul—one a poet, the other a prose writer—drew upon the work of two friends from Paris—one a poet, the other a prose writer—to weave together a story from the fall of the Ottoman Empire: the nationalism of the early republican years, its ruins, its westernizing project, its poetry, and its landscapes. The result of this somewhat tangled tale was an

image in which *İstanbullus* could see themselves and a dream to which they could aspire. We might call this dream—which grew out of the barren, isolated, destitute neighborhoods beyond the city walls—the "melancholy of the ruins," and if one looks at these scenes through the eyes of an outsider (as Tanpınar did) it is possible to see them as picturesque. First seen as the beauty of a picturesque landscape, melancholy also came to express the sadness that a century of defeat and poverty would bring to the people of Istanbul.

CHAPTER TWENTY-SEVEN

The Picturesque and
the Outlying Neighborhoods

In *The Seven Lamps of Architecture,* John Ruskin devotes much of the chapter entitled "Memory" to the beauties of the picturesque, attributing the particular beauty of this sort of architecture (as opposed to that of carefully planned classical forms) to its "accidental" nature. So when he uses the word *picturesque* ("like a picture") he is describing an architectural landscape that has, over time, become beautiful in a way never foreseen by its creators. For Ruskin, picturesque beauty rises out of details that emerge only after a building has been standing for hundreds of years, from the ivy, herbs, and grassy meadows that surround it, from the rocks in the distance, the clouds in the sky, and the choppy sea. So there is

254

nothing picturesque about a new building, which demands to be seen on its own terms; it only becomes picturesque after history has endowed it with accidental beauty and granted us a fortuitous new perspective.

The beauty I see in Süleymaniye Mosque is in its lines, in the elegant spaces beneath its dome, in the opening out of its side domes, in the proportions of its walls and empty spaces, in the counterpoint of its support towers and its little arches, in its whiteness, and in the purity of the lead on its domes—none of which could be called picturesque. Even four hundred years after it was built, I can look at Süleymaniye and see a mosque still standing in its entirety, just as it first did, and see it as it was meant to be seen. No one monument dominates the Istanbul skyline; it owes its magnificence not just to Süleymaniye but also to Hagia Sophia, Beyazıt, and Yavuz Sultan Selim, and the other great mosques in the heart of the city, together with the many little ones built by wives and children of sultans, and all the other stately old buildings that still reflect the aesthetic ideals its architects intended. It is only when we glimpse these buildings from a gap in the street or down an alley lined with fig trees, or when we see the light from the sea playing on one of their walls, that we can claim to take pleasure in the beauty of the picturesque.

In Istanbul's poor neighborhoods, however, beauty resides entirely in the crumbling city walls, in the grass, ivy, weeds, and trees still growing when I was a child from the towers and walls of the

fortresses of Rumelihisarı and Anadoluhisarı. The beauty of a broken fountain, an old ramshackle mansion, a ruined hundred-year-old gasworks, the crumbling wall of an old mosque, the vines and plane trees intertwining to shade the old blackened walls of a wooden house—these are accidental. But when I visited the city's back streets as a child, these painterly tableaux were so numerous it was difficult, after a point, to see them as unintended: these sad (now vanished) ruins that gave Istanbul its soul. But to "discover" the city's soul in its ruins, to see these ruins as expressing the city's essence, you must travel down a long labyrinthine path strewn with historical accidents.

To savor Istanbul's back streets, to appreciate the vines and trees that endow its ruins with accidental grace, you must, first and fore-

most, be a stranger to them. A crumbling wall, a wooden *tekke*—condemned, abandoned, and now fallen into neglect—a fountain from whose faucets no water pours, a workshop in which nothing has been produced for eighty years, a collapsing building, a row of homes abandoned by Greeks, Armenians, and Jews as a nationalist state bore down on minorities, a house leaning to one side in a way that defies perspective, two houses leaning against each other in the way that cartoonists so love to depict, a cascade of domes and rooftops, a row of houses with crooked window casings—these things don't look beautiful to the people who live among them; they speak instead of squalor, helpless hopeless neglect. Those who take pleasure in the accidental beauty of poverty and historical decay, those of us who see the picturesque in ruins—invariably, we're people who come from the outside. (It was much the same for the northern Europeans who lovingly drew the Roman ruins that the Romans themselves ignored.) So while Yahya Kemal and Tanpınar saw the back streets of "pure and remote Istanbul" as places where people still embraced the old traditions, while they struggled to do poetic justice to the beauties of such neighborhoods and worried

that their "pure" culture might disappear with Westernization—while they conjured up the lovely fiction that these neighborhoods were graced with the morality of the old guilds, the ethos handed down by our honorable and hardworking "fathers and ancestors"—Yahya Kemal was himself living in Pera, the place he once described as "the district where one never hears a call to prayer," while Tanpınar was residing in even more comfortable Beyoğlu, a district he sometimes mocked with near hatred.

Let us recall that Walter Benjamin said people from outside a city are most interested in its exotic and picturesque features. These two nationalist writers could see the city's "beauty" only in those parts

where they themselves were outsiders. One thinks of a story told
about the great Japanese novelist Tanizaki, who, long after extolling
the traditional Japanese house and describing its structure in loving
detail, told his wife that he would never live in one because it lacked
western comforts.

Istanbul's greatest virtue is its people's ability to see the city
through both western and eastern eyes. The first representations of
local history in the Istanbul press were exaggerations, of the sort so

loved by Sir Richard Burton, the translator of *A Thousand and One Nights,* and by Nerval, what the French call *bizarreries.* Koçu certainly excelled at conveying the history of the city through his "oddities," thereby making the reader feel he was reading about a distant and alien civilization. Even when I was a child, when the city was at its most run-down, Istanbul's own residents felt like outsiders half the time. Depending on how they were looking at it, they felt it was either too eastern or too western, and the resulting uneasiness made them fear they didn't quite belong.

While Yahya Kemal and Tanpınar were living on one side of the city (westernized Pera), they drew upon beautiful, nationalist, melancholy, and picturesque scenes from another part of the city (the poor neighborhoods of the Old City) to create an image of Old Istanbul for *İstanbullus* of later generations. This dream neighborhood first appeared in the 1930s and 1940s in conservative magazines and newspapers, accompanied by crude imitations of landscapes painted by western artists. Accompanying these anonymous tableaux—for it was never clear who had originally painted them or where they were situated, or even what century they depicted, nor were most newspaper readers aware that they conveyed a western viewpoint—were black-and-white sketches by local artists of the poor neighborhoods and line drawings of their back streets. I particularly liked the reproductions of the painter Hoca Ali Rıza's line drawings, the purest and least exotic in this genre, and indeed they were quite popular.

While the tourists arriving in Istanbul in the late nineteenth and early twentieth centuries were admiring its magnificent skyline and the way the light played on its seas and mosques, Hoca Ali Rıza was sketching the back streets, where the rush to westernization and modernization had been abandoned midway; and this perspective continues to be found in the photographs of Ara Güler. Ara Güler's photographs show Istanbul to be a place where traditional life carries on regardless, where the old combines with the new to create a humble music that speaks of ruin, poverty, and humility, and where there is as much melancholy in the faces of the city's people as in its views; especially in the 1950s and 1960s, when the last brilliant remnants of the imperial city—the banks, inns, and government buildings of Ottoman westernizers—were collapsing all around him, he caught the poetry of the ruins. In his *Vanished Istanbul,* with the marvelous photographs of Beyoğlu as I knew it as a child—its tramways, its cobblestone avenues, its shop signs, its tired careworn black-and-white *hüzün*—he also makes excellent use of the elements of the neighborhood picturesque.

This image of a black-and-white, broken-down, remote neighborhood, "where everyone is poor but honorable and knows who he is," is especially popular during Ramadan, when the papers adorn their HISTORY and ISTANBUL columns with new reproductions of the old engravings and line drawings that seem to get cruder with each new year. The master of this subsidiary art was Reşat Ekrem Koçu, who illustrated his *Istanbul Encyclopedia* and his popular newspaper history columns not with unattributed reproductions of engravings but with crude sketches of them. (It was a matter of convenience: To isolate the one or two desired clichés in a finely detailed engraving was expensive and technically more difficult.) Many of the engravings were themselves imitations based on watercolors by western artists, but when popular artists use these derived black-and-white engravings as the basis for their own illustrations (invariably printed on poor paper the color of mud), you never see at the bottom of the image the name of the original artist or even the artist who made the "original copy"; there is only a note indicating it was taken "from an engraving." In the fantasy of Old Istanbul, poverty was to be honored for preserving traditional identity, and it was therefore all the more attractive to the half-westernized, fervently nationalist, newspaper-reading bourgeoisie who had no interest in the harsh realities of urban life. As the dream of Old Istanbul came to define not just Istanbul's poor neighborhoods but every part of the city except its skyline, a literature arose to fill in the particulars.

When they wished to emphasize the Turkish or Muslim side of these poor but slowly westernizing neighborhoods, conservative writers created an Ottoman heaven where no one questioned the power or legitimacy of the pasha, where families and friends confirmed their ties to one another through rituals and traditional values (these of course being humility, obedience, and contentment with one's lot). Aspects of Ottoman culture that might offend westernized middle-class sensibilities—concubines, the harem, polygamy, the pasha's right to beat people—were tamed and softened by right-wing authors like Samiha Ayverdi, who showed pashas and their children as more modern than they actually were.

Ahmet Kutsi Tecer's much-loved play *Streetcorner* is set in a coffeehouse in a poor neighborhood on the outskirts of the city (modeled on Rüstempaşa); as in a Karagöz shadow play, all the city's greatest characters come together to amuse us, distract us from the city's harsh realities, and welcome us with open arms. This is a far cry from the novelist and short-story writer Orhan Kemal, who once lived in the back streets of Cibali (where his wife worked in a tobacco factory); he portrayed the same back streets as a place where the struggle to earn a living was so fierce even friends could come to blows. For me the lovely dream of a poor neighborhood was epitomized by the *Uğurlugil Family,* whose little adventures I enjoyed so much every evening on the radio; this family, as big, crowded, and modern as mine (though, unlike mine, a big *happy* family), somehow managed, despite its reduced circumstances, to find room for a black mammy.

Rooted as it was in the picturesque, in the melancholy of the ruins, the narratives of Old Istanbul were loath to examine the dark evils that might be lurking beneath the surface. This was, above all, a nationalist literature offering an innocent view of tradition, suitable for family enjoyment. So from the poor golden-hearted orphans who populated the books of Kemalettin Tuğcu, whose tales I loved so much when I was ten, the message was that even someone living in the poorest of the poor neighborhoods could, by dint of hard work and virtue (remember, these neighborhoods were identified as the very source of all the highest nationalist and moral values), find happiness one day; yet he was purveying this message during the seventies, even as the city around us was growing poorer every day.

Ruskin suggests that, because it is accidental, the picturesque can never be preserved. After all, what makes the scene beautiful is not the architect's intention but its ruin. This explains why so many *İstanbullus* do not like seeing old wooden mansions restored: When the blackened, rotten wood disappears under bright paint that makes them look as they did at the height of the city's glory and prosperity in the eighteenth century, their lovely degenerative con-

nection with the past is severed. For the image of the city that *İstanbullus* have carried with them over the past century is as the child of poverty, defeat, and ruin. When I was fifteen and doing my own paintings, it was especially when painting the back streets that I became troubled about where our melancholy was taking us.

CHAPTER TWENTY-EIGHT

Painting Istanbul

When I was fifteen, I began to paint local landscapes quite obsessively, but not out of any special love of the city. I knew nothing of still life or portraiture, and I had no desire to learn about them, so my only option was to portray the Istanbul I could see from my window or when I went out in the street.

I drew the city in two ways.

At first, I did Bosphorus scenes with the sea passing through the center of the city and the skyline in the background. Generally, these scenes owed a great deal to the "bewitching" landscapes produced by two hundred years of western travelers. I painted the

Bosphorus as seen between the gaps in the apartment buildings from our house in Cihangir, with Kızkulesi, Fındıklı, and Üsküdar in the background; later, I did the Bosphorus as seen from our subsequent house in the heights of Beşiktaş Serencebey—a sweeping view of the mouth of the Bosphorus, Sarayburnu, Topkapı Palace, and the silhouette of the Old City. I could do these drawings without ever leaving home. That I was painting the fabled "Istanbul view" was something I could never forget. Everybody already acknowledged the beauty of my subject, and because it was also real I was less inclined to ask why it was beautiful. When I finished my painting and asked myself the same question I would put to those around me so many thousands of times throughout my life—"Is it beautiful? Did I make it look beautiful?"—I could be sure that my choice of subject alone guaranteed me a "yes."

And so these paintings seemed to draw themselves, and I didn't feel I had to live up to the western artists who'd drawn the scene before me. I was not knowingly imitating any one of them in particular, but I used what I had gleaned from them in many of my touches. I would make the waves on the Bosphorus look as if they'd been drawn by a child, in the style of Dufy; I'd do my clouds in the style of Matisse; I'd cover up any areas I'd not been able to paint in detail with dots of paint "like the impressionists." I sometimes used scenes from postcards and calendars. My paintings were not markedly different from the Turkish impressionists who used impressionist techniques to paint all the great Istanbul views forty or fifty years after French artists had pioneered them.

Because I was painting something that everyone agreed was beautiful, and because this released me from the obligation of proving to myself and others that I was painting beautifully, I found painting relaxing. When that great deep urge overtook me, I would gather up my materials as fast as I could, but even as I assembled my paints and brushes around the canvas that would take me to the second world, I often had no idea what I was going to paint. That didn't matter. Painting was simply the means to an end; in my elation, any postcard view from one of the windows of our house would do. It did not bore me in the least to be doing the same view

I'd done a hundred times already in much the same way. The important thing was to delve at once into the painting's details and escape this world: to situate a ship passing down the Bosphorus in a way that suited the perspective (since Melling's time, the central preoccupation of all artists who have painted the Bosphorus). To lose myself in the particulars of the silhouette of the mosque behind it—to draw cypresses and car ferries accurately; to take my time on the domes, the lighthouse at Sarayburnu, and the men fishing from the shore—was to feel as if I were wandering among the very things I was painting.

Painting allowed me to enter the scene on the canvas. This was a new way into the second world of my imagination, and when I had penetrated the most "beautiful" part of that world—when the painting was all but done—a strange ecstasy would overtake me. The vision shimmering before me looked real. I would forget that I had painted a Bosphorus scene that everyone knew and loved; this was a wondrous thing of my own imagination. The joy I felt upon finishing a painting was so great that I wanted to touch it, pick out some detail to embrace, even take it into my mouth, bite it, eat it. If something got in the way of this fantasy, if I did not quite lose myself in my painting, if (as happened more and more often) the first world intruded to ruin my childish game, I'd be overcome by an urge to masturbate.

This first type of painting was akin to what the poet Schiller called "naïve poetry." My choice of subject was much more important to me than my style or my technique; most of all, I wanted to believe that my art was a spontaneous expression of something inside me.

With time, the childish, joyous, colorful, carefree world these Bosphorus paintings depicted began to look very naïve indeed, and my enjoyment of them diminished. Like so many of my favorite childhood toys—the miniature cars I had once parked so neatly on the borders of my grandmother's carpet, the cowboy guns, the train sets my father brought me from France—these bright naïve paintings could no longer rescue me from the boredom of everyday life. So it was that I turned my back on the city's famous views and began my second way of painting the city: quiet side streets, forgotten squares, cobblestone alleyways (heading down the hill to the Bosphorus, with the sea, Kızkulesi, and the Asian shore in the background), and domed wooden houses. These works, some of which were black-and-white drawings and some of them oil on canvas or cardboard, but still with very little color and a great deal of white, were born of two different influences.

I had been much affected by the black-and-white illustrations of poor neighborhoods, appearing ever more frequently in the "History" columns in newspapers and magazines and loved the silent melancholy poetry of the poor neighborhoods. So I painted the little mosques, the crumbling walls, the Byzantine arch just visible in the corner, the domed wooden houses, and, bowing to the rules of perspective I had only just mastered, the long rows of humble houses receding into the distance.

The other influence was Utrillo, whose work I knew from reproductions and a thrilling melodramatic novel based on his life. When I wanted to do a painting in the style of Utrillo, I chose a back street in Beyoğlu, Tarlabaşı, or Cihangir, where there were very few mosques or minarets. When the urge to paint overtook me, I would take out a few of the prints I had made of the photographs I'd taken

while strolling about the city streets; after contemplating them at length, I'd go on to paint a Beyoğlu scene, and—though they are very rare in Istanbul—I'd put Utrillo-like shutters on the windows of all the apartment houses. As I finished the painting, ecstasy would overtake me—just as it had in the old days, when I was younger—I'd feel as if the scene I'd painted was my own creation but also real. Even as I identified with the scene, I felt a degree of

detachment. To attain my ultimate goal—to leave myself behind—it was no longer enough to identify naïvely with the world in my painting; I had to make a spiritual leap as confusing as it was cunning: I'd become someone named Utrillo, who in Paris had once done paintings so very much like these. Of course I didn't really believe this; even when I was doing my Bosphorus paintings, I only half believed I had entered the world of my painting; now I only half believed I was Utrillo. But the new game was useful nevertheless, particularly if I was suffering an insecurity I could not begin to understand; if I doubted the value of the painting I had just done or was anxious for others to find it "beautiful" or "meaningful." By contrast, when the scene became too real, I felt my compass narrowing. In this case I would follow a pattern that would become more routine when sex entered my life soon afterward: As I was fin-

ishing a painting, a great wave of joy would crash over me and I would lose my bearings; this would give way to gloom and confusion and when this had receded, I'd take a rest.

Taking the still-wet painting I'd executed so hastily from one of my own photographs, I'd hang it on the wall at eye level and try to view it as if it were a painting by someone else. If I liked it, a haze of pleasure and security would settle over me; I had succeeded gloriously in capturing the melancholy of the back streets. But if—as happened more often—I judged my painting inadequate and deficient, I would examine it from other angles, standing farther away and then coming up closer, sometimes hopefully adding a few touches with my brush, struggling at last to accept the thing I had done. By now I could no longer believe I was Utrillo, no longer suppose there was something of him in my paintings. So just as I would do in later years after having sex, I'd fall into despair—it was not the view that was wanting but my painting. I was not Utrillo, but someone who had tried to do a painting *like* Utrillo.

I could not fend off that deepening melancholy; it spread like a stain. The almost-but-not-quite-shameful truth was that I could paint only when I thought I was someone else. I'd imitated a style; I'd imitated (though without ever using that word) an artist with his own unique vision and way of painting. And not without profit, for if I had somehow become someone else, I too now had "my" own style and identity. I would take a faint pride in this version. This was my first intimation of the thing that would nag at me in later years, the self-contradiction—a Westerner would call it the paradox—that we only acquire our own identity by imitating others. My unease at being under the influence of another artist was relatively light; I was still a child and I was painting to amuse myself. Another consolation, a simpler one, was that the city I had painted, the Istanbul I had photographed, itself exerted a more powerful influence on me than any artist could.

During the days when painting was my main escape, there would be a knock on the door and in would stride my father; if he found me caught up in the excitement of creation, he would face me just as respectfully as when he caught me as a child playing with my penis; without a hint of condescension, he'd ask, "So how are we doing today, Utrillo?" The implied joke reminded me that I was still child enough to get away with imitating others. I was sixteen when my mother, knowing how serious I was about painting, gave me per-

mission to use the Cihangir apartment, where we had once lived and where my mother and my grandmother now stored old furniture, as a studio. On weekends and sometimes in the afternoon, leaving Robert Academy, I would go to this cold empty apartment; having lit the stove and warmed myself up, I would choose one or two of the photographs I'd taken and, in a flash of inspiration, execute one or two huge paintings before returning home, tired and spent and full of a strange melancholy.

CHAPTER TWENTY-NINE

Painting and Family Happiness

Whenever I entered the Cihangir apartment my mother had arranged for me to use as a studio, I would huff and puff until I had lit the gas stove. (When I was eleven years old and living in this same apartment with my family, I'd been a committed pyromaniac—lighting fires wherever and whenever I could—but only now did I notice that this joy had left me long ago without so much as a goodbye.) By the time the high-ceilinged apartment was warm enough to take the chill off my hands, I'd have put on my paint-splattered smock—this more than anything defined me as someone who'd been painting for some time. It was, nonetheless, a somewhat mournful prospect, escaping into a painting I would not be able to show anyone, certainly not at once, though perhaps in one or two days. I'd turned the apartment into a gallery—my paintings hung on every wall—but no one, not my mother or even my father, ever came to admire them. And so it was in this apartment that I discovered a need not only to know my paintings would be seen, but also, while painting, to feel the presence all around me of those who'd be judging my work later. To be standing in a gloomy apartment full of chilly old furniture that smelled of dust and mold, painting scenes of Istanbul, made me feel gloomy too.

I would give a great deal if I could put my hands on some of those paintings (now lost) I did at home between the ages of sixteen and seventeen, depictions of "family happiness" in what we might call the Tolstoyan sense of the phrase. These paintings were hugely significant to me because—as you can see from the picture below, taken by a professional photographer who came to the house when I was seven—I sometimes had difficulty maintaining the "happy family" pose. Abandoning my usual Istanbul views and back streets, I painted "us" while my parents moved around me, doing the things they did every day. It was when tensions between my parents had softened somewhat—when no one was needling anyone else, and everyone was relaxed, and the radio or maybe a tape was playing in the background, when the maid was bustling in the kitchen as she cooked our supper, or just before we all set out together on an outing or a trip—that I would do these paintings, always in a single flash of inspiration.

My father would usually be stretched out on the sofa in the sitting room: It's where he spent most of his time at home, reading newspapers, magazines, or books (not the literary novels he'd enjoyed in his youth but books about bridge) or staring distractedly at the ceiling. If he was in a good mood and had put some orchestral music on the tape deck, say Brahms's First Symphony, he'd stand up on occasion to direct an imaginary orchestra, waving his arms as conductors do, which to me seemed angry, impatient, and obsessed. My mother, in her armchair right next to him, would raise her eyes from her newspaper or her knitting, with a smile, it seemed, of something between compassion and love.

It was an arrangement devoid of arresting detail, provoking no discussion, but this was why it attracted my attention. When this tableau made one of its rare appearances, I would whisper, "I'm going to do a painting" in a half-joking, half-ashamed voice, as if talking to a jinn that had taken up residence inside me; I would then rush to my room and grab my painting things—my oils or the 120 Guitar pastels my father had brought from England and a few sheets of the multicolored Schöler paper my aunt gave me every year for my birthday—and return to the sitting room, to arrange my father's desk in such a way that I could see them both when I sat down to dash off, very quickly, a picture of home.

Through it all, neither my father nor my mother would speak, and because they responded naturally to my sudden and irrepressible desire to do a painting, it seemed to me as if God had briefly stopped time just for me. (In spite of my general lack of interest, I still believed that She came to my aid at important moments.) Or perhaps my mother and father looked happy because they weren't speaking. For me, the thing called family was a group of people who, out of a wish to be loved and feel peaceful, relaxed and secure, agreed to silence, for a while each day, the jinns and devils inside them and act as if they were happy. Often as not they did so because they couldn't think of anything better to do and managed, in the end, to be convinced by their own pretense, but if, after holding the happy poses for some time, they had not been quite able to put their jinns and devils to sleep, my father's eyes would wander from the pages of his book as my mother continued her knitting with composed resignation and, looking out the window at the Bosphorus in the distance as though indifferent to its beauty, lose himself in thought. A magical silence would descend over the room as my mother and father stretched out, perfectly still, not saying a word but expressing what seemed a shared anguish; later, in the seventies, when like everyone else in the country we bought a television set and they somewhat sheepishly surrendered to its entertainments, there were no magical silences, and I never again had the desire to paint them. Because for me happiness occurred when the people who loved me were suppressing their demons and I was free to play.

Though they were posing as if for a photograph, not moving a muscle as my hand raced ever faster to finish my happy family scene, sometimes they conversed. One would mention something in the paper, and after a long silence, the other would offer up an analysis or say nothing at all. Sometimes my mother and I would be talking, and my father, who'd been lying on the sofa showing no interest in our conversation, would suddenly pipe up and prove he'd been listening all along. Sometimes, if one of us looked out the wide windows of our apartment in Beşiktaş Serencebey to see a strange and terrifying Soviet ship making its way up the Bosphorus, or if it was spring and a flock of storks on their way north from Africa crossed the sky, the long silence would be broken by a short superfluity, as in, "Those are storks!" But much as I loved these silences that fell over our sitting room, when we all sank into our own little worlds, I recognized the transience of their peace and happiness. Adding the finishing touches to my painting, I would notice fearsome details of my parents' bodies that I had missed altogether until seeing them with a painterly eye. I would look at my mother in her glasses, an expression half happy, half hopeful on her face, and at the yarn hanging from the knitting needles from which it dipped down first to her lap, then to her feet and into the plastic bag holding the skein. Next to this transparent bag, no less still when she was talking to my father than when she was lost in thought, was her slippered foot, and as I studied it long and carefully, a strange shiver would pass through me. There was something about people's arms, legs, and hands, something even about heads, that was lifeless, stolid as the vases in which my mother put gypsy holly—*kokino*—inanimate as the small table at her side or the Iznik plates she hung on the wall. Even though we had managed a happy family tableau, and even though I'd succeeded in suspending my disbelief, when the three of us sat, each in his own corner, something made us look like just three more pieces of furniture my grandmother had crammed into her museum room.

I reveled in these shared silences, which were as rare and precious as playing "the priest has run away" on special occasions, and our New Year's games of lotto. As I filled the page with, I imagined, Matisse's swift brushwork, dotting the carpets and curtains with the same little curves and arabesques Bonnard used in his domestic interiors, the sky outside would grow darker and I would notice that the light from the three-legged lamp next to my father had grown brighter. When evening had arrived for certain and the sky and the Bosphorus had assumed their deep gorgeous purple, and the light of the lamp had turned orange, I'd see that the windows no longer looked out over the Bosphorus or the car ferries or the ship crossing from Beşiktaş to Üsküdar or the smoke coming out of the chimneys of ships, but instead reflected upon us the inside of our house.

Either walking through the streets in the evening or looking out the window, I still loved looking through the orange halo of the streetlamps into other people's houses. Sometimes I'd see a woman sitting alone at a table reading her own fortune, striking just the same pose my mother did on those long winter evenings when my father did not come home, smoking cigarettes and patiently playing Patience. Sometimes I'd look into a humble little ground-floor apartment to see a family eating supper and talking all at once under the same orange light as in our house, and as I gazed at them from the outside I'd innocently decide they must be happy. Happy families viewed through windows—these are the pictures that tell us about our city; but in Istanbul, where, especially in the nineteenth century, visitors were rarely admitted to any room but the parlor, foreigners are seldom able to make sense of what they see.

CHAPTER THIRTY

The Smoke Rising from Ships on the Bosphorus

I n the mid-nineteenth century, steamships revolutionized sea travel, bringing closer the great cities of Europe; it made short visits to Istanbul possible. In time, some of those who committed their impressions to paper would inform a new idea of Istanbul created by a handful of local writers; but from the moment of their arrival, these steamships gave the city a new look. A company initially trading under the name of Şirket-i Hayriye and later known

as Şehir Hatları (City Lines) was set up, and soon every Bosphorus village had its own landing stage; as the ferries began to ply the strait, the city took on a faintly European aspect. (Let us remember that *vapeur*, the French word for *steam*, found its way into Istanbul Turkish and everyday life to become *vapur*, our word for *ship*.) Among the changes ferries brought with them were the busy *meydans* that grew up around the landing stages of the Bosphorus and the Golden Horn or the rapid growth of these villages that soon made them part of the city proper. (Until the ferries arrived, there were hardly any roads connecting them.)

As ferries began to carry passengers up and down the Bosphorus, they became as familiar to *İstanbullus* as Kızkulesi, Hagia Sophia, Rumelihisarı, and the Galata Bridge; soon they were such a part of everyday life that they assumed an almost totemic importance. Just as others become attached to Venice's vaporettos and love to show off their knowledge of the various shapes and models, so too do

İstanbullus dote on each and every ferry ever owned by City Lines; there are whole books devoted to them, complete with illustrations. Gautier wrote that every barber in Istanbul had a picture of a ferry hanging on his wall. My father could recognize every one put into service in his childhood just by its splendid silhouette, and if he couldn't remember at once, a moment later he would be reciting the names that still sound like poems to me: Fifty-three *İnşirah,* Sixty-seven *Kalender,* Forty-seven *Tarz-I Nevin,* Fifty-nine *Kamer.* . . .

When I asked him how he could distinguish ships that looked so much alike, he would enumerate the special features of each—say, when we had gone out for a drive along the Bosphorus or, if traffic made that impossible, in the sitting room of our house in Beşiktaş; but even after he had identified the uniqueness of each ship—this one had a hump, that one had an extra-long chimney, another had a hooked nose or a plump behind or leaned slightly to one side in a swift current—I still could not, even after close study, tell any of

them apart. But I did learn to distinguish the three ferries—two made in England and the other in Taranto, Italy, in 1952, the year of my birth—that were named after gardens; after studying their shapes and the width of their chimneys, I was finally able to tell the *Fenerbahçe* and the *Dolmabahçe* from the *Paşabahçe,* which I came to see as my lucky ship, so that whenever I happened to be walking through the city lost in thought and caught a glimpse of it when I looked down an alley or out the window, I would feel a little lift: I still do today.

The ferries' great gift to the skyline is the smoke from their funnels. I loved painting in their coal-dark clouds, which varied according to the ferry's position and make, the sway of the great Bosphorus currents, and, of course, the wind. Before I put in the

smoke coming out of the funnels with my frayed paintbrush, the painting had to be completely finished, even half dry. Like the signature I would later place into the lower righthand corner, the smoke coming out of a particular funnel seemed to me to be that ferry's special stamp. When the smoke thickened into a cloud, especially when rising from all the funnels of all the ships moored around Galata Bridge, it was as if my world was being wrapped in a black veil. Walking along the shores of the Bosphorus or traveling on a ferry, I loved passing under the swirling smoke of a vessel long departed. If the wind was right, a dry rain of millions of tiny black particles with the smell of burnt mineral would settle on my face like a cobweb.

Often, after I had brought a painting to a happy close and crowned it with just the right amount of smoke coming out of the ferries' funnels (sometimes I'd put in too much smoke and ruin the picture), I would consider the other ways I had observed smoke swirl, broaden out, and vanish, and then I'd file these images away, as if for future use. But with the last brushstrokes, the canvas before me would have so thoroughly assumed its own reality that I'd have already forgotten what I'd seen with my own eyes, what the smoke looked like in its true and natural form.

I find the perfect column of smoke comes with a light breeze, and after the smoke has for a time been rising at a 45-degree angle, it begins to run parallel with the ship without changing shape, as if someone has drawn an elegant line in the sky to indicate the ferry's course. The thin column of coal-dark smoke rising from a ferry docked on a windless day reminds me of smoke rising up from the little chimney of a hovel. When the ferry and the wind have

changed direction just slightly, the smoke rising from the funnel begins to swoop and swirl over the Bosphorus like Arabic script. But whenever I painted a Bosphorus scene with a City Lines ferry, I needed the smoke to convey the melancholy of the scene, so this joyful accidental shape, as much as I admired it, troubled me. On a day without wind, when dark smoke rising powerfully from a funnel lingers in the sky, there was an undeniable record of the melancholy the ferry had left in its wake as it curled its way from shore to shore. I loved to see thick black smoke sitting on the horizon and merging with the threatening clouds behind it, as in a Turner painting. But still, when finishing a painting with one or perhaps several ferries to furnish with smoke, it was not the shades of smoke I'd seen from the ferries themselves, but the smoke I'd seen in Monet, Sisley, and Pisarro that I called to mind—the bluish cloud in Monet's *Gare Saint-Lazare* or the happy ice-cream-scoop clouds from the very different world of Dufy—and that's what I'd paint.

In the opening lines of *Sentimental Education,* Flaubert has a beautiful description of smoke changing shape, and that is one of the reasons I love him. (There are other reasons too.) Here we end our hymn to smoke; by using this passage as a bridge to the next melody,

I have executed what was known in traditional Ottoman music as an *ara taksim*. The word *taksim* can mean to divide, to gather, or to channel water, and this is why the great field where Nerval saw vendors and cemeteries (and which also served as a water distribution center) came to be known to *İstanbullus* as Taksim. They still know it by the same name, and I've lived around it all my life. But it was not yet known as Taksim when Flaubert and Nerval passed through.

CHAPTER THIRTY-ONE

Flaubert in Istanbul:
East, West, and Syphilis

In October 1850, seven years after Nerval's visit to Istanbul, Gustave Flaubert arrived with his friend Maxime du Camp, the writer and photographer, as well as the case of syphilis he'd just caught in Beirut. He stayed here almost five weeks, and though, in a letter from Athens to Louis Bouilhet, he said, "One would have to stay [in Istanbul] at least six months," we should not take his claim too seriously, as Flaubert was a man who missed everything he left behind. As we can see very clearly from the letters carrying *Constantinople* next to the date, what he had been missing most since setting out on his journey was his house in Rouen, his study, and his dear mother, who'd wept copiously at his departure, and his dearest wish was to get home as soon as he could.

Following Nerval's itinerary, Flaubert had come to Istanbul via Cairo, Jerusalem, and Lebanon. Like Nerval, he'd grown tired of the harsh frightening ugliness and mystical exoticism of the East he glimpsed in these places; already bored with his own fantasies and overcome by the realities, which were more "oriental" than his dreams, he took little interest in Istanbul. (His original plan was to stay here for three months.) In fact, Istanbul was not the East he was looking for. In another letter to Louis Bouilhet, he recalled Lord Byron traveling through western Anatolia. The East that captured Byron's imagination was "the Turkish Orient, the Orient of the curved sword, the Albanian costume, and the barred window looking on the blue sea." But Flaubert preferred "the baked Orient of the Beduin and the desert, the vermillion depths of Africa, the crocodile, the camel, the giraffe."

Of all the places the twenty-nine-year-old writer had seen on his eastern voyage, it was Egypt that had fired his imagination, as it would do for the rest of his life. As he explained in letters to his mother and to Bouilhet, his mind was now on the future and the books he wished to write. (Among the imagined books was a novel called "Harel Bey," in which a civilized Westerner and an eastern barbarian slowly come to resemble each other, finally changing places.) From what he wrote to his mother, it is clear that all the elements later to form the Flaubert myth—his refusal to take seriously anything other than art, his contempt for bourgeois life, marriage, and making a living from trade—were already in place. A hundred years before my birth, as he was wandering the streets in which I would spend my life, a thought came to him that he would later set down on paper, and it would become one of the basic moral principles of modernist literature: "I care nothing for the world, for the future, for what people will say, for any kind of establishment, or even for literary renown, which in the past I used to lie awake so many nights dreaming about. That is what I am like; such is my character." (Letter from Flaubert to his mother, December 15, 1850, Istanbul.)

Why this fixation with the thoughts of western travelers, what they did on visits to the city, what they wrote to their mothers? It's partly that many times I've identified with a number of them (Nerval, Flaubert, de Amicis) and—just as I once had to identify myself with Utrillo in order to paint Istanbul—it was by falling under their influence and contesting with them by turns that I forged my own identity. It's also because so few of Istanbul's own writers have paid their city any attention whatsoever.

Whatever we call it—false consciousness, fantasy, or old-style ideology—there is, in each of our heads, a half-legible, half-secret text that makes sense of what we've done in life. And for each of us in Istanbul, a large section of this text is given over to what western observers have said about us. For people like me, *İstanbullus* with

one foot in each culture, the "western traveler" is often not a real person; he can be my own creation, my fantasy, even my own reflection. But being unable to depend on tradition alone as my text, I am grateful to the outsider who can offer me a complementary version—whether a piece of writing, a painting, or a film. So whenever I sense the absence of western eyes, I become my own Westerner.

Istanbul has never been the colony of the Westerners who wrote about it, drew it, or filmed it, and that is why I am not so perturbed by the use western travelers have made of my past and my history in their construction of the exotic. Indeed, I find their fears and dreams beguiling—as exotic to me as ours are to them—and I don't just look to them for entertainment or see the city through their eyes but also to enter into the full-formed world they've conjured up. Especially when reading the western travelers of the nineteenth century—perhaps because they wrote about familiar things in words I could easily understand—I realize "my" city is not really mine. Just as it is when I am contemplating the skyline and the angles most familiar to me—from Galata and Cihangir, where I am writing these lines—so it is, too, when I see the city through the words and images of Westerners who saw it before me; at times like

these I must face my own uncertainties about the city and my tenuous place in it. I will often feel as if I've become one with that western traveler, plunging with him into the thick of life, counting, weighing, categorizing, judging, and in so doing often usurping his dreams, to become at once the object and subject of the western gaze. As I waver back and forth, sometimes seeing the city from within and sometimes from without, I feel as I do when I am wandering the streets, caught in a stream of slippery contradictory thoughts, not quite belonging to this place and not quite a stranger. This is how the people of Istanbul have felt for the last 150 years.

Allow me to illustrate this with a story about Flaubert's penis, a matter of some concern to him during his stay in Istanbul. In a letter to Louis Bouilhet on the second day of his visit, our troubled author confessed that the seven chancres that had appeared on his penis after he caught syphilis in Beirut had now merged into one. "Every night and morning I dressed my wretched prick!" he wrote. First he thinks he might have caught it from a Maronite, or "perhaps it was a little Turkish lady. The Turk or the Christian?" he asks, and in the same mocking tone goes on to observe, "*Problème!* Food for thought! That's an aspect of the 'Eastern Question' the *Revue des*

Deux Mondes doesn't dream of!" Around this time, he was also writing to his mother that he would never marry, but this wasn't owing to his illness.

Even though grappling with the syphilis that would result in such a sudden hair loss that even his own mother would not recognize him on his return, Flaubert managed to visit Istanbul's brothels. But when one of the dragomen [guide translators] who always took western travelers to the same places showed Flaubert a place in Galata that was "filthy" and the women were "ugly," Flaubert expressed a wish to leave at once. By his account, the madam, by way of appeasement, offered him her own daughter, a sixteen- or seventeen-year-old Flaubert found very attractive. But the daughter refused to go with him. The residents of the house had to force her—the reader is left to wonder how they managed this feat—and when the two were finally alone, the girl asked Flaubert in Italian if he could show her his organ so she might be sure he was not sick. "Since on the lower part of my glans I still have an induration and was afraid she would see it, I acted the monsieur and jumped down from the bed, saying loudly that she was insulting me, that such behavior was revolting to a gentleman; and I left," Flaubert writes.

When, at the beginning of his journey, a doctor in a Cairo hospi-

tal had demonstrated with one gesture how he ordered patients to pull down their trousers and display their chancres for the benefit of visiting western physicians, Flaubert had studied them all meticulously and made careful notes about them in his notebook, remarking with satisfaction—as he would when describing the height, stance, and dress of a dwarf in the courtyard of Topkapı Palace—that he had seen yet another eastern oddity, another filthy eastern custom. If he had come to the East to see beautiful unforgettable spectacles, Flaubert's desire to survey its diseases and odd medical practices was no less intense. Still, he had no intention of exposing his own lesions or his own odd habits. In his brilliant *Orientalism,* Edward Said makes much of the opening scene in the Cairo hospital when analyzing Nerval and Flaubert, but he fails to mention the Istanbul brothel where the drama ends; had he done so, he might have prevented many Istanbul readers from using his work to justify nationalist sentiment or to imply that, if it weren't for the West, the East would be a wonderful place. Perhaps Said chose to omit it because Istanbul was never a colony of the West and therefore not central to his concerns. (Although nationalist Turks would later claim the disease to have spread throughout the world from America, western travelers of the nineteenth centuries called syphilis *"frengi,"* or "French," knowing it was the French who carried the infection to other world civilizations. Fifty years after Flaubert's visit to Istanbul, Şemsettin Sami, the Albanian who brought out the first Turkish dictionary, would simply write that *"frengi* came to us from Europe." But in his *Dictionary of Accepted Ideas,* Flaubert would still take the view he had when first asking himself how he'd caught this disease; without succumbing to another East-West joke, he concludes that it had caught more or less everyone.)

With no qualms about admitting to an interest in the strange, the frightening, the filthy, and the queer, Flaubert writes at length in his letters about the "cemetery whores" (who serviced soldiers at night), about the empty stork nests, the cold, the Siberian winds whipping

down from the Black Sea, and the city's great crowds. Like so many other visitors, he was specially fascinated by its cemeteries: He was the first to note that the gravestones one saw all over the city were, like the memories of the dead themselves, slowly sinking into the earth as they aged, soon to vanish without a trace.

CHAPTER THIRTY-TWO

Fights with My Older Brother

Between the ages of six and ten, I fought with my older brother incessantly, and as time went on the beatings to which he subjected me grew more and more violent. There were only eighteen months between us, but he was considerably bigger and stronger, and because it was (and perhaps still is) considered normal, even healthy, for two brothers to fight and come to blows, no one saw the need to stop us. I saw the beatings as personal failures and blamed them on my weakness and lack of coordination; during the first few years, when my brother angered or belittled me, I was often the first to strike, and half believing that I deserved the beatings, of course I wasn't going to challenge violence in principle. If one of our fights ended with broken glass and windowpanes and me bruised and bleeding, my mother's complaint when she finally intervened was not that we had hit each other and not that I'd been beaten up, but that we'd messed up the house—and that because we'd been unable to settle our differences peaceably, the neighbors would complain yet again about the noise.

Later, when reminded of those brawls, my mother and my brother claimed no recollection of them, saying that, as always, I'd invented them just for the sake of something to write about, just to give myself a colorful and melodramatic past. They were so sincere that I was finally forced to agree, concluding that, as always, I'd been swayed more by my imagination than by real life. So anyone reading these pages should bear in mind that I am prone to exaggeration. But what is important for a painter is not a thing's reality but its shape, and what is important for a novelist is not the course of events but their ordering, and what is important for a memoirist is not the factual accuracy of the account but its symmetry.

So the reader who has noted how I have described Istanbul when describing myself, and described myself when describing Istanbul, will have already figured out that I am mentioning these childish but merciless fights to prepare the scene for something else. After all, children have a "natural" inclination to express themselves with violence; boys will be boys. There were games we'd invented

for ourselves, common games with specially adapted rules. In our dark and shadowy house, we played Hide and Seek, Catch the Handkerchief, Snake, Sea Captain, Hopscotch, The Admiral Has Sunk, Name the City, Ninestone, Scare, checkers, chess, table ball (on a table made for children), and Ping-Pong (on our collapsible dining table), to name only a few. When my mother was out, we'd scrunch up newspaper and play soccer all over the house until we were worked up into a sweaty frenzy, and often these games would turn into fights.

Whole years of our lives were devoted to "marble matches" that echoed the tactics and legends from the male world of soccer.

Using backgammon pieces as our players, placing them on the field following the rules of soccer, we would imitate defensive and offensive strategies we'd observed, and as we grew more dexterous, these games grew more animated. We'd arrange our two teams of backgammon pieces (or marbles) in formation on the carpet that served as our playing field, and then, following the fine and varied rules we had established after hundreds of fights, we'd shoot for the goalposts a carpenter had made for us. Sometimes the marbles were named after the great soccer players of the day, and like people who have no trouble telling their beloved striped kittens apart, we could distinguish our marbles with a single glance. We'd comment on the match to an imaginary crowd in the manner of Halit Kıvanç, the greatest sportscaster of the day, and when we scored we'd shout "go-o-o-oal" as people in the stands do at a real match, and then we'd imitate the rumblings in the crowds. We included comments from the soccer federation, the players, the press, and even the fans (but never the referee); eventually, we would forget that it was just a game of a game and enter into vicious and deadly combat. Most of the time I'd crumble under the first blows.

These early fights were sparked by defeat, excessive teasing, and cheating, but it was rivalry that fueled them. They were fought not to establish who was in the right but which of us was stronger, more skillful, more knowledgeable, more clever. And they expressed an anxiety we felt about having to learn the rules of the game—and indirectly the rules of the world—where in an instant we would be called upon to prove our agility and our mental prowess. In these rivalries were the shadows of the culture that drove my uncle to assault us with crosswords and mathematics problems whenever we entered his apartment, the same culture that brought us that half-serious jockeying between the different floors of the building—each of which supported a different soccer team—and that we found in those textbooks of ours that exaggerated the victories of the Ottoman Turks and books we received as gifts, like the *Encyclopedia of Discoveries and Inventions.*

My mother may have had her hand in it too, because, perhaps to make her daily life easier, she turned everything she could into a con-

test. "Whoever puts on his pajamas and goes to bed first gets a kiss," my mother would say. "Whoever gets through the whole winter without catching a cold or falling ill, I'll buy him a present." "Whoever can finish his supper first without spilling anything onto his shirt, I'll love him most." These motherly provocations were designed to make her two sons more "virtuous," quiet, and cooperative.

But behind my hopeless fights with my brother was the insistent competitiveness of my heroes, all of whom were committed to winning, coming out on top, however improbable the result. So—just as we would raise our hands in class, to prove we were not like all those dunces—my brother and I would give our all to vanquishing and crushing each other to fend off the fear we kept hidden in the darkest corner of our hearts: the melancholy and desolation of sharing Istanbul's shameful fate. When *İstanbullus* grow a bit older and feel their fates intertwining with that of the city, they come to welcome the cloak of melancholy that brings their lives a contentment, an emotional depth, that almost looks like happiness. Until then they rage against their fate.

My older brother was always better at school than I was. He knew everyone's address and could hold figures, telephone numbers, and mathematical formulas in his head like a secret melody (whenever we went out together, I would spend my time looking at the shopwindows, at the sky, at whatever struck my fancy, and he would look at the street numbers and the names of the apartments); he loved reciting soccer regulations, match results, the capitals of the world, and sports statistics, just as, forty years later, he enjoys rattling off the deficiencies of his academic rivals and how little space they take up in the Citation Index. Although my interest in painting came partly from my desire to spend time alone with my pencils and my paper, it also had something to do with my brother's total lack of interest in it.

But after hours of painting, if I had not found the happiness I'd been seeking, and when the darkness of the heavily curtained and overfurnished house began to seep into my soul, I would, like all *İstanbullus,* long for a quick route to victory and enter into a contest that might make one possible; whatever game it was that we were interested in at that moment—a marbles match, chess, a game of wits—I'd try to talk my brother into playing it again.

He would raise his head from his book and say, "So you're itching for it, are you?"—referring to the game I lost most times we played, not the brawling that came after. "The defeated wrestler never tires of a fight!" he'd say, thinking back on my most recent loss. "I'm doing another hour of work, and then we'll play." He'd return to his book.

His desk was as neat and organized as mine was messy, like the scene of an earthquake.

If our early fights helped us master the ways of the world, our later quarrels were more sinister. Once we'd been two brothers growing up together under the worried eyes and the constant shower of admonitions of a mother trying to fill the void left by an often absent father, hoping that if she denied this void she could somehow keep the melancholy of the city from seeping into the house. But now we began to act like two bachelors, each determined to carve out his separate domain. Such rules and regulations as we had established over the years to keep the peace—which parts of the cupboards were whose, what books belonged to whom, who got to sit next to our father in the car and for how long, who was to close our bedroom door at bedtime, who would turn off the light in the kitchen, and, when the latest issue of *History* magazine arrived, who got to read it first—even these settled protocols became sources of argument, insults, taunts, and threats. A single intemper-

ate remark—"That's mine, don't touch it!" or "Watch out or you'll be sorry!"—would lead to a skirmish, a twisting of arms, punching, beating, violence. To protect myself, I'd grab wooden hangers, fire tongs, a broomstick, anything I could use as a sword.

Formerly, we'd used a game we had seen in real life (like a soccer match) and imitated it with marbles; if questions of pride and honor arose, we would settle them with a fight, but it was the game we cared about; now we had thrown aside that pretext and were fighting to settle questions of pride and honor drawn directly from life. We knew each other's weaknesses intimately, and we began to exploit them. Above all, our fights were no longer angry outbursts that descended into violence; they were mercilessly planned acts of aggression.

Once, when I'd managed to hurt him, my brother said, "Tonight, when our parents go to the cinema, I'm going to beat you to a pulp!" At the supper table that night, I implored my parents not to go, repeating my brother's threats, but they still left me, as blindly confident as a peacekeeping force that thinks it has resolved a dispute between warring parties.

Sometimes, when we were alone in the house—giving everything we had to one of our intense battles and dripping with sweat—the bell would ring and, like a husband and wife who'd been caught fighting by neighbors, we'd cut our fevered amusement short and politely usher the neighbor, the unnecessary guest, into the house with all the appropriate pleasantries—"Please come in, sir," we'd say, "please sit down"—gleefully winking at each other, we'd explain that our mother would be back soon. But later, when we were alone again, we'd never rush back into our fight as a bickering couple might; instead, we'd act as if nothing had happened and return to our happy, idle pursuits. Sometimes, if I'd been roughed up very badly, I would lie down on the carpet and cry like a child imagining his own funeral, before falling fast asleep. My brother, no less humane or good-hearted than I, would, after working for a while at his desk, begin to feel sorry for me; he'd rouse me and tell me to get changed and go to bed, but when he'd gone back to work, I'd go to bed still dressed to wallow in dark self-pity.

The melancholy I itched for—and would later claim—that mood that spoke to me of defeat, obliteration, and degradation, also allowed me a respite from all the rules that needed to be learned, all the mathematics problems that needed to be solved, all the sections of the Karlowitz Treaty that needed to be memorized. To have been beaten and humiliated was to feel free. There were times when, in spite of myself, I wanted to be beaten, as my brother sensed when he said I was itching for it. Sometimes it was because he sensed it, and because he was cleverer and stronger, that I'd want to fight him with all my strength and get my thrashing.

After every beating, a dark feeling would catch up with me when I was alone in bed, as I berated myself for being so clumsy, guilty, and lazy. *What's up?* a voice inside me would ask. *I'm bad,* I'd reply. In an instant, this answer would grant me a dizzying freedom; a bright new world would open up before me. If I was prepared to be as bad as I could be, I'd be able to paint whenever I liked, forget about my schoolwork, sleep in my clothes. At the same time, there was the strange comfort I took in the defeat, the damage, the bruises on my arms and legs, the split lips, the bloody noses: My battered body was proof that I could not fight a good enough fight, that I deserved to be defeated, degraded, crushed. Perhaps it was while I was entertaining such thoughts that bright daydreams began blowing through my head like summer breezes and I was entranced to think that one day I would do something great. These dreams had a potency that belied the violence and injured pride that had given rise to them. The second world now shimmering before me, promising a happy new life, was fed above all by the violence I had just endured, and that made my imaginings all the more vibrant and lifelike. As I'd feel the city's melancholy-*hüzün* settling into me, I discovered by chance that when I put pencil to paper at times like this, I liked what I did much more; as I forgot the world and played about with my melancholy, its darkness would begin to fade away.

CHAPTER THIRTY-THREE

A Foreigner in a Foreign School

If you include the year I spent learning English in preparatory school, I spent four years at Robert Academy. It was during this time that my childhood came to an end, and I discovered the world to be more confusing, inaccessible, and distressingly boundless than I had ever suspected. I'd spent my entire childhood inside my close-knit family in a house, a street, a neighborhood that for me was, for all I knew, the center of the world. Until I started at the lycée, my education had done nothing to disabuse me of the notion that the heart of my personal and geographical universe also set the standards for the rest of the world. Now, at lycée, I discovered that I did not, in fact, live in the center of the world, and the place where I lived was not—this was more painful—the world's beacon. Having discovered the fragility of my place in the world, and at the same time the vastness of that world (I loved getting lost in the low-ceilinged labyrinths of the library built by the American secular Protestants who had founded the college, breathing in the pungency of old paper), I felt lonelier and weaker than ever before.

For one thing, my brother was no longer there. When I was sixteen, he left for America, to study at Yale. We may have fought incessantly, but we'd also been soulmates—discussing the world around us, categorizing, placing things, passing judgment—and my bond with him was stronger even than my bonds with my mother and my father. Released from the never-ending contests, taunts, and thrashings that did so much to fire my imagination and promote my idleness, I hardly had much cause to complain. But especially when melancholy descended, I'd miss his company.

It seemed that some core inside me had disintegrated, but my head could not quite fathom where this core was. This seemed to be the reason I could not give myself wholly to my lessons, my home-work, or anything else. Sometimes it would break my heart that I could no longer be at the head of the class without a special effort, but it was as if I had lost the ability to be too upset or too pleased about anything. During my childhood, when I had thought myself happy, life was soft as velvet, diverting as a fairy tale. By the time I was thirteen or fourteen, this fiction had fragmented. From time to time I would manage to believe in one of these fragments with all my heart; I would then resolve to devote myself to it utterly, only to find myself drifting again—just as, at the start of every school year, I would decide to be first in the class, only to fall short of the mark. Sometimes the world seemed to grow more distant, a sensation I felt most keenly when my skin, my mind, my antennae were most desirously alert to it.

Amid all the confusion were the never-ending sexual fantasies, reminders of the other world in which I could always take shelter. I knew sex not as something you shared with another person but as a dream you created by yourself. Like the machine that set itself up inside my head to sound out every letter for me, once I'd learned how to read, now there was a new machine that would extract a sex-ual dream or a passing pleasure from almost anything and portray the arousing spectacle in technicolor with shocking clarity. Nothing was sacred—the machine fed on everyone I knew and every picture I saw in newspapers and magazines, and when it had cut and pasted the required details into a sexual fantasy, I would shut myself up in my room.

As I wallowed in guilt afterward, I would recall a conversation I'd had in my old middle school with two classmates. One was very fat and the other stuttered. Struggling to find his words, the stutterer asked me, "Do you ever do it?" Yes, I was already doing it in middle school, but my shame was so great it was all I could do to mutter an answer that might have been no and might have been yes. "Oh, but you shouldn't, not ever!" the stutterer cried, his face reddening at the thought that someone as clever, quiet, and hardworking as I would fall so low. "Masturbating is a fearful habit; once you start you can never stop." At this point, I recall my very fat friend gazing at me with pained and mournful eyes—although he too urged me in whispers to avoid masturbation (or *thirty-one,* as it was known among us)—for he too had discovered this habit-forming drug. He now believed himself damned, just as he knew himself doomed to be fat, and so he wore the expression of one bowing to God's will.

Mixed in with my memories of these years is something that caused me the same guilt and loneliness and that I continued to do when I went on to the Technical University to study architecture. But it was hardly a new habit: I'd been skipping class since primary school.

At first it was a matter of boredom, or shame at some imagined shortcoming no one had noticed, or the simple knowledge that I'd have too much to do if I went in to school that day. The reasons might have had nothing to do with school: an argument between my parents, pure laziness or irresponsibility, an illness during which I'd been shamelessly babied. A poem I had to memorize, the prospect of being bullied by a classmate, and (at lycée and university) my deep boredom, my melancholy, my existentialist despair—these too served as excuses. Sometimes I skipped school because I was a house pet, because—when my brother went off to school alone— the things I did in the solitude of my own room were done better— and besides, I'd long known that I would never be as good a student as my brother. But there was also something deeper, and it came from the same source as my melancholy.

Just as his inheritance from his father was about to run out, my father found a job in Geneva; that winter he went there with my mother, leaving us with our grandmother, and it was under her spineless governance that I started skipping school in earnest. I was eight years old; every morning, when İsmail Efendi rang the bell to take us to school, my brother would head out with his book bag while I would mumble some excuse for delay: I hadn't packed my book bag yet, I'd just remembered something I'd forgotten (could my grandmother give me a lira?), and, by the way, my stomach ached, my shoes were wet, I needed to change my shirt. My brother, knowing full well what I was up to and not wanting to be late for school, would say, "Let's just go, İsmail. You can come back for Orhan later."

Our school was a four-minute walk from home. By the time İsmail Efendi had dropped off my brother and come back for me, class was about to start. I'd drag my feet a bit more, find someone else to blame for the thing missing or unready, pretend that my stomach was aching so badly I hadn't noticed İsmail Efendi ringing the bell. By now, because of the strain of all these lies and tricks and thanks to the dreaded vile milk they made me drink every morning—boiling hot, its stink still in my nostrils—my stomach would in fact be aching a little. After a while my oatmeal-hearted grandmother would give in.

"All right, İsmail, it's awfully late, the bell must have rung by now; we'd better keep him at home." Then, raising her eyebrows, she'd turn to me and say, "But listen, tomorrow you're definitely going to school, do you understand? If you don't, I'll call the police. I'll write a letter to your parents."

Years later, when I was in lycée and there was no one to check up on me, skipping school was more fun. Because I paid for my guilt with every step I took in the city streets, I was better able to appreciate the experience and could see things only a truly aimless and idle idiot would notice: the broad-brimmed hat that woman over there was wearing, the burnt face of a beggar I'd missed despite passing him every day, the barbers and their apprentices reading the papers in their shops, the girl in the marmalade advertisement on the wall of the apartment building across the street, the workings of the clock in Taksim Square, which was shaped like a piggy bank (I would have missed this entirely if not for passing by just as they were repairing it). The empty hamburger shops, the locksmiths in the back streets of Cihangir, the junk dealers, the furniture repairmen, the grocery stores, stamp dealers, music shops, antiquarian booksellers, seal makers, and typewriter shops of Yüksekkaldırım—everything was as real and beautiful and irresistible as it had been

when I was a child, wandering these same streets with my mother. The streets would be full of vendors selling *simits,* fried mussels, pilaf, chestnuts, grilled meatballs, fish bread, doughballs, *ayran*—a yogurt drink—and sherbets, and I would buy whatever struck my fancy. I'd stand on the corner, a bottle of soda in hand, watching a group of boys playing soccer (were they skipping school like me or did they not go to school at all?); I'd walk down an alley I'd never seen before and experience a moment of great happiness. There were other times when my eyes would be on my watch, and I'd think about what was going on at school right then, and my guilt would make my melancholy all the stronger.

During my lycée years, I explored the back streets of Bebek and Ortaköy, the hills around Rumelihisarı, and the landing stages of Rumelihisarı, Emirgân, and İstinye, which were still in use in those days, and the fishermen's coffeehouses and rowboat mooring stations around them; I would take ferries to all the places that the ferries went then, enjoy all the pleasures a ferry could offer as I took in the other towns of the Bosphorus: the old ladies dozing at their windows, the happy cats, and the back streets where you could still find old Greek houses that didn't lock their doors in the morning.

Having committed my crimes, I would often resolve to return to the straight and narrow: become a better student, paint more regularly, go to America and study art, stop provoking my American teachers (who, despite the best intentions, had all turned themselves into caricatures), and stop trying to annoy my lethargic and malevolent Turkish teachers for annoying me so much. In a very short time, my guilt turned me into an ardent idealist. In those years the sins most common among the adults in my life—and these were the sins I could least excuse—were dishonesty and insincerity. From the way they asked after one another's health to the way they threatened us students, from their shopping habits to their political pronouncements, it seemed to me that their every expression in life was two-faced, and that "experience in life"—the thing they were forever telling me I didn't have—meant the ability, after a certain age, to be hypocritical and manipulative without trying and then to be able to sit back and pretend innocence. Let me not be misunderstood: I too played plenty of tricks, changed my story to suit the person, and told packs of lies, but afterward I would be plagued with such violent guilt, confusion, and fear of being found out that for a time I'd wonder if I'd ever again feel balanced and "normal"; this gave my own lies and dissimulations a certain consequence. I would then resolve to tell no more lies and to cease being a hypocrite—not because my

conscience wouldn't allow it or because I thought telling a lie and being two-faced were one and the same thing, but rather because the confusion that followed my transgressions exhausted me.

These pangs, ever more intense, did not just come to me after I'd dissembled, they could hit me any time: while joking around with a friend, waiting alone in a cinema queue in Beyoğlu, holding the hand of a beautiful girl I'd just met. A great eye would swing out of nowhere to hang in the air before me—like some sort of security camera—and subject whatever I was doing (paying the woman in the booth, searching for something to say to the beautiful girl after I'd held her hand), and whatever banal, insincere idiocy I was uttering ("One please, in the middle section, for *From Russia with Love*"; "Is this the first time you've come to one of these parties?") to merciless scrutiny. I'd be at once my film's director and its star, in the thick of things but also watching from a mocking distance. Having caught myself in the act, I could maintain a "normal" demeanor for only a few seconds, after which I'd plunge into a deep and confused anguish—I'd feel ashamed, afraid, terrorized, and terrified of being marked as alien. It was as if someone were folding my soul over and over on itself like a piece of paper, and as my depression deepened, I could feel my insides beginning to sway.

When this happened, there was no remedy but to go into a room and lock the door behind me. I would lie back and review my hypocrisy, repeat my shaming banal cant to myself, over and over. Only by gathering up pens and paper and writing or painting something could I exit the loop, and only if I painted or wrote something I liked could I return to "normal."

Sometimes, even when I hadn't done anything false, I would suddenly see I was a fake. Catching a glimpse of myself in a shopwindow or, in Beyoğlu, sitting in the corner in one of the city's suddenly ubiquitous hamburger and sandwich shops, treating myself to a sausage sandwich after a film, I'd see myself in a mirror on the opposite wall and think my reflection too real, too crude to bear. These moments were so excruciating I'd want to die, but I'd continue eating my sandwich with ravenous anguish, noting how much I resembled Goya's giant—the one who ate his son. The reflection was a memento of my crimes and sins, confirmation that I was a loathsome toad. It was not just because the reception rooms in the unlicensed brothels in the back streets of Beyoğlu had these same huge framed mirrors hanging on their walls: I disgusted myself because everything around me—the naked bulb above my head, the grimy walls, the counter at which I was sitting, the cafeteria's sickly colors—spoke of such neglect, such ugliness. And I would know then that no happiness, love, or success awaited me: I was doomed to live a long, boring, utterly unremarkable life—a vast stretch of time that was already dying before my eyes even as I endured it.

Happy people in Europe and America could lead lives as beautiful and as meaningful as the ones I'd just seen in a Hollywood film; as for the rest of the world, myself included, we were condemned to live out our time in places that were shabby, broken-down, featureless, badly painted, dilapidated, and cheap; we were doomed to unimportant, second-class, neglected existences, never to do anything that anyone in the outside world might think worthy of notice. This was the fate for which I was slowly and painfully preparing myself. Because only the very rich of Istanbul could live like Westerners, and this at the cost, it seemed, of unbearable soullessness and artificiality, I grew to love the melancholy of the back streets; I spent my Friday and Saturday evenings wandering them alone and going to the cinema.

But at the same time that I was living in this world of my own— reading books I shared with no one, painting, acquainting myself with the back streets—I'd also made some evil friends. I joined a set of boys whose fathers were in textiles, mining, or some other industry. These friends would drive to and from Robert Academy in their fathers' Mercedes-Benzes, and as they drove through Bebek and Şişli, they'd slow down every time they saw a beautiful girl, to invite her into the car, and if they managed to "scoop her," as they liked to put it, they'd immediately start dreaming of the great sexual adventures before them. They were older than I, these boys, but utterly brainless. They'd spend their weekends trawling Maçka, Harbiye, Nişantaşı, and Taksim for more girls to scoop into their cars; every winter, they'd spend ten days skiing on Uludağ with everyone else who went to the foreign private lycées, and in the summer they tried to meet the girls who summered in Suadiye and Erenköy. Sometimes I would go out hunting with them, and it would shock me how some girls could tell from one glance that we were innocuous children just like them and fearlessly step into the car. On one occasion, two girls got into a car I was in, acting as if it were the most normal thing in the world to get into some stranger's luxury sedan that happened to be passing in the street. I engaged them in a random conversation, and after going together to a club where we drank lemonade and Coca-Cola, we all went our separate ways. Aside from these friends, who lived in Nişantaşı like me and with whom I regularly played poker, I had a few others with whom I occasionally played chess or Ping-Pong or met to discuss painting and art. But I never introduced them to one another or met them together.

With each of these friends I was a different person, with a different sense of humor, a different voice, a different moral code. I had never set out to become a chameleon; there was no clever, cynical plan. Most of the time, these identities sprang up by themselves as I conversed with my friends and got excited about whatever they were saying. The ease with which I could be good with the good, bad with the bad, and strange with the strange did not produce in me the disaffection I observed in so many of my friends; by the time I was twenty, it had cured me of cynicism. Whenever something interested me, a part of me would embrace it absolutely.

But earnest interests did not cure me of the urge to mock everyone and everything. At Robert Academy, when my classmates showed more interest in the spicy jokes I was whispering to them than in the teacher, it pleased me to be proven a good storyteller. The main butts of my jokes were the boring Turkish teachers, some

of them uneasy about teaching in an American school and fearful that "spies" among us were "informing" on them to the Americans; other Turkish teachers were given to long nationalist orations and because, compared with the Americans, they seemed apathetic, tired, old, and depressed, we felt they didn't like us any more than they liked themselves or life itself. Unlike the friendly and well-meaning American teachers, their first impulse was always to make us memorize the textbook and punish us if we didn't, and we hated them for their bureaucratic souls.

The Americans were mostly younger and, in their zeal to teach their Turkish students, took us to be far more innocent and wide-eyed than we were. Their almost religious fervor when explicating the wonders of western civilization would leave us caught between laughter and despair. Some had come to Turkey hoping to teach the illiterate children of the impoverished third world; most were leftists born in the 1940s who would read to us from Brecht and offer up Marxist analyses of Shakespeare; even when they were reading us literature, they were trying to prove that the source of all evil was a society created by good people who had taken the wrong path. One teacher who made a point of explaining the fate of a good person who refused to bow to society, often used the phrase "You are pushed," and a few of the jokers in the class kept saying, "Yes, sir, you are pushed," the teacher never the wiser about a Turkish word that sounded just like "pushed" and meant queer; when the whole class tittered, we weren't insulting him, but our veiled resentment of our American teacher was acknowledged among us. Our timid anti-Americanism was in keeping with the nationalist leftist mood of the time, and it worried the school's bright Anatolian scholarship students the most. They'd taken difficult exams to earn the right to study at this exclusive school and were mostly brilliant and hard-working boys from poor provincial families; while they had grown up dreaming of American culture and the land of the free—most of all, they longed for the chance to study at an American university and perhaps settle in the States—even so, they were troubled by the war in Vietnam and not immune to resentment, and from time to time their anger at Americans bubbled over. The Istanbul bourgeoisie and my rich-kid friends weren't particularly troubled by all this. For them, Robert Academy was simply the first step toward the future that rightfully awaited them as managers and owners of the country's biggest companies or as Turkish agents of big foreign firms.

I wasn't sure what I was going to be, but if anyone asked I said I would stay in Istanbul and study architecture. It wasn't just my idea, my family had reached a consensus to this effect some time before. As I had a good mind like my grandfather, my father, and my uncle, I too was meant to study engineering at Istanbul Technical University, but since I had such a keen interest in painting, it was decided that it would be more fitting for me to study architecture at the same institution. I cannot remember who first applied this simple logic to the question of my future, but by the time I was at Robert Academy it was a settled plan and I'd made it my own. Never once did I entertain

the idea of leaving the city. This wasn't owing to any great love of the place where I lived, but rather a deep-seated reluctance to abandon habits and houses that had made me the sort who was just too lazy to try out anything new. I was, as I had begun to discover even then, the sort who could wear the same clothes and eat the same things and go for a hundred years without getting bored so long as I could entertain wild dreams in the privacy of my imagination.

At the time, my father was the head of Aygaz, Turkey's leading propane company, so sometimes he said he had to go out to Büyükçekmece to inspect a few depots or filling stations that were under construction in Ambarlı. We would take the car for a Sunday morning spin there, or we'd go to the Bosphorus, or we'd go out to buy something or visit my grandmother—whatever the reason, he'd put me in the car (a German Ford, a 1966 Taunus), turn on the radio, and put his foot on the accelerator. It was on these Sunday morning excursions that we discussed the meaning of life and what I was to do with mine.

In the 1960s and early 1970s, the main streets of Istanbul were empty on Sunday mornings, and as we drove through neighborhoods I'd never seen before, we'd listen to "light western music" (the Beatles, Sylvie Vartan, Tom Jones, and suchlike) and my father would tell me that the best thing a person could do was to live by his own lights—money could never be the object, but if happiness depended on it, it could be a means to that end—or he would tell me how once when he had left us he had gone to Paris, had written poems in his hotel room, and had also translated Valéry's poems into Turkish, but years later, while he was traveling in America, the suitcase in which he kept all his poems and translations had been stolen. As the music rose and fell in rhythm with the city streets, he would would adjust his stories to the beat—he spoke of having seen Jean-Paul Sartre many times in the streets of Paris during the 1950s, of how the Pamuk Apartments in Nişantaşı had come to be built, of the failure of one of his first businesses—and I knew I would never forget anything he told me. From time to time he'd pause to admire the view or a beautiful woman on the pavement, and while I listened to his offerings of gentle and understated wisdom and advice, I would gaze at scenes of the leaden winter morning as they flashed across the windshield. As I watched the cars crossing the Galata Bridge, the back neighborhoods where a few wooden houses still stood, the narrow streets, the crowds heading to a soccer match, or the thin-funneled tugboat pulling coal barges down the Bosphorus, I'd listen to my father's wise voice telling me how important it was that people followed their own instincts and passions; that actually life was very short; and that also it was a good thing if a person

knew what he wanted to do in life—that, in fact, a person who spent his life writing, drawing, and painting could enjoy a deeper, richer life—and as I drank in his words, they would blend in with the things I was seeing.

Before long, the music, the views rushing past the window, my father's voice ("Shall we turn in here?" he'd ask), and the narrow cobblestone streets all merged into one, and it seemed to me that while we would never find answers to these fundamental questions, it was good for us to ask them anyway, that true happiness and

meaning resided in places we would never find and perhaps did not wish to find, but—whether we were pursuing the answers or merely pleasure and emotional depth—the pursuit mattered no less than the attainment, the asking as important as the views we saw through the windows of the car, the house, the ferry. With time, life—like music, art, and stories—would rise and fall, eventually to end, but even years later those lives are with us still, in the city views that flow before our eyes, like memories plucked from dreams.

rushes home to take shelter from that storm, that earthquake, that death, I too long to be back within my own four walls.

I don't like afternoons in spring when the sun suddenly comes out full strength, mercilessly illuminating all the poverty, disorder, and failure. I don't like Halaskârgazi, that great avenue that stretches from Taksim through Harbiye and Şişli and goes all the way to Mecidiyeköy. My mother, who lived in this area as a child, speaks longingly of the mulberry trees that once lined its avenues; now they're lined with apartment buildings constructed during the sixties and seventies in the "international style"; they have huge windows and walls covered with ugly mosaic tiles. There are back streets in Şişli (Pangaltı), Nişantaşı (Topağacı), and Taksim (Talimhane) that make me want to flee at once: These are places, far from anything green and without the sliver of a Bosphorus view, where family quarrels have caused the small lots to be parceled out into yet smaller ones, from which apartments rise up in crooked misery.

In the days when I walked up and down these airless and down-hearted streets, I'd think that every aunty looking down from her window and every old mustachioed uncle hated me—and, more-over, that they were right to do so. I hate the back streets between Nişantaşı and Şişli with their clothing stores, the streets between Galata and Tepebaşı with their lighting and chandelier stores, the area around Taksim Talimhane when it was still mostly stores selling spare automotive parts. (During the roller-coaster years, when my father and my uncle were gleefully investing my grandfather's legacy in one lackluster venture after another, they too had opened such a store here, but being unable to get it off the ground, they forgot about car parts and amused themselves with practical jokes, like get-ting their errand boys to "sample Turkey's first canned tomato juice" after they had doused it heavily with pepper.) As for the pot-makers that have invaded the streets around Süleymaniye, causing an endless din of hammers and machine presses, I hate them as much as I hate the taxis and little trucks that service these places and clog up the traffic. I see them, and the anger brewing up inside me makes me hate the city as much as I hate myself, all the more so when I look at the huge and brilliantly colored letters of signs by which the gentlemen of the city advertise their names, businesses, jobs, professions, and successes. All those professors, doctors, surgeons, certified financial consultants, lawyers admitted to the bar, Happy Döner Shops, Life Groceries, and Black Sea food stores; all those banks, insurance agencies, detergent brands and newspaper names, cinemas and jeans stores; the posters advertising soft drinks; the stores where you can buy drinking water and tickets for soccer pools for the lottery; the stores that announce themselves as licensed retailers of propane gas in signs festooned above their names in huge proud letters—all these give me to know that the rest of the city is as confused and unhappy as I am and that I need to return to a dark corner, to my little room, before the noise and signs pull me under.

AKBANKMORNINGDÖNERSHOPFABRICGUARANTEED-DRINKITHEREDAILYSOAPSIDEALTIMEFORJEWELSNURIBA-YARLAWYERPAYINSTALLMENTS

So in the end I'll escape the terrorizing crowds, the endless chaos, and the noonday sun that brings every ugly thing in the city into relief, but if I'm already tired and depressed, the reading machine inside my head will remember every sign from every street and repeat them, run together like a Turkish lament.

SPRINGSALESELAMIBUFFETPUBLICTELEPHONESTAR-BEYOĞLUIPNOTARYALEMACARONIANANKARAMARKET-SHOWHAIRDRESSERHEALTHAPTRADIOANDTRANSISTORS

Count the French and English words on billboards and posters, in shop signs, magazines, and businesses; this is indeed a city moving westward, but it's still not changing as fast as it talks. Neither can the city honor the traditions implied by its mosques, its minarets, its calls to prayer, its history. Everything is half formed, shoddy, and soiled.

RAZORSPLEASEPROCEEDATLUNCHTIMEPHILIPS-
LICENSEEDOCTORDEPOTFOLDTHECARPETS-
PORCELAINFAHIRATTORNEYATLAW

To escape this hybrid lettered hell, I conjure up a golden age, a
pure and shining moment when the city "was at peace with itself,"
when it was a "beautiful whole." The Istanbul Melling painted, of
western travelers like Nerval, Gautier, and de Amicis. But as my reason reasserts itself, I remember that I love this city not for any purity
but precisely for the lamentable want of it. And that same inner
pragmatist, the one who will pardon me my defects too, warns me
against the *hüzün* hanging over the city, its telegraphy still tapping
away inside my head.

STREETYOURMONEYYOURFUTUREINSURANCESUN-
BUFFETRINGTHEBELLNOVAWATCHESARTIN-
SPAREPARTSVOGUEBALIVIZONSTOCKINGS

I've never wholly belonged to this city, and maybe that's been the
problem all along. Sitting in my grandmother's apartment, drinking
beer and liqueur with my family after a holiday feast, or tooling
around the city on a winter's day with my rich would-be playboy
friends from Robert Academy in their fathers' cars, I felt the same
way I feel now if I'm walking the streets on a spring afternoon: The
idea rises up inside me that I'm worthless and belong nowhere, that
I must distance myself from these people and go hide in a corner—
it's almost an animal instinct—but it's the desire to flee the very
community that has opened its arms to me, it's God's all-seeing, all-
forgiving gaze, that induces such deep guilt.

When I started lycée, loneliness seemed a transitory thing; I was
not yet mature enough to see it as my fate. I would dream of a good
friend to accompany me to the cinema, sparing me the worry of
standing about idle and alone during the intermissions. One day, I
dreamed, I would meet intelligent and cultivated people with whom
I could discuss the books I read and the paintings I painted, and
never for a moment would I feel fake. One day, too, sex would cease

to be a solitary pursuit; I would have a beautiful lover with whom I would share my forbidden pleasures. Though certainly of an age to fulfill such ambitions, I was paralyzed by longing, shame, and fear.

In those days, misery meant feeling out of place, in one's home, one's family, and one's city. It was this greater community—where strangers addressed you as an elder brother, where everyone said *we* as if the entire city were watching the same soccer match—from which I'd cut myself off. Fearful that this condition would become a way of life, I'd resolve to be like other people. In my late adolescence, I succeeded in becoming the sort of sociable young wise guy who was everyone's friend, easygoing and insipid. I joked incessantly, told anecdotes, made everyone in class laugh by imitating the teacher; my pranks became family legends. When I took the game too far, I was an able diplomat, dignifying nefarious deeds with fine euphemisms. But afterward, when I shut myself up in my room, the only way I knew to escape from the world's duplicity and my own hypocrisy was to masturbate.

Why were the little rituals of friendship so much harder for me than for everyone else? Why did I have to clench my teeth to push myself through ordinary niceties and then hate myself, and why, when I made friends, did I feel like I was playing a part? Occasionally I would embrace a role with such manic energy I'd forget I was just acting; I'd enjoy myself, for a time, like everyone else, but then a melancholy wind would blow in out of nowhere, and I'd want to return to my house, my room, my darkness, and curl up in a corner. The more I turned my mocking gaze inward, the more it was directed at my mother, my father, my brother, and the horde of relations—harder and harder for me to call my family—my school friends, various other acquaintances, the entire city.

I sensed that what had plunged me into this wretched state was Istanbul itself. Not just the Bosphorus, the ships, the all-too-familiar nights, lights, and crowds; of that I was sure. There was something else that bound its people together, smoothing their way to communicate, do business, live together, and I was simply out of harmony with it. This world of "ours"—in which everyone knew everyone, both good points and limits, and all shared in a common

identity, respecting humility, tradition, our elders, our forefathers, our history, our legends—was not a world in which I could "be myself." Wherever I was the performer and not the spectator, I could not feel at home. At a birthday party, for example, after a while—even as I went around the room smiling benevolently, asking "How's it going?" and patting people's backs—I would begin to observe myself from the outside, as if in a dream, and I would recoil at the sight of this pretentious idiot.

After I had gone home and spent some time reflecting on my duplicity ("Why do you always lock your room now?" my mother had started to ask), I would conclude that this flaw, this flair for deception, resided not just in me but in the spirit of the community that had created these relations; it was in the "we," and only someone who had gone crazy enough to see the city from the outside could recognize it as the city's "communal ideology." But these are the words of a fifty-year-old writer who is trying to shape the chaotic thoughts of a long-ago adolescent into an amusing story.

To continue: Between the ages of sixteen and eighteen it wasn't just myself I despised but my family, my friends, and their culture; the official and unofficial political statements that purported to explain what was happening around us; the newspaper headlines;

and the way we all wanted to look different from who we were and basically never understood ourselves at all. Throbbing in my head

were all the letters from the street signs and billboards. I wanted to paint, I wanted to live like the French painters I'd read about in books, but I lacked the strength to create such a world in Istanbul, nor did Istanbul lend itself to the project. Even the worst paintings of the Turkish impressionists—their views of mosques, the Bosphorus, wooden houses, snowy streets—pleased me, not as paintings but as likenesses of my city. If a painting looked like Istanbul, then it wasn't a good painting; if it was a good painting, it didn't look enough like Istanbul to suit me. Perhaps this meant I had to stop seeing the city as art, as a landscape.

Between the ages of sixteen and eighteen, part of me longed, like a radical Westernizer, for the city to become entirely European. I held the same hope for myself. But another part of me yearned to belong to the Istanbul I had grown to love, by instinct, by habit, and by memory. When I was a child, I was able to keep these two wishes apart (a child has no qualms about dreaming in the same moment of becoming a vagabond and a great scientist), but, as time wore on, this ability faded. At the same time, the melancholy to which the city bows its head—and at the same time claims with pride—began to seep into my soul.

But maybe its source was neither the poverty nor the destructive burden of *hüzün*. If from time to time I wanted to curl up in a corner alone like a dying animal, it was also to nurse an anguish that came from within. So what was this thing whose loss was causing me such misery?

CHAPTER THIRTY-FIVE

First Love

B ecause this is a memoir, I must hide her name, and if in naming her I offer a clue in the style of the Divan poets, I must also hint that this clue, like the rest of my story, might be misleading. Her name meant Black Rose in Persian, but as far as I could ascertain, no one on the shores from which she jumped joyfully into the sea, and none of her classmates at the French lycée, were aware of this—because her long shiny hair was not black but chestnut and her brown eyes only one shade darker. When I cleverly told her this, she raised her eyebrows as she always did when she became suddenly serious, and, pushing out her lips just a little, she said that of course she knew what her name meant and that she'd been named after her Albanian grandmother.

According to my mother, though, the girl's mother (whom my mother referred to as "that woman") must have married very young, because when my brother was five and I was three and my mother took us out on winter mornings to Maçka Park in Nişantaşı, she'd seen the child with her mother, who looked like a young girl herself, my mother said, pushing her around in an enormous pram and trying to get her to go to sleep. My mother once hinted that the Albanian grandmother had come out of the harem of a pasha who had either done something very bad during the armistice years or disgraced himself by opposing Atatürk, but I had no interest then either in the Ottoman mansions that were burning down all around us or in the families that had once lived in them, so I've forgotten the exact story. My father, meanwhile, told me that the little Black

Rose's father, with the help of a few intimates influential in government circles, had become the agent for a few American and Dutch companies and struck it rich overnight, but there was nothing in his tone to suggest he disapproved.

Eight years after our meetings in the park, when my family bought a house in the Bayramoğlu neighborhood, a summer resort to the east of the city, very fashionable among the nouveau riche for a time during the 1960s and 1970s, I would see her riding her bicycle. During the town's heyday, when it was still small and empty, I'd spend my time there swimming in the sea, going out in boats to trawl for fish, catching mackerel and scad, playing soccer, and, on summer evenings after I'd turned sixteen, dancing with girls. Later, however, after I had finished lycée and had begun to study architecture, I preferred to sit on the ground floor of our house, painting and reading. How much did this have to do with my rich-kid friends, who called anyone who read anything other than a textbook an intellectual or a shady character "riddled with complexes"? This last slur they applied indiscriminately—it could mean you had psychological problems, or it could mean you were worried about money. I was more worried about being labeled an intellectual, so, hoping to convince them I was not an effete snob, I began to say I read my books—my Woolf, Freud, Sartre, Mann, Faulkner—"just for fun," though they'd ask why I underlined passages.

It was my bad reputation that attracted the Black Rose's attention late one summer—this despite the fact that all that season, and all the ones before when I'd spent more time with my friends, we'd hardly noticed each other. When my friends and I would go to discos in the middle of the night as one big happy group, racing (and sometimes crashing) someone's Mercedes, Mustang, or BMW to Bağdat Avenue (then known as the Asian city's Park Avenue and only half an hour away), or when we'd take their speedboats out to some desolate cliff, lining up empty soda and wine bottles to shoot at with their fathers' chic hunting guns, scaring the girls (when they screamed, we boys hushed them); or when we were listening to Bob Dylan and the Beatles while playing poker and Monopoly, the Black Rose and I took no interest in each other.

This young and noisy crowd gradually dispersed as summer drew to a close, and then there were the *lodos* storms that lashed these shores every September, always shattering one or two rowboats and putting yachts and speedboats at peril. While the rain continued pelting down, the seventeen-year-old Black Rose began to pay visits to the room in which I painted and which, taking myself too seriously, I called my studio. All my friends dropped by from time to time, to try a hand with my paper and my brushes or to examine my books with the usual suspicion, so this was not particularly unusual. Like most people living in Turkey, rich or poor, male or female, she needed conversation to pass the time and fill her days.

In the beginning, we shared the last of the summer's gossip—who was in love with whom and who had made whom jealous—though that summer I hadn't paid much attention. Because I had paint on my hands, she sometimes helped me make tea or open a tube of color before going back to her place in the corner, kicking off her shoes, and stretching out on the sofa, using one of her arms as a pillow. One day, without telling her, I did a sketch of her lying there. I saw this pleased her, so the next time she came I did another. The next time, when I said I was going to draw her, she asked, "How shall I sit?" like a starlet who's never been in front of the camera before, thrilled and yet unsure of where to put her arms and her legs.

When I studied her long thin nose so that I could draw it right, the hint of a smile would form on her little mouth; she had a broad forehead, she was tall, with long suntanned legs, but when she came to see me she wore a chic long closed skirt handed down to her by her grandmother, so I could see only her small straight feet. When while sketching I studied the contours of her small breasts and the extraordinarily white skin of her long neck, a shadow of shame would flit across her face.

During her first visits, we spoke a lot, and she did most of the talking. Because I'd pointed out a cloud I'd seen in her eyes and lips and said, "Don't look so miserable!" she told me, with a directness I hadn't expected, about her parents' quarrels and the endless fights among her four younger brothers; she told me how the family sometimes got around her father's punishments—house arrest, a speedboat ban, a few slaps—and how sad her mother was that her father chased other women; she also told me that because our mothers were bridge partners and had confided in each other, she knew my father did likewise—and as she told me all this, she looked straight into my eyes.

Slowly we sank into silence. She would walk in and go to her usual place, or she would pose for the painting (heavily influenced by Bonnard), or she would open one of the books that happened to be lying around and stay on the same divan reading, in various positions. Later, whether or not I was drawing her, we fell into a routine: She'd knock on the door, come in without saying much, stretch out on the divan in the corner, pose as she read her book, or sometimes, out of the corner of her eyes, she would watch me sketching her. Every morning, after I'd been working for a while, I remember I'd start to wonder when she'd come, and I remember that she never kept me waiting long but would wear that same shy smile as she made her way almost apologetically to stretch out in her usual place.

One subject of our ever-less-frequent conversations was the future. In her view I was very talented and hardworking and so destined to become a world-famous painter—or did she say a famous Turkish painter?—and she would come to my crowded opening in Paris with her French pals and proudly tell everyone she was a "childhood friend."

One evening, with the excuse of looking at the clear sky and a rainbow that had appeared over the other side of the peninsula following a rainstorm, we left my dark studio to walk together through the town for the first time; we walked for a very long while. I remember that we said nothing. We were worried about being seen by the few acquaintances who remained in the now half-empty resort and about the possibility of running into our mothers. But the thing that made this walk wholly "unsuccessful" was not that the rainbow disappeared before we had a chance to see it but the unacknowledged tension between us. It was while we were on this walk that I noticed for the first time just how long her neck was and what a pleasing way she had of walking.

On our last Saturday evening, we decided to go out together, and we met without telling any of the handful of curious and unimportant friends still at the resort. I'd borrowed my father's car, and I was tense. She'd put on makeup and a very short skirt, and a lovely perfume that stayed in the car for some time afterward. But before we even got to the amusing place we were headed for, I could already sense the ghost that had made our first walk unsuccessful. It was at the half-empty but still much too noisy discotheque, while we were trying to recapture the effect of the long and peaceful silences we'd enjoyed in my studio—it was only now I realized how deep they'd been—that we recovered our composure.

But still we danced, to slow music. Because I'd seen others doing it, I put my arms around her, and then I pulled her closer as if by instinct, and noticed that her hair smelled of almonds. I loved the little movements of her lips when she ate and how she looked like a squirrel when she was worried.

As I was about to take her home, I broke the silence in the car by saying, "Are you in the mood for a painting?" Without showing much enthusiasm, she agreed, but when we walked hand in hand into our dark garden and saw that the studio lights were on—was there someone inside?—she changed her mind.

She visited me every afternoon over the next three days: stretching out on the sofa—gazing at my painting, at the pages of her book, at the little curled waves in the sea outside—and then leaving as unobtrusively as she had come.

It did not cross my mind to get in touch with her in Istanbul that October. The books I was reading so passionately, the paintings I did in such haste, my radical leftist friends, the Marxists who were killing one another in the corridors of the university, the nationalists, and the police—they all made me ashamed of my summer friends and their rich resort with its barricaded entrance and its watchmen.

But one evening in November, after the central heating was on, I phoned her house. When her mother picked up the phone, I hung up without speaking. The next day I asked myself why I had made that ridiculous phone call. I did not realize I had fallen in love, and I had not yet discovered what I would have to learn again and again every time this happened: I was possessed.

A week later, on another cold dark evening, I phoned again. This time she answered. In words I had prepared in advance in some corner of my mind, without the rest of my mind knowing it, I spoke with rehearsed spontaneity: That painting I'd begun at the very end of the summer, did she remember? Well, I was hoping to finish it now, so could she come and pose for me one afternoon?

"Should I wear the same clothes?" she asked.

I hadn't thought of this. "Yes, wear the same clothes," I said.

So the following Wednesday I went to the gates of Dame de Sion, where my mother had once been a pupil, to pick her up; I kept my distance from the crowd of mothers, fathers, cooks, and servants waiting near the door, preferring, like a number of other young men, to hide behind the trees to the side. Hundreds of girls were pouring past the threshold, all wearing this French Catholic school's uniform—a navy blue skirt with a white shirt—and when she emerged from the crowd, she looked as if she'd shrunk; her hair was tied back, in her arms were her schoolbooks, and in a plastic bag she was carrying the clothes she would be posing in.

When she found out that I was not taking her home so my mother would offer her tea and cake, but to the apartment in Cihangir that my mother was letting me use as my studio, she grew anxious. But after I had lit the stove there and pulled out a divan like the one in the summerhouse and she saw that I was "serious" about the painting, she relaxed, changed modestly into her long summer dress, and stretched out on the divan.

It was in this way, and without announcing itself as a love affair, that the relationship between a nineteen-year-old artist and his even younger model began to dance in harmony with a strange music whose notes we did not even understand. In the beginning she came to the Cihangir studio once a fortnight, later it was once a week. I started doing other paintings in the same mode (a young girl reclining on a sofa). By now we were speaking even less than we had during the last days of the summer. My real life was very crowded, what with my studies at the architecture faculty, my books, and my plans to become a painter; I was afraid some intrusion into the purity of this second world would ruin it, so I didn't discuss my everyday troubles with my sad, beautiful model. It wasn't because I thought she wouldn't understand, I just wanted to keep my two worlds separate. I had lost interest in my summer friends and my lycée classmates who were preparing to take over their fathers' factories, but—by now I could no longer hide it from myself—seeing the Black Rose once a week made me very happy.

On rainy days, just as when I'd been staying in this same Cihangir apartment as my aunt's guest, the pickup trucks and American cars struggling up Chicken Can't Fly Alley would skid on the wet cobblestones and we would hear them. During the ever longer but not at all unpleasant silences between us while I painted, we would sometimes come eye to eye. In the beginning, because she was still enough of a child to be happy about such a thing, she would smile, and then, fearing that she had ruined the pose, she would immediately return her lips to their former shape and her dark brown eyes would stare into mine with the same silence for a very long while. Toward the end of these strange silences, as I studied her face, she could see from my expression the effect she had had on me, and as I continued to look straight into her eyes without breaking the stare, I understood from the curve that began to appear at the corners of her lips—which she could not keep from turning into a smile—that my long stare had pleased her. Once, as she smiled in this half-happy, half-sullen way, bringing a smile to my lips too (my brush now floating aimlessly across the canvas), my beautiful model was overcome by the urge to let me know why she had smiled—and broke her pose.

"I like it when you look at me like that."

Actually, this explained not just why she'd smiled but why she'd been coming to this dusty Cihangir apartment once a week. A few weeks later, when I saw the same smile forming on her lips, I put down my brush and went over to sit next to her on the sofa, and as I'd been dreaming of doing for several weeks, I dared to kiss her.

Because the sky was black and the dark room had made us more comfortable, this late-breaking storm swept us up and carried us along without impediment. From the divan on which we were lying, we could see the searchlights of the Bosphorus boats traveling stealthily across the dark waters to the walls of the apartment.

We continued meeting, without breaking our ritual. By now I was very happy with my model, but why did I hold back all the impulses I would display so lavishly in the future in situations like this: the sweet nothings, the attacks of jealousy, the panics, the bungling, and other emotional reactions and excesses? Because I didn't feel them. Perhaps this was because our artist-model relationship—the thing that had made us notice each other and that still bound us together—required silence. Or perhaps it was because—and I had thought about this with a childish shame in the most obscure corner of my mind—I knew that if I ever married her, I would have to become a factory owner, not an artist.

After nine Wednesdays of silent painting and silent lovemaking, a much simpler worry came between the happy painter and his model. My mother, who could not go for long without checking on her son, went to the studio apartment in Cihangir that she also used for storing old furniture; as she looked over my paintings, Bonnard's influence did not prevent her from recognizing my beautiful model. Each time I'd finish a painting, my chestnut-haired love would break my heart by asking, "Is that supposed to look like me?" (not important, the wise guy would tell her), so while we were probably both pleased that my mother had recognized her—it answered her question once and for all—at the same time we were worried that my mother would ring hers and prattle happily about how close we'd become. (For her part, the Black Rose's mother thought her daughter was spending her Wednesdays in a drama class at the French consulate.) As for the temperamental father, let's not mention him at all.

We ended our Wednesday meetings at once. A short while afterward, we began to meet on other days, on afternoons when she got out of school early or on some mornings when I skipped class. Because my mother's raids continued, because we no longer had enough time to paint and enjoy our long silences, and because I let a classmate who was being hunted down by the police—for, it was insisted, a political crime—hide out there, we stopped going to the

Cihangir apartment altogether. Instead, we walked the streets of Istanbul, staying away from Nişantaşı, Beyoğlu, Taksim, and all the other places we were likely to run into the acquaintances we called "everyone"; instead, we'd meet at Taksim—a four-minute walk from the Dame de Sion in Harbiye and also from my university in Taşkışla—and board a bus that took us farther afield.

We began with Beyazıt Square, where the Çınaraltı Café had retained its old look (even after political skirmishes around the front gates of Istanbul University had become commonplace, the boy waiters never lost their composure); pointing at the Beyazıt National Library, I boasted that it contained "one copy of every book ever published in Turkey"; I took her to the Sahaflar Secondhand Book Market, where on colder days the old booksellers crouched around the gas and electric stoves in their little stores; I showed her the unpainted wooden houses of Vezneciler, the Byzantine ruins, and the streets lined with fig trees; and I took her to the Vefa Boza Shop, where my uncle had sometimes taken us on winter evenings to sample this famous fermented millet drink, and where I pointed out to her Atatürk's personal *boza* glass, now inside a frame on the wall. That a rich "Europeanized" girl from Nişantaşı who knew all the fashionable shops and restaurants of Bebek and Taksim should, of all the things I had shown her in poor old melancholy back-street Istanbul beyond the Golden Horn, pay the most attention to a *boza* glass that had not been washed for thirty-five years didn't bother me. I was pleased with my companion, who put her hands in her coat pockets just like I did and liked to walk very fast, like me, and looked at things as carefully as I had done two or three years earlier when first exploring these neighborhoods on my own. I felt myself closer to her than ever, and my stomach began to ache in a way I had not yet discovered was another symptom of love.

Like me, at first she was perturbed by the centuries-old wooden houses of the poverty-stricken back streets of Süleymaniye and Zeyrek, which looked as if the tiniest tremor would cause them to collapse. She was bewitched by the emptiness of the Museum of Painting and Sculpture, a mere five minutes from the *dolmuş* stop right across from her school. The disused fountains of the poor neighborhoods; the white-bearded skull-capped old men who sat in the cafés watching the streets; the old aunties at their windows, staring at passing strangers as if they might be slave merchants; the neighborhood people who would try and guess who we were in voices loud enough for us to hear (*What do you think about these two, big brother? They're brother and sister, can't you see? Look, they've taken the wrong turn*)—all this awakened in her the very shame and melancholy it awakened in me. We'd be chased by children trying to sell us trinkets or simply to talk (*Tourist, tourist, what is your name?*), but she didn't get upset, as I did, or ask, Why do they think we're foreigners? Even so, we stayed away from the Covered Bazaar and the markets of Nuruosmaniye. When the sexual tension became too much to bear—she still didn't want us to go back to paint in Cihangir—we'd return to Beşiktaş, which we visited all the time because of the Museum of Painting and Sculpture, and get on the first ferry (54 *İnşirah*), going as far down the Bosphorus as time allowed, to watch the leafless groves, the sea that trembled before the *yalıs* when the north wind blew, the fast-running waters that changed color as the wind pushed the clouds across the sky, and the surrounding gardens full of pine trees. Years later, I asked myself why it was that we never held hands, during these walks and sea trips, and came up with many reasons: (1) We were two timid children who took to the streets of Istanbul not to feel our love but to hide it; (2) lovers who hold hands in public are happy and want everyone to see they are happy, whereas I, though I was willing to accept that we were happy, was afraid of appearing superficial; (3) this sort of happy gesture would turn us into tourists who had come to these poor ruined conservative districts for "careless pleasure"; and (4) the melancholy of the poor neighborhoods, of ruined, ravaged Istanbul, had long since engulfed us.

When this melancholy sat heavily on me, I would want to rush back to Cihangir to do a painting that somehow paralleled these Istanbul views, though I had no idea how such a painting would look. I soon discovered that my beautiful model sought a very different cure for her melancholy, and this was my first disillusionment.

"I'm feeling very low today," she said, when we met in Taksim. "Would you mind if we went to the Hilton Hotel to drink some tea?

If we go to any of those poor neighborhoods today, I'm only going to feel worse. Anyway, we don't have enough time."

I was wearing one of those army coats that leftist students wore in those days; I hadn't shaved, and even if they did let me into the Hilton Hotel, did I have enough money to pay for tea? I dragged my feet for a while, and then we went to the hotel. In the lobby, we were recognized by a childhood friend of my father's who came every afternoon to drink tea and pretend he was in Europe, and after shaking my melancholy love's hand in a most pretentious way, he whispered into my ear that my young lady friend was very lovely. We were both too preoccupied to pay him much attention.

"My father wants to take me out of school here and send me to Switzerland," my beloved told me, as a tear rolled from one of her enormous eyes and dropped into the teacup in her hand.

"Why?"

They'd found out about us. Did I ask who they meant by *us*? Had the boys she'd loved before me aroused such anger and jealousy in her father? Why was I so much more important? I can't remember whether I asked these questions. Fear and self-interest had blinded my heart, and I was too worried about protecting myself. I dreaded losing her—while still without an inkling of the great pain that awaited me—but I was also angry that she now refused to stretch out on my divan and pose for me and let me make love to her.

"We can speak more easily in Cihangir on Wednesday," I said. "Nuri's left. The place is empty again."

But the next time we met, we went to the Museum of Painting and Sculpture. We'd made this a habit because it was easy to get there quickly from her school and easy also to find an empty gallery where we could kiss. Above all, it saved us from the city's cold gloom. But after a while the empty museum and its mostly abominable paintings delivered us to a melancholy even stronger than the city's. By now the watchmen knew us and had begun to follow us from room to room, and because this exacerbated the tensions between us, we stopped kissing at the museum too.

But we quickly fell into a routine that stayed with us throughout the joyless days that followed. We would show our student cards to the two old watchmen, who, like all watchmen in Istanbul's museums, would give us sour looks, as if to ask, *What could you possibly want to see in this place?* With false cheer, we would ask them how they were, before going straight to see the museum's little Bonnard and tiny Matisse. Reverently whispering their names, we'd move quickly past the anguished but uninspired paintings of Turkish academicians, reciting the names of the European masters they imitated: Cézanne, Léger, Picasso. What we found disillusioning was not that these artists, most of whom came from military schools and had studied in Europe, had allowed themselves to be influenced by western artists, but that they captured so little of the feel, touch, and soul of the city about which we had wandered, so in love and so cold.

But still, the main reason we came to this building, originally built for Dolmabahçe Palace's crown prince and only a few paces from the room in which Atatürk died—the very thought that we had kissed so close to this spot made our skin crawl—was not that the galleries were empty or convenient, and not that the late Ottoman splendor of the high ceilings and wonderful wrought-iron balconies was refreshing after the tiring poverty of Istanbul, and not that the Bosphorus views from its large windows were much more beautiful than most of the paintings on the walls; what kept us coming back was our favorite painting.

This was Halil Pasha's *Reclining Woman*. On our first meeting after our visit to the Hilton lobby, we bypassed the rest of the museum, heading straight to this painting; its model was a young woman who had, as I noticed with surprise on first inspection, kicked off her shoes to stretch out on a blue divan and stare sadly at the painter (her husband?), using one of her arms as a pillow, just as my model had done so many times. It was not only this strange resemblance that drew me to this painting; during our first visits to the little side gallery where it hung, she had watched us kiss. Whenever we heard one of the suspicious old watchmen creaking his way across the parquet floors, we'd stop, sit up straight, and launch into a serious conversation about her, so we knew every detail of the painting well. To this we'd add whatever we'd found on Halil Pasha in the encyclopedia.

"The girl's feet must have grown cold after sundown," I said.

"I have more bad news," said my love; every time I looked at this painting, she looked more like Halil Pasha's model. "My mother's asked a matchmaker over, and she wants me to meet her."

"So will you?"

"It seems ridiculous. The man she's suggesting is someone or another's son and he's studied in America." In a mocking whisper, she told me his rich family's name.

"Your father's ten times richer than they are."

"Don't you understand? They're doing this to get me away from you."

"So are you going to meet the matchmaker when she comes for coffee?"

"That's not important. I don't want trouble at home."

"Let's go to Cihangir," I said. "I want to do another painting of you, another *Reclining Woman*. I want to kiss you and kiss you."

My love, slowly discovering my obsessions and beginning to fear them, tried to address the question that was gnawing at both of us. "My father's in a bad way because you want to be an artist," she said. "You'll become a poor drunken painter, and I'll be your nude model. . . . That's what he's afraid of."

She tried to smile but couldn't. Hearing our watchman creak slowly but powerfully across the parquet floor, we turned, by habit, even though we'd not been kissing, to the subject of the *Reclining Woman*. But what I really wanted to ask was, Why does your father have to know what sort of career awaits every boy his daughter "goes out with" (the expression was just coming into use in Turkish around this time) and when he plans to marry her? I also wanted to say, Tell your father I'm studying to be an architect! But even as I struggled to answer her father's fears, I knew that doing so would be condemning myself to become a weekend artist from this moment on. Every time I asked her to come back with me to Cihangir and she refused—this went on for weeks—my head, fast losing its capacity for cold-blooded reason, would urge me to shout, And what's so wrong about being an artist? But the empty rooms of these ostentatious apartments—built for the heir apparent and now housing Turkey's first museum of painting and sculpture—like the wretched paintings on its walls, were answer enough. Having just read a book about Halil Pasha, I knew that he was a soldier who had not been able to sell any paintings at all as he advanced in years, so he and his sad wife, also his model, had lived in army quarters and eaten frugal meals in their canteens.

When we met after that, I would try very hard to amuse her, showing her Prince Abdülmecit's solemn paintings (*Goethe in the Harem, Beethoven in the Harem*) to make her smile. Then I would ask, "Shall we go to Cihangir?" despite having promised myself not to. We would hold hands and fall silent. "Am I going to have to kidnap you?" I asked, assuming an air borrowed from some film I'd just seen.

During a later meeting, which had been very difficult to arrange because it was so hard for us to speak on the phone, when we were sitting in the museum in front of the *Reclining Woman,* my sad and beautiful model told me, with tears flowing down her cheeks, that her father, who regularly thrashed her brothers badly, also loved his daughter to a degree that could be said to be pathological; he was insanely jealous, and she was afraid of him; at the same time, she loved him dearly. But now she had realized that she loved me even more, and in the seven seconds it took the old museum watchman to creak his way down the corridor, we kissed with an intensity and abandon that I had never before known. As we kissed, we held each other's faces in our hands as if they were as fragile as porcelain.

Halil Pasha's wife stared sadly down at us from her magnificent frame. When the watchman appeared at the door, my lovely said, "You can kidnap me."

"Then I will."

I had a bank account I'd opened up years earlier to save an allowance I had from my grandmother; I also owned a quarter of a shop on Rumeli Avenue—this had been settled on me after one of my parents' fights—and I also had a number of securities, although I had no idea where they were. If I could manage to translate an old novel by Graham Greene in a fortnight, I could take it to a publisher friend of my friend Nuri (no longer wanted by the police); according to my calculations, I could, with the money I earned from the translation, put down two months' rent on a small apartment like my studio in Cihangir and live there with my beautiful model. Or perhaps, after I'd kidnapped her, my mother (who'd been asking me why I seemed so troubled lately) would take pity on us and give us the Cihangir apartment.

After a week of deliberations only slightly more realistic than those of a child who plans to grow up to be a fireman, we arranged to meet in Taksim, but for the first time she failed to turn up, though I waited for an hour and a half. That evening, knowing I would lose my mind if I didn't talk to someone, I called up my friends from Robert Academy, whom I had not seen in a very long time. Happy to see me in love, in agony, and beyond help, they smiled to see me drunk out of my mind in a Beyoğlu *meyhane,* where they reminded me that even if I didn't marry the underage girl without her father's consent, even if I just lived in the same house with her, I'd still be thrown into prison; then, upon hearing me spout more nonsense, they asked me how I expected to become an artist if I had to abandon my studies and work to support her—it didn't upset me when they said this—and finally, in a spirit of friendship, one of them offered me the key to an apartment where I could lie with my "reclining woman" whenever I wished.

After waiting twice outside the crowded gates of Dame de Sion, hiding in a distant corner, I was able to kidnap my lycée student lover. I promised her that if she came back with me to my friend's apartment (which I had already visited and tried to tidy), no one would disturb us. Finally I managed to persuade her. As I was later to discover, it wasn't just my thoughtful Robert Academy friend who used this *garçonnière* but also his father, and it was such a dreadful place I sensed at once that my Black Rose would never want to strike a pose there to suggest a painting, if only to make us feel better. On the great bed in this apartment, whose only other furnishings were a bank calendar hanging on the wall and a shelf, where, between two bottles of Johnnie Walker, sat all fifty-two volumes of the *Encyclopedia Britannica,* we thrice made sad and angry love. When I saw that she loved me more than I had thought, when I saw how she shook when we made love, when I saw how easily and often she burst into tears, the pain in my stomach grew more severe, but when I tried to fend it off I felt even more helpless than before. Because every time we met, she told me about her father's plans to take her to Switzerland during the February vacation for a supposed ski trip and then enroll her in a fancy school full of rich Arabs and cracked Americans. The panic in her voice made me believe her, but when I tried to cheer her up by imitating a tough guy from a Turkish film and vowing to kidnap her, seeing the happy look on my love's face, I would believe myself too.

At the beginning of February, at our last meeting before the school holiday, to put the looming disaster out of our minds and also to thank him for giving us the key to his house, we met with my good-hearted friend. Some other classmates joined us, and that evening was the first time any of them had seen my love; as each friend tugged at a different part of me, I had cause to remember why I had so instinctively chosen never to mix my various circles of friends. Things went wrong between my Black Rose and my college friends from the moment they met. Trying to establish a rapport with her, they made gentle fun of me, but she wouldn't play along; later, to appease them, she joined in on jokes that might have been fine at another time but now sounded impossibly silly. Upon being asked about her mother and her father, what they did and where they lived, and all the other questions about wealth and property, she cut the conversation short to show she despised such talk, and for the rest of the evening, aside from looking at the Bosphorus from the Bebek restaurant and talking about soccer or some consumer brand or other, the only moment in which she took any evident pleasure was when we stopped at the narrowest point of the Bosphorus, the Aşiyan, to watch yet another wooden mansion burning on the opposite shore.

It was one of the most beautiful Bosphorus *yalıs,* in Kandilli, very close to the point, and to see it better I got out of the car. My lovely had tired of watching my friends enjoying the fire so she came to stand beside me, her hand in mine. To get away from the cars and the crowds that had gathered to sip tea and to get a better view of this, one of the last remaining Ottoman mansions, as it went up in flames, we walked to the other end of Rumelihisarı. I told her how when I was in lycée and skipped classes, I had often taken a ferry to the other side and explored those streets too.

Standing in front of the little cemetery in the dark cold night, feeling the tumultuous strength of the Bosphorus currents in our very bones, my love whispered that she loved me very much and I said I would do anything for her and then I embraced her with all my might. We kissed; whenever I paused to open my eyes, I'd see the orange light of the fire on the other side playing on her soft skin.

On the way home, we held hands in the back of the car, saying nothing. When we got to her apartment, she rushed to the door like a child. It was the last I would see of her. She didn't show up for our next assignation.

Three weeks later, when the school holidays were over, I started going to the gates of Dame de Sion when school let out. From a distance, I watched the girls coming out one by one and waited for the Black Rose to appear. Ten days later, I was forced to accept that the effort was useless and I had to stop, but every afternoon my legs would still take me to the lycée gates, where I would stay until the crowds had dispersed. One day, her eldest and favorite brother emerged from the crowd, told me that his sister sent me her fondest regards from Switzerland, and handed me an envelope. In her letter, which I read in a pudding shop while smoking a cigarette, she told me she was very happy with her new school but that she missed me and Istanbul a lot.

I wrote her nine long letters, seven of which I put into envelopes and five of which I posted. I never received an answer.

CHAPTER THIRTY-SIX

The Ship on the Golden Horn

In February 1972, when I was in my second year of studying architecture, I found myself going to class less and less. How much did this have to do with the loss of my beautiful model and the lonely melancholy into which I withdrew afterward? Sometimes I wouldn't leave our Beşiktaş house at all but spent the whole day reading. Sometimes I would take a thick book (*The Possessed, War and Peace, Buddenbrooks*) with me and read it during class. After the Black Rose

disappeared, my pleasure in painting continued to wane. When drawing on canvas or paper or when brushing on paint, I no longer felt that sense of play, that sense of victory I had had as a child. Painting had started as a happy childish amusement and now, mysteriously, I was losing that joy, and as I had no idea what might replace it, a dense cloud of unease engulfed me. To live without painting, to have no escape from the real world—what other people called "life"—was turning into a prison. If my dread overpowered me—and if I'd been smoking to excess—it became difficult to breathe. Being short of breath in ordinary life made me feel as if I were drowning. I'd be overcome by a desire to do myself harm or else run away from this class I was in, this school.

But still I went to my studio from time to time and did my best to forget my almond-scented model—or to do the opposite and try to conjure her up with another painting. But there was something missing. My mistake was to persist in the delusion that painting could still offer me such pleasure as only a child can enjoy, when I was no longer a child. In the middle of a painting, I'd see where it was going and, deciding it was not good enough, leave it half finished. These bouts of indecision led me to conclude that if every new painting was to bring me the happiness art had brought me as a child, I would have to settle my purpose before I started. But I had no idea how I might go about thinking about painting in such a way. Perhaps because until now I'd always felt happy while painting, I did not understand that I had to suffer to paint, that this pain might in fact help develop my art.

It also scared me to see my disquiet spread to other interests: After years of claiming that architecture was an art, I realized that architecture had no more to offer me than painting. I had never been particularly interested in it as a child, unless I counted the games I'd played with sugar cubes and wooden blocks. And as my mostly uninspired teachers at the Technical University possessed the souls of engineers, had no sense of play, and took no creative pleasure in architecture, their classes began to seem a waste of time, distractions from the things I really should be doing, the "truer" life I thought I should be living. Everything around me palled when thoughts like these came to me—the lecture I was attending, the bell I longed to ring, the teachers strutting about their classrooms, the students joking and smoking between classes—they'd turn into their own ghosts, trapped as I was inside this aimless, false, and suffering world that promised me only self-loathing and suffocation. I would feel my allotted time slipping away and my destination receding, as happened so often in my dreams. To fight off this nightmare, I would write a few things or do a few drawings in my notebooks during class: I would sketch my professor and the backs of his more attentive students, and I would write parodies, pastiches, simple rhyming couplets, about what was going on in class. . . . Soon I had an audience that anxiously awaited each installment, but in spite of this the sense of time slipping away—and my dread that my life was even now voiding itself of meaning—grew so powerful that if I entered the architecture faculty in Taşkışla intending to spend the whole day there, an hour later I'd be bolting out of the building as if for my life (and heedless of whether I was stepping on the cracks between the pavement slabs); having thrown myself outside, I would escape into the Istanbul streets.

The back streets between Taksim and Tepebaşı, through which I'd passed as a child when my mother and I would go home in a *dolmuş* and which had seemed to a six-year-old like a distant land, and the Pera neighborhoods so masterfully built by Armenians that they were still standing—these were the places I now began to explore. Sometimes I would go straight from the Architectural Faculty to Taksim, board any bus, and go wherever my fancy or my feet happened to take me: the mean narrow streets of Kasımpaşa; Balat, which on my first visit had looked fake, like a film set; the old Greek and Jewish

neighborhoods that new immigrants and poverty had changed beyond recognition; the very Muslim, very bright back streets of Üsküdar, which were full of wooden houses right up until the 1980s; the eerie old streets of Kocamustafapaşa, ruined by hastily con-

structed and sinister-looking concrete apartment buildings; the beautiful courtyard of Fatih Mosque, which never failed to delight me; the area around Balıklı; the neighborhoods of Kurtuluş and Feriköy, which, as they got poorer, seemed older, giving one the impression that middle-class families had been there for thousands of years, changing language, race, religion as the oppressive state required (in fact it had been only fifty); the poorer neighborhoods perched on the lower slopes (just as in Cihangir, Tarlabaşı, and Nişantaşı)—I made my way through all these places aimlessly. In the beginning the point was not to have a point, to escape the world in which everyone had to have a job, a desk, an office. But even as I explored the city wall by wall, street by street, I poured my own angry, evil melancholy into it. Even now, if I happen to pass through the same streets and see a ruined neighborhood fountain or a ruined wall belonging to a Byzantine church (Pantocrator, Küçük Ayasofya) that looks somehow older, or when I look down an alley and see the

Golden Horn shimmering between the wall of a mosque and an apartment building covered with ugly mosaic tiles, I will remember how troubled I was the first time I looked at this view from the same angle and notice how different the view looks now. It's not my memory that's false; the view looked troubled then because I myself was troubled. I poured my soul in the city's streets, and there it still resides.

If we've lived in a city long enough to have given our truest and deepest feelings to its prospects, there comes a time when—just as a song recalls a lost love—particular streets, images, and vistas will do the same. It may be because I first saw so many neighborhoods and back streets, so many hilltop views, during these walks I took after I lost my almond-scented love, that Istanbul seems such a melancholy place to me.

When the loss was still new, I saw my mood reflected everywhere—a full moon would become a clock face; everything was some symbol of the sort that would later make a dream. In March 1972 I boarded a *dolmuş* (just as I had done with the Black Rose), alighting, as it was still possible to do in those days, where I wished, which in this case was the Galata Bridge. The sky was a low, dark, grayish purple. It looked as if it might be about to snow, and the bridge walkways were empty. Spotting the wooden stairs on the Golden Horn side of the bridge, I descended to the pier.

Here I found a small city ferry that was about to leave. The captain, the machinist, and the rope man had all gathered on the landing like the crew of an ocean liner, greeting the handful of passengers as they smoked and sipped tea and chatted among themselves. When I stepped on board, I adapted to my new circumstances and greeted them too, and immediately felt as if my tired fellow passengers, with their dull coats, their skullcaps, their scarves, and their string bags, were old acquaintances and I was just another commuter who traveled up and down the Golden Horn on this ferry every day. When it slipped quietly into motion, I felt this sense of belonging, this sense of sitting now in the heart of the city, and I felt it with such intensity that I also felt something else. Above us, on the bridge (where I could see bank advertisements and the antennae of trolleybuses) and on the city's main roads, it was around

noon on a day in March 1972; but here, in the world below, we belonged to an older, broader, weightier time. It seemed to me that in scrambling down the stairs to the ferry that I'd noticed only by chance, I'd gone back thirty years to the days when Istanbul was more isolated from the world, poorer, and more nearly in harmony with its melancholy.

Through the trembling windows in the rear of the ship's upper deck, I watched the Golden Horn's landings slowly flowing past, and its hills, covered with the wooden houses of old Istanbul, and its

cypress-filled cemeteries; alleyways, dark hills, shipyards, rusting hulls; an endless string of little factories, shops, and chimneys; ruined Byzantine churches; the most magnificent Ottoman mosques rising above the dingiest and narrowest streets; the Church of the Pantocrator in Zeyrek; the great tobacco warehouses of Cibali; even the shadow of Fatih Mosque far in the distance. Through the ship's clouded, trembling windows, this midday scene seemed, like the Istanbul views I saw in disintegrating old movies, as dark as midnight.

The ferry's engine made a noise like my mother's sewing machine, cutting out abruptly as it approached a landing; the windows would stop trembling, and the still waters of the Golden Horn, the old aunties boarding the ship with fifty baskets, chickens and roosters and the narrow streets of the old Greek neighborhoods behind them; the little factories and warehouses and barrels; the old car tires; the horse-drawn carriages that wandered about the city—they all looked as finely and clearly drawn as in hundred-year-old postcards, and they all looked black and white. When the ferry moved away from the shore and the windows began to tremble again, as we moved toward the cemeteries of the opposite shore, the black smoke from the ship's funnel would veil the view in a

melancholy that made it look even more like a picture. At times the sky seemed pitch black, but then, just like a corner in a film that suddenly comes aflame, a cold snow light would appear.

Is this the secret of Istanbul—that beneath its grand history, its living poverty, its outward-looking monuments, and its sublime landscapes, its poor hide the city's soul inside a fragile web? But here we have come full circle, for anything we say about the city's essence says more about our own lives and our own states of mind. The city has no center other than ourselves.

So how did I come to feel so much at one with my fellow *İstanbullus* on that day in March 1972 when I skipped class to ride down the Golden Horn on that old ship all the way to Eyüp? Perhaps it was that I wished to convince myself that, next to the great *hüzün* of the city, my own heartbreak and the loss of my love for painting—

the love I thought would carry me through life—were not important. That by looking at Istanbul, so much more defeated, ruined, and sorrowful, I would forget my own pain. But to say such a thing would be to talk in the language of Turkish melodrama, like a hero who is already afflicted with melancholy when the film begins and

so destined to lose "in life and in love"—and it won't do to use the city's melancholy to explain away my own. In fact, no one in my family or my circle of friends had taken my ambitions to be a poet-painter at all seriously. As for the city's poets and painters, most had their eyes so firmly pinned on the West that they couldn't even see their own city: They were struggling to belong to the modern age, the world of the trolleybuses and bank advertisements on top of the Galata Bridge. I had not yet attuned myself to the melancholy that gave the city its gravitas—because of the happy, playful child inside me I was perhaps the person most removed from it; until now, I'd had no desire to embrace it; feeling it inside me, I'd run the other way to take refuge in Istanbul's "beauties."

Why should we expect a city to cure us of our spiritual pains? Perhaps because we cannot help loving our city like a family. But we still have to decide which part of the city we love and invent the reasons why.

As the ferry approached Hasköy, it occurred to me, in my sad confusion, that if I had come to feel deeply connected to my city, it was because it offered me a deeper wisdom and understanding than

any I could acquire in a classroom. Through the ship's trembling windows I could see the ruined old wooden houses; the old Greek neighborhood of Fener, still half abandoned due to relentless state oppression; and among these ruined buildings, looking more mysterious than ever under the dark clouds—Topkapı Palace, Süleymaniye Mosque, and the silhouette of Istanbul's hills, mosques, and churches. Here amid the old stones and the old wooden houses, history made peace with its ruins; ruins nourished life and and gave new life to history. If my fast-extinguishing love of painting could no longer save me, the city's poor neighborhoods seemed prepared, in any event, to become my second world. How I longed to be part of this poetic confusion! Just as I had lost myself in my imagination

to escape my grandmother's house and the boredom of school, now, having grown bored with studying architecture, I lost myself in Istanbul. So it was that I finally came to relax and accept the *hüzün* that gives Istanbul its grave beauty, the *hüzün* that is its fate.

I rarely returned to the real world empty-handed. I would bring home a serrated telephone token of a type no longer in circulation or some obscure object I'd jokingly tell my friends could be used "either as a shoehorn or a bottle opener"; I'd bring back a chip of a brick that had fallen off a thousand-year-old wall; a wad of Imperial Russian banknotes, which all the city's junk dealers had in abundance at that time; I'd bring back the stamp from a company that had gone under thirty years earlier; weights from a street vendor's scale; the cheap old volumes I'd buy at the end of almost every trip, when my feet would take themselves to Sahaflar Secondhand Book Market. . . . I craved books and magazines about Istanbul—any type of printed matter, any program, any timetable or ticket was valuable information to me, and so I began to collect them. A part of me knew I could not keep these things forever; after I had played with them for a while, I would forget them. And so I knew I would never become one of those obsessive collectors whose work is never done, or even an insatiable collector of knowledge like Koçu, though in the early days I told myself that eventually it would all form part of a great enterprise—a painting or a series of paintings or a novel like those I was then reading by Tolstoy, Dostoyevsky, and Mann. There were times—when every strange memento seemed saturated with the poetic melancholy of lost imperial greatness and its historical residue—that I imagined myself to be the only one who had unlocked the city's secret; it had come to me as I watched through the windows of the Golden Horn ferry, and I had embraced the city as my own—no one had ever seen it as I did now!

Once I had mastered this new poetic outlook, I chased with unchecked ardor after anything and everything connected with the city. Everything I touched in this state of mind, every piece of knowledge, every artifact, seemed like a work of art. Before my elation subsides, let me describe one such ordinary thing, that ferry with the trembling windows.

It was called the *Kocataş*. It was built in 1937 in the Golden Horn, in Hasköy shipyard, along with its sister ship, the *Sarıyer*. They'd been fitted with two engines made in 1913 and salvaged from a yacht named the *Nimetullah,* formerly the property of Hıdiv Hilmi Paşa. Can we deduce from the trembling windows that the engine didn't suit the ferry? Such details allow me to feel myself a true *İstan-*

bullu and give depth to my melancholy. After it had dropped me off in Eyüp, the little *Kocataş* would continue operating for another twelve years, to be taken out of service in 1984.

The objects I brought back from my aimless walks, my attempts at "getting lost"—a few old books, a calling card, an old postcard, or a strange piece of information about the city—these things were indispensable proof that the walk I'd taken was "real." Like the Coleridge hero who wakes to find himself holding the rose of his dreams, I knew these objects were not of the second world, which had brought me so much contentment as a child, but of a real world that matched my memories.

The trouble with Eyüp, where the *Kocataş* left me, was that this perfect little village at the end of the Golden Horn did not seem real at all. As an image of the inward-looking, mysterious, religious, picturesque, and mystical East it was so perfect as to seem like someone else's dream, a sort of Turkish Eastern Muslim Disneyland planted on the edge of the city. Was this because it was outside the old city walls and therefore without the Byzantine influence or the many-layered confusions you saw elsewhere in the city? Did the high hills bring night earlier to this place? Or had Eyüp decided out of religious and mystic humility to keep its buildings small, keep its distance from the greatness of Istanbul, and keep its complex power—the power it derives from its dirt, its rust, its smoke, its wrecks, its cracks, its remains, its ruins, its filth? What makes Eyüp so close to western dreams of the East and makes everyone love it so? Is it its continuing ability to derive full benefit from the West and westernizing Istanbul, while still keeping itself distant from the center, the bureaucracy, the state institutions and buildings? This was why Pierre Loti loved the place, finally buying a house and moving here—because it was unspoiled, a perfect, beautiful image of the East—and for the same reasons I found it irksome. When I arrived in Eyüp, the delicious melancholy that had come to me from the view of the Golden Horn, with its ruins and its history, vanished into thin air. I was slowly coming to understand that I loved Istanbul for its ruins, for its *hüzün,* for the glories once possessed and later lost. And so, to cheer myself up, I left Eyüp to wander around other neighborhoods in search of ruins.

CHAPTER THIRTY-SEVEN

A Conversation with My Mother: Patience, Caution, and Art

For many long years, my mother spent her evenings alone in the sitting room, waiting for my father. My father spent his evenings at his bridge club, and from there he would go on to other places, returning so late that my mother would have already tired of waiting and gone to bed. After my mother and I had sat across from each other to eat supper (my father would have rung by then: *I'm very busy,* he would have said, *I'll be home late; you go ahead and eat*), my mother would spread her cards across the cream-colored tablecloth and read her future. As she turned over each card in each fifty-two-card deck—one at a time, trying to order them by value, with red following black—there was no great desire to search the cards for signs, nor did she take pleasure in fashioning the signs offered by the cards into a story that gave the future a pleasing shape. For her this was a game of patience. When I'd come into the sitting room and ask whether she'd read her fortune yet, she always gave me the same answer:

"I'm not doing this to read my fortune, darling, I'm doing it to pass the time. What time is it? I'll do one more and then I'm going to bed."

As she said this, she would glance over at the old film playing on our black-and-white television (a new thing in Turkey) or the discussion about the Ramadans of yesteryear (in those days, there was only one channel, expressing the state's point of view), and she would say, "I'm not watching this; turn it off if you like."

I would spend some time watching whatever was on the screen; it could be a soccer match or the black-and-white streets of my childhood. I was less interested in the show than I was in a respite from my inner turmoil and my room, and while I was in the sitting room I did as I did every night and spent some time chatting with my mother.

Some of these chats turned into bitter arguments. Afterward I would return to my room and shut my door, to read and wallow in guilt until morning. Sometimes, after arguing with my mother, I'd go out into the cold Istanbul night and wander around Taksim and Beyoğlu, chain-smoking through the dark and evil back streets until I could feel the chill in my bones, and after my mother and everyone else in the city had gone to sleep I would return home. I fell into the habit of going to bed at four in the morning and sleeping till noon; I would keep to this routine for the next twenty years.

The thing my mother and I argued about in those days—sometimes overtly and sometimes without admitting it—was my uncertain future; for in the winter of 1972, in the middle of my second year studying architecture, I'd stopped attending classes almost entirely. Aside from the few I had to attend to avoid removal from the roll and expulsion, I was hardly ever seen at the Taşkışla architecture faculty.

Sometimes I would tell myself, sheepishly, "Even if I never become an architect, I'll still have a university diploma," an observation much repeated by my father and my friends, who all had some influence on me, making my situation, at least in my mother's eyes, only more precarious. I'd seen my love of painting die and felt the painful void it left behind, so I could tell in my heart of hearts that I would never make it as an architect. At the same time, I knew I could not go on forever reading books and novels until morning or spending my nights wandering the streets. I would sometimes panic and rise abruptly from the table, trying to get my mother to face facts. Because I didn't know why I was doing this, much less quite what it was I was trying to get her to accept, it sometimes seemed as if we were fighting each other blindfolded.

"I was like you when I was young," my mother would say, just—

I would later decide—to annoy me. "I'd run away from life, just like you. While your aunts were at university, living among intellectuals or having fun at parties and balls, I'd sit home like you and spend hours gazing stupidly at *Illustration,* that magazine your grandfather liked so much." She'd pull on her cigarette and look at me to judge whether her words were having any effect. "I was shy, afraid of life."

When she said this, I knew she meant *like you,* and as anger boiled up inside me, I'd try to calm myself with the thought that she was saying these things "for my own good." But my mother was expressing a deep and widely held view that it broke my heart to know she shared. As my eyes moved from the television to the ferry search-lights moving up and down the Bosphorus, I would repeat this orthodoxy to myself and think how much I hated it.

I knew it not from my mother, who never expressed it openly, but from the lazy Istanbul bourgeoisie and like-thinking newspaper columnists who would conclude, in their moments of greatest and most insolent pessimism, "Nothing good can come out of a place like this."

This pessimism is fed by the melancholy that has for so long broken the city's will. But if the melancholy flows from loss and poverty, why do the city's rich embrace it too? Perhaps it is because they are rich by chance. It may also be because they have created nothing brilliant of their own to rival the western civilization they hope to imitate.

There was in my mother's case, however, some basis to this destructive, cautious, middle-class cant she had spoken all her life. Soon after they married, after my brother and I were born, my father mercilessly set out to break her heart. His absences, the family's slow impoverishment—when she married she hadn't the faintest idea that she'd have to grapple with such things, and I always felt that these misfortunes had forced her to mount a sustained defensive posture in the face of society. During our childhood years, whenever she took my brother and me shopping in Beyoğlu, to the cinema, or the park, and she noticed men were looking at her, her guarded expression told me of the extreme caution she exercised with anyone not a member of our family. If my brother and I began to argue in the street, I'd see, along with her anger and distress, a desire to protect us.

I sensed this caution most keenly in my mother's constant entreaties to "be normal, ordinary, like other people." This plea carried a great deal of traditional morality—the importance of being humble, of accepting what little you had and making the most of it, practicing the Sufi asceticism that had left its mark on the entire culture—but this outlook hardly helped her understand why anyone might suddenly leave school. In her view, I was wrong to exaggerate my importance, to take my moral and intellectual obsessions so seriously; such passionate concern was better reserved for cultivating honesty, virtue, diligence, and being like everyone else. Art, painting, creativity—these were things only Europeans had the right to take seriously, my mother seemed to be saying, not we who lived in Istanbul in the second half of the twentieth century, in a culture that has fallen into poverty, thereby losing its strength, its will, and its appetite. If I was forever mindful that "nothing good can come out of a place like this," I wouldn't live to regret it.

At other times, to dignify her position, my mother would tell me that she'd named me Orhan because, of all the Ottoman sultans, it was Sultan Orhan she had loved most. Sultan Orhan had not pursued grand projects and had never drawn attention to himself; instead, he had lived an ordinary life without excess, which was why the history books spoke so respectfully and so sparingly about this second Ottoman sultan. Although my mother smiled as she told me this, it was clear that she wanted me to understand why she thought these to be important virtues.

On those evenings when my mother waited for my father and I came from my room to argue with her, I knew my part would be to resist the broken-down, humble, melancholy life that Istanbul was offering and with it the comforting ordinariness my mother wanted for me. Sometimes I would ask myself, Why am I going out there to have this argument again? and in failing to find a convincing answer, I sensed an inner turmoil I could not begin to understand.

"You used to skip class in the old days too," my mother would say, turning her cards over faster and faster. "You'd say, 'I'm ill, I have a stomachache, I have a fever.' When we were in Cihangir, you made quite a habit of this. So one morning, when you said, 'I'm ill, I'm not going to school,' I shouted at you, do you remember? I said, 'Whether you're ill or not, you are leaving right now and going straight to school. I don't want you at home!' "

At this point in the story, which she told me as often as she could, my mother would pause and—perhaps knowing it infuriated me—she would smile; there would follow a pause as she took a drag from her cigarette, and then, without looking me in the eye but always with a lilt in her voice, she would add, "After that morning, I never again heard you say, 'I'm ill; I'm not going to school.' "

"Then I'm saying it now!" I said rashly. "I'm never setting foot in the architecture faculty again."

"So what are you going to do then? Are you just going to sit at home like me?"

Slowly there rose up the urge to push this argument to the limit and then slam the door and go off for a long, lonely walk in the back streets of Beyoğlu, half drunk, half mad, smoking cigarettes and hating everyone and everything. The walks I took in those years sometimes lasted hours, and sometimes, if I had wandered long enough—gazing at shopwindows, restaurants, half-lit coffeehouses,

bridges, fronts of cinemas, advertisements, letters, filth, mud, rain-
drops falling into the dark puddles on the pavement, neon lights, car
lights, and packs of dogs overturning the rubbish bins—sometimes
another urge would come to me: to go home and put these images
into written words, find the language to express this dark spirit, this
tired and mysterious confusion. This was an urge as irrepressible as
that happy old yearning to paint, but I was not sure what to make of it.

"Is that the lift?" my mother asked.

We both stopped to listen, but we couldn't hear anything to suggest a lift. My father was not on his way up. As my mother again
concentrated on her cards, turning them over with a renewed
energy, I watched her in astonishment. She had a certain way of
moving that was very soothing to me as a child, though when she'd

withdrawn her affections, watching her move this way had caused
me pain. Now I was no longer sure how to read her. I felt myself
caught between unbounded love and anger. Four months earlier,
after a long investigation, my mother had tracked down the place in
Mecidiyeköy where my father met with his mistress; skillfully
extracting the key from the janitor, she'd gone into the empty apartment to meet with a scene that she would later cold-bloodedly

describe to me. A pair of pajamas that my father wore at home was sitting on the pillow in this other bedroom, and on the bedside table stood a tower of bridge books, just like the one he'd built on his side of the bed at home.

For a long time, my mother had told no one what she'd seen; it was only months later, on one of those evenings of playing patience, smoking, and watching television out of the corner of her eye, that I had come out of my room to talk to her and she had suddenly blurted out the story. Seeing my distress, she cut her tale short. Still, every time I thought about it later, the notion of another house my father visited every day could not help but make me shudder; it was as if he had done what I had never managed—he'd found his double, his twin, and it was this creature, not his lover, he went to this other house every day to be with; the illusion only reminded me that something in my life, in my very soul, was wanting.

"In the end, you're going to have to find a way to finish university," my mother would say, as she dealt herself a new hand. "You can't support yourself painting; you'll have to get a job. After all, we're not rich like we used to be."

"That's not true," I said, having long ago worked out that even if I did nothing in life my parents could still support me.

"Are you trying to tell me you can support yourself painting?"

From the way my mother angrily stubbed out her cigarette in the ashtray, from her half-mocking, half-condescending tone and the way she could continue playing cards even while talking about a matter so important, I sensed where we were heading.

"This isn't Paris, you know, it's Istanbul," my mother said, sounding almost happy about it. "Even if you were the best artist in the world, no one would pay you the slightest attention. You'd spend your life alone. No one would understand why you'd given up a brilliant future to paint. If we were a rich society that respected art and painting, then—well, why not? But even in Europe, everyone knows that Van Gogh and Gauguin were cracked."

Certainly she'd heard all my father's stories about the existentialist literature he'd loved so dearly during the fifties. There was a encyclopedic dictionary—its pages now yellowed, its cover tattered—to which my mother had referred a great deal to check facts, a custom that now furnished me with a sarcastic retort.

"So does your *Petit Larousse* say that all artists are crazy?"

"I have no idea, my son. If a person is very talented and hard-working, and if he's lucky, perhaps he can become famous in Europe. But in Turkey you'd just go crazy. Please don't take this the wrong way. I'm saying all this to you now so you won't be sorry later."

But I was sorry now, and all the more so to think she could say such hurtful things while continuing to play patience and read her fortune.

"What exactly is supposed to have offended me?" I asked, possibly hoping that she'd say something to wound me further.

"I don't want anyone to think you're having pyschological difficulties," my mother said. "That's why I won't tell my friends that you're not attending classes. They're not the sort of people who would understand why someone like you would decide to leave university to become a painter. They'd think you'd taken leave of your senses; they'd gossip behind your back."

"You can tell them whatever you like," I said. "I'd give up anything not to be imbeciles like them."

"You will do no such thing," my mother said. "In the end you'll do the same thing you did when you were little: pick up your bag and patter off to school."

"I don't want to be an architect, I know this for sure."

"Study for two more years, my son, get yourself a university diploma, and after that you can decide if you want to be an architect or a painter."

"No."

"Shall I tell you what Nurcihan says about your giving up on architecture?" my mother said, and I knew that in ushering in the opinion of one of her worthless friends she was trying to hurt me. "You're troubled and confused because of these fights between me and your father, because he's always running around with other women—that's what Nurcihan thinks."

"I don't care what your bird-brained society friends think about me!" I cried. Even knowing she was trying to provoke me, I still walked into her trap, willing myself to slip from playacting into a real rage.

"You're very proud, my son," my mother said. "But I like that about you. Because the important thing in life is not this art nonsense but pride. There are a lot of people in Europe who become artists because they're proud and honorable. In Europe they don't think of an artist as a tradesman or a pickpocket, they treat artists as if they're special. But do you really think you can be an artist in a country like this and still keep your pride? To be accepted by people here, who understand nothing of art, to get these people to *buy* your work, you'd have to toady to the state, to the rich, and, worst of all, to semiliterate journalists. Do you think you're up to this?"

My fury gave me a dizzying vitality that pushed me out of myself; I felt a wondrous ambition—so vast it surprised even me—to leave the house and run out into the street. But I resisted, knowing that if I held on here awhile longer to continue this war of words, destroying as much as I could, rebelling with all my might, giving pain and accepting pain in return, then, after we had each uttered our worst, I could still burst out the door into the dark dirty evening and run out into the back streets. My legs would take me up and down the uneven pavements, past streetlamps with pale lights or none at all, to the melancholy of the narrow cobblestone alleys,

and there I would enjoy a perverted happiness at belonging to such a sorrowful, dirty, and impoverished place. Walking without end, fired by rage, ideas and images filing past me like figures in a play, dreaming of the great things I would do someday.

"Look at Flaubert, he lived in the same house as his mother his entire life!" my mother continued in her half-compassionate, half-condescending manner, carefully examining her new cards. "But I don't want you to spend your whole life lounging around the same house with me. That was France. When they say someone is a great artist, even the water stops running. Here, on the other hand, a painter who leaves school and spends his life at his mother's side ends up either drunk or in the nuthouse." And then, another tack: "If you had a profession, believe me, you'd get a lot more pleasure out of painting."

Why was it that in such moments of unhappiness, anger, and misery, I could find pleasure in nocturnal walks through the desolate streets with only my dreams to keep me company? Why, instead of the sun-drenched postcard views of Istanbul that tourists so loved, did I prefer the semidarkness of the back streets, the evenings and cold winter nights, the ghost people passing through the light of the pale streetlamps, the cobblestone views, their loneliness?

"If you don't become an architect or find some other way to make a living, you'll become one of those poor neurotic Turkish artists who have no choice but to depend on the mercy of the rich and the powerful—do you understand that? You do, of course—no one in this country can get by just by painting. You'll be miserable, people will look down on you, you'll be plagued by complexes, anxieties, and resentments till the day you die. Is that the sort of thing someone like you—as clever, as lovable, as full of life as you—really wants to do?"

I'd walk down to Beşiktaş and all the way along the Dolmabahçe Palace walls as far as the stadium, as far as the *dolmuş* stop. I liked walking along these high thick old mossy palace walls at night. I would feel that energy of the anger pulsating in my forehead getting more violent by the minute until I got to Dolmabahçe, and then I'd go up an alley and be in Taksim in twelve minutes.

"When you were little, even when things were at their worst, you were always smiling, joyful, optimistic—oh, you were such a sweet child. Everyone who saw you had to smile. Not just because you were cute, but because you didn't even know what sadness was. You were never bored; even at the worst times you'd just invent something and play happily for hours; you were always so cheerful. For someone like this to become a troubled, miserable artist who is always bowing to the rich—even if I weren't your mother, I couldn't bear it. That's why I want you to listen to me carefully and not take offense at what I say."

On my way up to Taksim, I'd stop for a moment to look at the lights of Galata in the half-dark view, and then I'd head for Beyoğlu to spend a few minutes browsing through the bookstalls at the beginning of İstiklâl Avenue, and after that I'd stop for a beer and vodka in one of those beerhalls where the television drowns out the noisy crowd, and smoke a cigarette, as everyone else was doing (I'd look around to see if there happened to be any famous poets, writers, or artists sitting nearby), and when I felt I was attracting too much attention from all those mustachoied men—because I was looking around me, and alone, and had a child's face—I would go out again to mingle with the night. After walking down the avenue for a little, I'd head into the back streets of Beyoğlu, and when I had reached Çukurcuma, Galata, Cihangir, I would pause to gaze at the halos of the streetlamps and the light from a nearby television screen flickering on the wet pavements, and it would be while peer-

ing into a junk shop, a refrigerator that an ordinary grocer used as a window display, a pharmacy still displaying a mannequin I remember from my childhood, that I would realize how very happy I was. The sublime, dizzying, pure anger I felt right now at listening to my mother would leave me after an hour of wandering the back streets of Beyoğlu—or should I go to Üsküdar, or try the back streets of Fatih?—wherever I went, as I got colder and colder, I'd be warmed by the furious flame of my brilliant future. By then my head would be light from the beer and the long exertion, and the mournful streets would seem to flicker as in an old film, a moment I would want to freeze and hide away—the way I used to hide a precious seed or a favorite marble in my mouth for hours on end—and at that same moment I'd want to leave the empty streets and return home to sit down at my desk with pencil and paper to write or draw.

"That painting on the wall over there—Nermin and Ali gave it to us as a wedding present. When they got married, we went to see the same famous painter to see if we could buy one of his paintings for them in return. If you could have seen how thrilled Turkey's most famous artist was that some people had finally turned up at his door to buy a painting, or what ridiculous airs he put on to hide his pleasure, or how he practically swept the floor with his bowing as we left with his painting in our hands, or how unctuously he bade us farewell, you wouldn't wish becoming a painter on anyone in this country, my son. That's why I'm not

ABOUT THE PHOTOGRAPHS

I relived much of the excitement and puzzlement of writing this book while choosing the photographs. Most were taken by Ara Güler; during my time searching in his home-studio-archive-museum (in Beyoğlu, where he has spent most of his life), I came across many treasured but long-forgotten images (for example, the tugboat on 284 with its funnel lowered to pass under the Galata Bridge), as beguilingly familiar to my adult eye as they were strange. When I happened on the view of the snow-covered Galata Bridge on 316 it was as if my own memory had been projected onto a screen; there were other moments like that, when I would be seized by a frenzy to capture and preserve this dreamscape or to write about it. Ara Güler's vast and seemingly endless archive, while first and foremost a tribute to his art, is also a superb record of Istanbul life from 1950 to the present day and will leave anyone who knew the city during those years drunk with memories.

The following photographs are by Ara Güler: pages 29, 31, 35, 40 (top and bottom), 42 (bottom), 43 (bottom), 49 (bottom), 52, 53 (right), 93 (top and bottom), 95 (top), 96, 97, 99, 100, 102, 105, 106, 109, 112, 142, 174, 175, 181, 202, 222, 229, 231, 247, 249, 250, 252, 256, 257, 258, 260, 263, 279, 280, 281, 283, 284, 293, 307, 316, 322, 323, 324, 345, 347, 348, 349 (top), 350 (bottom), 351, 352, 359, 363, 366, 367.

In the archives of Selahattin Giz (born 1912), exploring his photographic record of the streets of Beyoğlu (begun while still a student at Galatasaray Lisesi and continued during his forty-two years at *Cumhuriyet*) was like gaining entry to a private world of enchantment. Perhaps this is because, as his photographs show, Giz loved the city's empty, lonely, snowy streets as much as I do: pages 28, 33, 34, 41 (top and bottom), 49 (top), 51, 53 (left), 56, 58, 59, 86, 95 (bottom), 110, 130, 139, 140, 144, 145, 146, 170, 171, 209, 211, 239, 241, 243, 246, 248, 251, 278, 292, 306, 315 (top), 365.

I would like to thank the Istanbul City Council for permission to include from their collection the photographs of another news photographer, Hilmi Şahenk: pages 36, 42 (top), 43 (top), 48 (top), 60, 98, 143, 201, 208, 236, 282, 308, 315 (bottom), 344, 349 (bottom), 350 (top).

The photograph of Hagia Sophia on 226 was taken by James Robertson in 1853.

The photographs on 225, 228, and 232 (bottom) were taken by the Abdullah Brothers, who ran a photographic agency in Istanbul during the last quarter of the nineteenth century.

While researching this book, I discovered that the postcard artist Max Fruchtermann also used some of the Abdullah Brothers' photographs. The illustrations on pages 48 (bottom), 50 (top), 55, 57, 230, 232 (top), 244, 254, and 255 are taken from Max Fruchtermann's postcards, as is the city panorama on pages 288–291, a five-postcard stone print following the fashion of the time.

The old photographs on pages 133, 135, 137, 156, 158, 219, 233, and 253 came to me secondhand and my efforts to find out who took them have not been successful.

I would like to thank the Foundation le Corbusier for the drawing by Le Corbusier on 38.

The engraving on 45 is by Thomas Allom, the painting on 259 is by Hoca Ali Rıza, and the painting on 337 is by Halil Pasha.

The enlarged details on pages 62–73 and 218 are by Melling.

As I describe in Chapter 28, the photographs of Beşiktaş and Cihangir between pages 268 and 272 were taken by me; I still like the picture I took as a fifteen-year-old boy of the cobblestone alley seen from Cihangir (page 87).

———

I would like to thank Esra Akcan and Emre Ayvaz for their careful editing and helpful comments.

INDEX